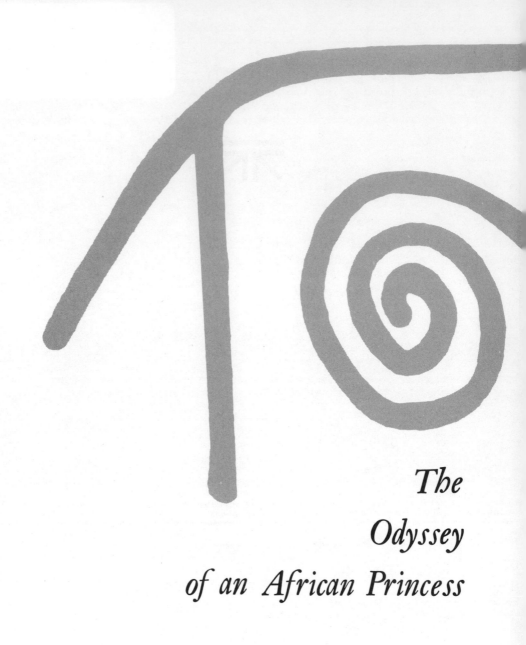

The
Odyssey
of an African Princess

A TOUCHSTONE BOOK

Published by Simon & Schuster Inc.
New York London
Toronto Sydney Tokyo

ELIZABETH
of
TORO

An Autobiography by
Elizabeth
Nyabongo

SIMON AND SCHUSTER/TOUCHSTONE
Simon & Schuster Building
Rockefeller Center
1230 Avenue of the Americas
New York, New York 10020

Designed by Nina D'Amario/Levavi & Levavi
Manufactured in the United States of America

1 3 5 7 9 10 8 6 4 2
3 5 7 9 10 8 6 4 2 Pbk.

Library of Congress Cataloging in Publication Data
Elizabeth, Princess of Toro.
Elizabeth of Toro.

(A Touchstone book)
Rev. ed. of: African princess, 1983.
Includes index.
1. Elizabeth, Princess of Toro.   2. Diplomats—
Uganda—Biography.   3. Uganda—Princess and princesses—
Biography.   I. Elizabeth, Princess of Toro. African
princess.   II. Title.
DT433.28.E44A3   1989   967.6′04′092 [B]   89–10078
ISBN 0–671–67395–5
0–671–67396–3 Pbk.

To Wilbur

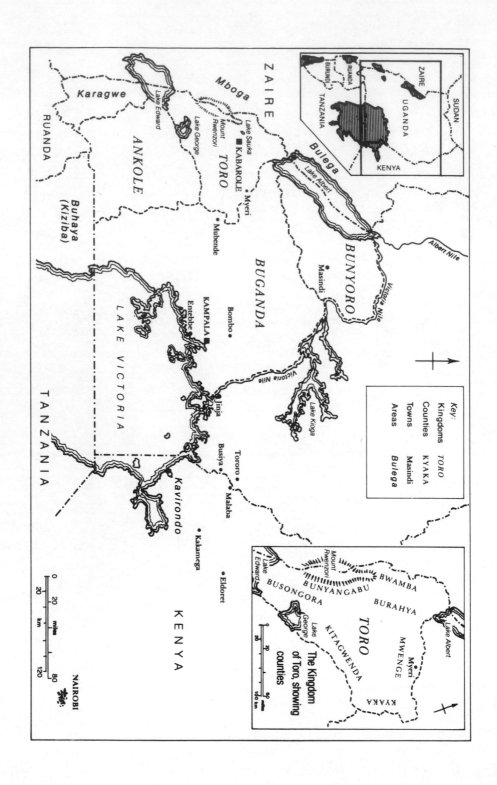

Key:
Kingdoms   *TORO*
Counties   KYAKA
Towns   Masindi
Areas   *Bulega*

The Kingdom
of Toro, showing
counties

Contents

Contents

Acknowledgments

There are many people without whose encouragement and help this book would not have been written. To my American publishers—Dan Farley and Sol Skolnick—and to my British publisher—Christopher Sinclair-Stevenson—I owe a great debt of gratitude for their support. For their help with the original research, which was published in my first book, *African Princess*, and which remains integral to *Elizabeth of Toro*, I would like to thank Dorothy Allan, Babuza, John Bell, Margaret Bolton, Asanasiyo Byanrungu, Dr. Byaruhanga, Joan Cox, Janet Glover, Ailsa Hamilton, Samali Kabaseke, Mr. and Mrs. Kahwa, John Kalisa, Kajabago Karusoke, Stephanie Keil, Father Kisembo, Kisoro, Dr. John Lonsdale of Trinity College, Cambridge, Mary-Christian MacEwen, Bishop Magambo, Prince George Mawanda, Caroline Montagu, my mother, Stephen Nabeta, Dorothy Nyakato, Canon Rubale, Mr. Rwakabuguli, Mary Stuart, Sheila Warren, and Nicholas Fairbairn, M.P. In addition, my sincere thanks go to Harry Reasoner and Patti Hustler of *60 Minutes*, Barbara Feinman, Gayla Cook, Dr. Ibulahimu Kakoma, Jackie Trescott, Henry Brandon, Dr. John Brademas, Dr. Hans Peter Kaul, Antonio Monroig, and Phillis Byrne who made important contributions to the present volume. I am indebted to the late Dr. Schofield, and to many Batoro, for the unique photographs used in this book. In this respect British and American *Vogue* also deserve thanks.

My warmest appreciation goes to my executive editor Carole Hall

Acknowledgments

for her sympathetic help; and to Malaika Adero, Patricia Eisemann, Renée Rabb, Joanne Lauro, Deirdre Amthor, Nina D'Amario, Beatrice Cunningham, Stephanie Bowling and Geri Freeman, also of Simon and Schuster.

Prologue

It was still dark when I reached the Uganda-Kenya border, and I watched the dawn break as other travelers arrived, forming a line behind me. By the time the customs officials opened their office and sleepily began going through the motions of inspecting my papers, I could not bear to wait one more minute. I said to the man holding my papers, "Please help me. My husband has died in a plane crash and I've got to get to Casablanca."

He stared at me almost as if he were seeing me for the first time. I thought to myself, "How idiotic of him to just stand there and stare at me senselessly." Moments passed before he stamped my papers. To my surprise, he followed me outside. "Akiiki," he called to me. "I am from Kihwera. I am your husband's uncle."

So that was it. The poor man had been frozen by the news. I explained what had happened to Wilbur and why I was making this journey. "But are you going alone, Akiiki?" he asked, his voice filled with grief.

"Yes, I am, Uncle. Wilbur and I did not share our love or life with anybody. And that's how I want it in death. I want to be alone with him."

I bid him good-bye as gently as I could, struggling to remain focused on the next step of the journey. Eventually my friend Godfrey Kavuma in Nairobi, and Uganda and Moroccan embassy officials would help me locate Wilbur's body, which was being guarded in

Casablanca. They would book or charter flights for me so that I could bring Wilbur back home to Toro. But crossing the Ugandan border, I felt utterly alone, holding together the remaining pieces of my life. Nothing I had experienced before had hurt so much—not the terror of the tyrant Milton Obote, not exile or the twisted mind of Idi Amin.

Months later, I recalled a sunny, happy morning in London when I started singing, "After the thrill of life is gone, life continues on," as I moved from our bedroom to the kitchen to make our usual breakfast of tea and bread. On the way, I had passed Wilbur, who stopped to listen. Ironies always struck a sensitive cord within him.

Those words would, one day, become my reality. Sometimes, I wonder whether Wilbur was just a beautiful dream, yet without his love my life would have amounted to much less. Even though I wonder if the spirit of mankind survives or if we control our destiny, I am resigned to be driven forward by an uncontrollable force until I am laid next to Wilbur.

I

LIVING HISTORY

1

Behind a Mask
of Silence

The air was fresh from the mist in the atmosphere and from the dew that had settled on the leaves and the grass overnight. I felt the blood run faster through my veins in anticipation.

My father had received some stark advice from my headmistress, "That child will never achieve her potential until she leaves the kingdom." Indeed, it was wise counsel. He had decided I should be sent to Gayaza High School in Buganda, one of Uganda's four former kingdoms.

Yet on the day of departure, hope and fear, excitement and terror, jostled for places in my heart. My father, the king of Toro, was going to deliver me himself into the safekeeping of the Kabaka, king of Buganda. The Kabaka, my uncle, was to be my guardian while I was away at school, just as his father had been guardian to my father, who in turn was guardian to the Kabaka.

Since it was a long and perilous journey of two hundred miles, we had to conform to the procedures of any other safari. Tradition required us to rise at 4:00 A.M., in the dark, as my father had done in his childhood when he made the journey on foot, at a time when lions and elephants roamed freely on the road.

All was done in silence, for it would have been bad manners to wake those who were neither bound for school nor "hunt." The whole caravan assembled in the breakfast room, like a shooting party—drivers, secretaries, attendants, princes, princesses, and the king, who alone sat on a chair while the rest ate their pawpaws, bananas, and other fruit, sitting on the floor. The convoy, with food prepared, stood ready at the door. The king issued his last orders—as a military man, everything had to be handled with military precision, for it was an important mission to accompany two young princesses— my cousin Angeline and I—to school! We were each a bag of nerves.

The whole company prepared to mount the waiting Land-Rovers, laden with our baggage. My father drove his own Land-Rover, nick-named "*Kapala*." His flag was unfurled on the front, and I climbed into the back. We set off, like an army patrol, eastward in the dark.

The road followed the contour exactly along the old elephant tracks that for generation after generation had been used by the elephants in their search for the easiest way to food and water. We were traveling through a remnant of the vast equatorial rain forest that once covered the whole of Uganda, and passed Toro's sole sawmill (owned by Grenvil Singh—a third-generation Ugandan Sikh, whose family had always kindly supplied us with firewood). I felt dwarfed by the immense height of the *Mvules* (the African oak) and their attendant creepers, some twisting crazily skywards, others suspended in midair. Then the forest came to an abrupt end and a panorama of undulating, grassy hills unfolded before us. This was Mwenge County—the heart of the tea-growing area in Uganda. I gazed with amazement at this man-made emerald-green sea of acres and acres of well-manicured tea plantation, belonging for the most part to the Eu-ropean settlers.

Toro, with its high altitude and correspondingly temperate climate, had attracted Uganda's only small settler community. My father had told us many tales of the past about these men, every one of whom had become his personal friend. In one story Kelsall, the pioneer of Kiko, Toro's oldest tea estate, was dragged from his bed by a lion but grabbed a pistol from under his pillow, and when the lion loosened its grip on his leg momentarily, he shot and killed the beast. His African houseboy rushed to his aid and summoned help. Kelsall was carried on a litter for some one hundred miles to the nearest hospital.

We drove on to Kyaka, the great cattle district of Toro, which is peopled by the Banyakyaka. We stopped for an hour at a small trading center, where the people gathered round to show my father their love and loyalty, and to tell him of their progress and their problems. Meanwhile, Angeline and I resorted to the calming influence of a glass of milk each.

Eventually, we reached the Great Rubicon, the border between the kingdoms of Toro and Buganda, and it suddenly came home to me that I was being sent away. The convoy halted, and the driver got out and removed my father's royal pennant from the masthead of his car. Princesses are not supposed to show fear, so I disguised my emotions behind a mask of silence.

We drove on to Mubende, a trading place in Buganda, where we stopped for tea with an Indian friend of my father's, and then we proceeded to Kampala. I had never been in a town before, far less a city. It seemed so strange and busy and huge. In Kabarole, our home, you could count the buildings. The Kabaka's palace was bigger than my father's, covering perhaps two or three square miles. We passed the main gate and instead turned left through a little gate called *Kalala* (every gate had a name). It was the Kabaka's special gate, reserved only for his fellow kings.

In the palace we were greeted by princes and princesses and sat on the floor waiting for the Kabaka. Only my father sat on a chair. The Kabaka came in almost unnoticed and sat down beside him. He wore simple clothes and spoke in a low voice. The two kings did most of the talking. Some of the people there related stories, and my father laughed loudly. Finally, he and the Kabaka went off to the Kabaka's private office and the princesses showed Angeline and me to our royal quarters.

The next day my father left. Angeline and I were taken to say good-bye to him. As we knelt, I wanted to burst into tears, but princesses never, never cry. He went off with his entourage—and I was on my own. Now I was to find that many of the assumptions upon which I had previously based my life had to go. I had for a start moved into the territory of another tribe, so I had two alienating characteristics: I was foreign as well as being royal.

Fortunately, once we reached school, I found immediate consolation in the headmistress, Nancy Corby. She was a Methodist missionary and rejoiced in music and Christianity, both of which enabled her to project an aura of peace and optimism that I found very reassuring.

However, as with everyone who is sent away to school, there were some people and some activities that had traumatic effects on me. One of the greatest of these was digging. On arrival at the school, I had been handed bucket No. 19 and a hoe. We went to our small iron beds in the dimly lit dormitory, but I hardly slept. In the morning when the drum rolled, we jumped out of bed, took our buckets, and ran to fetch the water with which to wash ourselves. Then the drum sounded again and we were sent to dig with our hoes in the banana plantations. First, we had to clear the elephant grass. I hated doing that; it was so sharp and cut my hands. But I hated the digging even more. I couldn't do it properly, but we were made to go on digging till we had each finished our allotted patch.

All night long I would dread the arrival of morning, bringing as it did the infernal and eternal digging. I hated getting water, too, from the distant bore hole. Some of the girls could carry three buckets at a time, two of them on their heads, but I couldn't, so I had to go back and back again. I used to feel so helpless, but nobody would ever offer to help me. That was one of the main differences between my life in Toro and my life away at school. At home everyone had been there to wait on me, but now there was no one. In this painful way I learned self-help. Angeline and I stuck together as much as possible, but she was in another dormitory, so at night we were exposed to the mercies of girls from another tribe. They mocked me about the way I spoke their language, and they teased me about being royal and arriving and leaving in the Kabaka's Rolls Royce. There was one person to whom I could always turn, though: the drummer, who came from Toro like me. His rather inappropriate name was Nakuzabasajia ("Woe of Men") and he lived with his wife in a little house at the main gate. Whenever we were troubled, we would run to him and he would tell us what to do. He had been at the school for forty years, and he is there still. I owe a great deal to that man.

There was another person from Toro, a teacher in the secondary school, called Nesta Mukeri, who was a relation of ours. So on weekends we used to go to see her, creeping through the woods like leopards, as it was against the rules. Her house was the nearest thing to home the two of us had. Actually, we did have an excuse to go there because she looked after our pocket money, but we were really only allowed to collect it on Saturdays. We decided that a week of Saturdays was our type of week!

However, we transgressed at our peril. The prefects were all from Buganda and they could easily sentence you to digging—which I was so bad at that I sometimes had to stay behind during the holidays, after school had broken up, to finish. The prefects could also make you cook and peel green bananas, which stained your hands with purple, or they could command you to sit for hours at a time on top of rocky ground, which meant you missed prep and earned the scorn of the other girls.

Digging was always followed by breakfast and then the dignified and reassuring recitation of prayers led usually by Nancy Corby. Afterwards, we went to our lessons, wearing our English school dresses—dark blue with a star on the chest and the proud initials G.H.S., which we had to sew on ourselves. (I always sewed mine on askew and had to do them all over again. Somehow, I was forever last at everything!) During the afternoon, we younger children had a siesta, and then would come tea at four o'clock when we could get together with our friends. Tea was followed by games, which I enjoyed tremendously. I was specially good at basketball (I had the height for it), and it made a welcome change to excel in something.

By the time I left the primary school, I was much more confident and able to stand up for myself. I was more fluent in the language and had even become proficient at hoeing. (I was not very good at handicrafts and cooking, though—I have never been able to cook, unlike my sisters.) I was finding it far easier to make friends, and luckily there were quite a few other girls from Toro at secondary school—among them Catherine Kabaseke and Vanisi Nyakake, who became my staunch supporters, and Margaret Semugeshi, who later married my brother Stephen.

I still encountered difficulties born of tribal jealousy. Once I was even suspended for three weeks. Our class had decided to tease the teacher when she came in and pretend that instead of her teaching us, we would teach her. For reasons which I naïvely mistook for popularity, I was chosen to be the ringleader. When the teacher came in, the others egged me on: "Go on, Elizabeth." So, with mounting hesitation, I walked to the blackboard, took the chalk from the teacher's hand, told her to sit down, and proceeded to conduct the lesson. She stormed out in a rage, and after being hauled before an incredulous and angry staff, I was banished for three weeks. None of the other conspirators ever received so much as a reprimand.

My father was incensed; how could a princess bring down such disgrace on the royal house? I was clapped off to my mother's house, but a week later the king sent for me and caned me mercilessly. (My back had to be massaged for two weeks as I lay in bed.) I returned to school much chastened and contrite, and the incident was never brought up again. However, I had learned one lesson: not to trust those who flattered.

Even the Kabaka could not protect me from the jealousy of some of the girls. My father was anxious that I should learn to stand on my own two feet, so I spent two of the three school holidays in Buganda at the home of the queen mother of Buganda, the Kabaka's mother. And every year on November 19, I would be collected in his Rolls Royce to attend his birthday celebrations. I always made sure I brought back some sherry and wine for the other girls—I thought it would make up for the privileges I had—but there was always some spiteful girl who would report me.

I remember there was one little girl in our class who was extremely poor (her family lived in a grass hut), but Mary Mawano was always top in geometry, chemistry, and English. The headmistress, Joan Cox, took us for English. She was a woman of great erudition and inspired respect from everyone. One day she walked into class and at once asked someone to spell the word "psychology." We all began with an "s" until Mary Mawano advanced timidly to the blackboard and wrote the letter "p." We roared with laughter—and received a stony look from Miss Cox.

Gradually I moved upwards in the school. I excelled as a singer and actress (playing a very tall, thin Julius Caesar), became a prefect, and worked hard. Toward the end, school was actually becoming fun. At long last, we thought, we are about to leave school behind us—and we became more adventurous. We were all in a hurry to taste forbidden fruits, to indulge in the worldly pleasures which up until that time had been denied us. Soon, we would be free to grow our hair like women and not have it cropped to the regulation stubble; soon, we would be able to dance and drink and smoke and have boyfriends.

As soon as we left school and got back to the Kabaka's palace, Angeline and I decided to sneak out to meet two boys. They were from King's College, Budo, the Eton of Uganda, and they took us off to dance and exchange photographs and sing at a secret rendezvous in Kampala. But as they brought us back to the gate, *Kalala*, in their little black car, who should turn up but the Kabaka! I dropped to my knees; he swept pass. But he had noticed, and he told my father, who summoned me home.

Once more I was to be exiled, and this time it was to England.

2

To Crown
My Days

"*Oraire ota, mwana wange*" ("Good morning, my child"), a voice from behind greeted me in Rutoro, startling me out of my mournful reverie. I turned and saw Mrs. Schofield, the guardian my father had chosen for me. No one had warned me that she spoke our native tongue. I began kneeling to return the greeting when she put out a hand to prevent me, saying with a smile, "You'll cause such a commotion if you do that. I'm afraid we don't do that in England."

At Heathrow Airport my "mother country"—as England was known to us—gave me a chilly if typical reception with snow, ice, and freezing rain. I felt extremely miserable.

"Elizabeth, this is Margaret Kabahenda, my daughter," said Mrs. Schofield.

Amused by my puzzled expression, she continued, "Do you know the meaning of 'Kabahenda,' Elizabeth?"

I confessed my ignorance. She explained, "When Margaret was born in Toro Hospital, the nurses called her 'Kabatoro,' meaning 'of the Batoro.' But when I took my baby daughter to see your grandfather and told him she had been named 'Kabatoro,' he said: 'She is our child, hence she will be known as "Kabahenda," meaning 'of the royal.' "

Mrs. Schofield smiled with pride as she finished her story. "You will find a lot to remind you of Toro in our home, but now we must hurry back. Kabahenda has very kindly brought her coat and a pair of boots for you." When I inquired why I had to wear such strange-looking footwear, she said: "Have you never seen snow before?" I told her that I had seen it from a distance on top of the Mountains of the Moon.* She laughed. "Come, I will show you." I followed her outside, and there I saw my first proper snow. I felt frozen to the marrow! "Come on, Elizabeth. In England you must learn to bear up. You will be better off in the car than standing out here," Mrs. Schofield said.

"Do you want to sit with Nanka in the back or come with me in the front?" she asked me.

"Good heavens," I thought, "even the family dog has a Kitoro name." I accepted her invitation to sit in the front, using as an excuse that I was allergic to cats and dogs. "Right you are. Take the rug from the front seat and wrap yourself up well. It's six hours' drive to Melksham."

I felt my heart sink at the mention of Melksham. I had comforted myself that the excitement of living in London would in part compensate me for my banishment from Toro, but instead I was being taken to a small village in Wiltshire, where I would have to settle into the monotonous routine of a missionary home (it might just as well have been a nunnery): English breakfast, sewing name tapes on my school clothes, lunch, an afternoon rest, taking Nanka for a walk, tea, drawing-room conversation, supper, prayers, and bed. Apart from one day's shopping expedition to Bath in Somerset with Mrs. Schofield to buy my school uniform and some personal clothes, and the occasional country drive, this routine remained unaltered until the day Mrs. Schofield delivered me to Sherborne School for Girls in Dorset, one of the top schools in Britain with the foremost headmistress in Britain, Dame Diana Reader Harris.

* The Mountains of the Moon, a sixty-mile range higher than the Alps, straddle the border between Uganda and Zaïre.

Today I realize that for my father, Sherborne was a dream come true. As a devout Christian, he had always entrusted me to the care of good Christian homes during my school holidays. Sherborne, which had a tradition of evangelical Christianity, appeared to him to be ideal.

The Chinese Revolution was inadvertently responsible for the fact that the opportunity arose. For many years Sherborne had enjoyed an exchange arrangement with a distinguished private school in Peking. But Mao's Revolution ended that congenial contract, and so the indomitable headmistress, Dame Diana Reader Harris, sought another international alternative. In 1957 she visited Gayaza High School. I do not remember her visit to our classroom, but she did not forget me. She was so struck by my presence that she asked who I was and all about me. She did not allow her initial impression to fade; it seemed she was determined to have me at Sherborne.

My father's decision to commit me to its care was influenced by the personality of his longstanding missionary friend, Mrs. Georgina Schofield, an old girl of the school, who had devoted her life to good works and selfless service in Toro and throughout Uganda. To him, she personified the standards of honor and commitment which he wished me to emulate as the future Batebe.

According to ancient tradition in Toro, as in ancient Egypt, the king ascends the throne with his sister the princess royal, who is known as the *Batebe*. As my great-aunt Bagaaya had been the Batebe to my grandfather, King Kyebambe, and my aunt, Ruth Komuntale, had been to my father, so was I destined to be the Batebe to my brother, Patrick Kaboyo Olimi, when he succeeded my father. My father was determined that I should be trained for this role.

Our bond to Christianity was old and deep. Of all its evidence I had been given, none astounded me more than the blood pact contracted between King Kyebambe's mother, Queen Victoria, and Père Achete, a French Catholic missionary. In accordance with tradition, it was celebrated early one morning at the house of one of the parties—in this case Queen Victoria's palace—and before either party had eaten anything. Père Achete was brought to the palace and seated in the queen's reception room. A special mat was brought in and spread on the floor, and a basket containing two coffee beans and a knife was placed in the middle of it. The queen, accompanied by members of her family and clan, entered and sat at one end of the mat. Achete sat at the other end, facing the queen, and the ceremony began. Queen Victoria took the knife and made an incision in her stomach. She dipped one of the coffee beans into the blood and gave it to Achete, who swallowed it. Achete then made an incision in his own stomach, dipped the remaining coffee bean in his blood and gave it to the queen, who swallowed it.

Then each of them swore to be loyal, truthful, and to support the other and his or her offspring forevermore.

A bond had been contracted and sealed in blood between them—*Omukago*, the ancient institution of blood brotherhood. It is an eternal and irreversible bond which must be strictly observed, not only by the parties to it but by their offspring. Any betrayal of this bond is an offense and will bring down a curse on the traitor, his clan, his offspring, and his neighborhood. It was an insurance against personal, clan, or tribal feuds because, once contracted, forgiveness is automatic. The parties to it and their offspring become blood relatives; consequently no marriage could occur between them.

That the queen was able to conclude a blood pact with a white, male Roman Catholic missionary at that time is an amazing occurrence, an act whose revolutionary content is unsurpassed by any other. It defied all past rules by cutting across time, race, sex, class, and religion.

When Christian missionaries later banned the institution of blood brotherhood as cannibalistic and barbaric, they sliced through the moral fiber of our society. In pre-colonial times, betrayal of one's country, clan, tribe, or neighborhood was anathema. In the aftermath, betrayal became rampant.

But these thoughts would not occur to me until years later. At that moment, I simply found myself looking forward to going to school as a relief from the boredom of Melksham.

My initial encounter with Sherborne came as a severe shock. I was extremely conscious of being the only black student. I felt that I was on trial and that my failure to excel would reflect badly on the entire black race. With only one year to prepare for and take the entrance examination for Cambridge or Oxford—my companions had had two years for the same task—I was handicapped from the word go. On top of this, I had a problem with communication. English had always been my strong point at my former school, but the English spoken by the Sherborne girls was quite different from mine. They spoke the Queen's English, while I spoke English as it is spoken in Africa. And I found the pace of our daily routine so demanding that one day I collapsed and was discovered in the house kitchen sound asleep at the table. To me, the other girls seemed to move at supersonic speed; they talked fast, walked fast, ran fast, gobbled their food and played fast.

Every morning, the first bell rang at 7:10, when we had to jump out of bed and grab our jugs to fetch water from the bathrooms. The second bell went at 7:20, when we had to be back in our cubicles and strip-wash from the waist upward in silence. By the third bell at 7:30, we had to be dressed, our hair brushed, beds stripped down, and then make a dash to breakfast. If we were late, we had to report to matron or the head of the house or a prefect to offer an explanation. After breakfast we tidied our cubicles before hurrying off to school.

During my early terms at Sherborne, I would be reduced to tears every morning as I ran in all directions, appealing to someone to help me knot my school tie. If there is one thing that could have turned me into a female militant, it was this masculine streak in English female education, which demanded that girls should be as good as boys—but on boys' terms! Fortunately, I was living in Alderhelmsted West, the house nearest the school building, so I didn't have to cycle or walk long distances to school, as some girls from other houses did.

In my turbulent frame of mind, the school prayers at the beginning of each morning used to have a soothing effect on me before I had to face the daily pressure of academic work. Latin and French provided mental torture. It was a prerequisite of successful entrance to Oxford and Cambridge that every candidate had to have two foreign languages other than English. In spite of what I thought were persuasive and compelling arguments to the contrary, Oxbridge* decided that English should count as my mother tongue and that I would have to learn two additional foreign languages. (This made me wonder whether these two seats of learning were not a little wanting in logic.)

I discovered that the approach to education at Sherborne differed fundamentally from that in African schools. In post-colonial Africa,

* Oxbridge means the universities of Oxford and Cambridge.

education has become a means to an end: namely, to pass an examination in order to qualify for university or other institution of further education. Teachers are regarded as people with secrets which it is the combined role of teacher and pupil to find out. Because the European concept of education is alien to our culture, the result is that students are spoon-fed. Notes are dictated. Students are guided and tested frequently. At Sherborne, on the other hand, the aim behind our education was to allow the pupil to discover herself through interaction with her teacher; we were encouraged to value the significance of facts above mere fact-finding. Sherborne's long tradition of "O"- and "A"-level (Ordinary and Advanced) successes spanned more than half a century, while in Uganda we were still pioneering this system of examination. Furthermore, in Uganda we had no television, radio, or newspapers at school to provide us with educational backup, and therefore I found the girls at Sherborne much more academically mature than myself.

But if the academic work was causing me mental stress, school games drove me to utter despair. If *mens sana in corpore sano* is not written into every school motto in the British public school system, it ought to be. I suppose it stems from the nineteenth-century belief that one is more morally pure if one has a healthy body. However, while there might have been, in the last century, sound justification for training boys in such a manner as to help them in conquering the world for the British Empire, I failed to see any need for such English excesses in the twentieth century, with an almost nonexistent empire!

Doggedly determined, I set out to protect myself from this peculiarly English obsession. My excuses that exposure to the unfamiliar English climate was causing my hair to fall out and myself to feel ill proved of no avail. Alas, I was forced to endure interminable games of hockey and lacrosse.

Ultimately I was rescued by my other tormentors—Latin and French. The school was forced to recognize that I needed to put in extra hours in these two languages if I were to reach the required standard—after all, many of my classmates had been studying these subjects for at least six years. I was spared school games on condition that I went for walks or runs instead, and extra coaching was arranged for me.

Once the pressure of work eased, I was able to participate more in Sherborne's varied activities. My real personality, suppressed by the strain I had been under, surfaced again, and my African background proved an asset both to myself and the school. In African schools, children are exposed to a healthy mixture of backgrounds, from the very poor peasants to royal children. This does not apply in English public schools. At Sherborne the girls came from one social class and most of them lived very sheltered lives. In my experience, the depth of understanding of humanity is more profound in an African pupil than in an English public school student. I believe this explains why teachers and girls at Sherborne used to tell me that I was more mature, more spontaneous, in my attitude toward life and exhibited more enthusiasm about everything than my English counterparts, who were brought up to show less emotion. I laughed a lot as my self-confidence increased, so much so and so heartily that, on occasions, the other girls would panic, fearing they would never be able to stop me. Laughter helped me to triumph over my English teasers. I was able to laugh at being called "Baggy" instead of sulking as I had initially, and I no longer took to heart derogatory remarks about Africa or the black race. As a result, I made many friends who often invited me out with their parents. My love of music also found an outlet and I took piano lessons and joined the school choir. In the school music festival, Alderhelmsted West sang a Rutoro song I had taught them, accompanied by me on an African traditional drum.

As Dame Diana Reader Harris recalls, at the end of every school lecture, she could rely on finding me waiting in her study ready to fire questions at the guest lecturer. It was through these lectures that I met Father Trevor Huddleston, who came to lecture to us about South Africa. For the first and only time in my life, I experienced God's presence in a human being. Years later, when I became a refugee from Amin's Uganda, it was to this saintly man that I turned for advice and direction.

I was made a school and house prefect, signifying that my presence in the school was considered of some value. When a telegram arrived summoning me to an interview at Cambridge, I was struck mute—even more so when a second message arrived with the news that I had been admitted to Girton College.

To crown my days at Sherborne, I became one of the first three African women to be admitted to Cambridge, and the first African woman from the east and central regions. (My two colleagues were Olu Abisogom from Nigeria and Lulu Coker from Sierra Leone.)

All my academic endeavors had been worthwhile. I telegraphed my father, who received the news of my admission with disbelief. After all, his daughter had opened a new chapter in African history.

Who could have predicted the twists and turns of history that had brought me to Cambridge less than one hundred years after four hundred years of slave trade and the first invasion of Uganda by the Imperial British East Africa Company, headed by Captain F. D. Lugard?

As I recalled that history, I searched for lessons that would strengthen me in this new stage of my life in England. I remembered in particular the king of Bunyoro, Kabalega, who mobilized almost the whole of the country against the British. Kabalega fought on to the bitter end, but he was finally captured and exiled to the Seychelles Islands. From captivity, the valiant king wrote to his son: "Only my sons who resisted and fought the British should call themselves Babito [princes]. Those who did not should never call themselves Babito, and they should rightly be ruled for ever more."

However, from Toro's point of view, Kabalega was a more deadly menace than the British. At the time of Lugard's arrival in Uganda, Toro had already been overrun by Kabalega, who had invaded as soon as he heard the news of my great-grandfather King Nyaika's death, and before a new king could be installed. Thousands of men, women, children, weapons, and cattle were captured and removed wholsesale to Bunyoro.

Miraculously, Queen Victoria, along with her one-year-old son (the future King Kyebambe of Toro) and many others, escaped in 1875 to the kingdom of Ankole, where they were granted asylum. They had believed Ankole would provide them with a safe haven because Kiboga, the mother of the reigning king Ntare, was a Toro princess. So they settled in a place called Sema, about thirty miles from Mbarara, the capital.

When Kabalega learned that Kiboga had given refuge to the Toro princes, he knew that as long as they were alive his hold on Toro was insecure. So he sent a message to Kiboga, asking her how she could offer protection to "our common enemy." By "common enemy" he was reminding Kiboga of the historical fact that not only did she come from Busongora, a former dukedom, but that she herself had been given in marriage to the Ankole king as the price to buy peace beteen Ankole and Toro.

Between them, Kabalega and Kiboga hatched a plot to murder all the Toro princes in Ankole. The murders would take place at a feast given by Kiboga which the princes were to attend. On the day of the feast, Kiboga's messengers arrived at Sema to collect the princes, including little Kyebambe, who was then about ten years old. As the princes were being led away, Queen Victoria suddenly snatched her son by the hand and made off unobserved. Meanwhile, all the other princes were murdered as Kiboga had planned. Thomas Kato, a loyal Mutoro who had accompanied the princes to the feast, lay under the body of each prince as he was being killed so that the royal blood wouldn't flow on the ground!

Queen Victoria herself, however, with her infant son and her entourage walked through the jungle, finally reaching the kingdom of Buganda where they were given asylum by the king. The only thing Queen Victoria had managed to bring with her was the perfumed ointment contained in the horn of a cow, which she used to massage daily into her young son's body. In Buganda they stayed at Kabula near Masaka about a hundred miles from Kampala.

They were there when Captain Lugard arrived in Uganda. When Queen Victoria heard the news about Lugard's gun and its superior power over traditional weapons, she lost no time in establishing contact with him. She sent a messenger bearing a special wooden vessel containing a sample of salt from the crater lakes of Toro, and the message that if Lugard helped to restore her son to his kingdom, he could have a share in Toro's salt and other mineral wealth.

Lugard was swift to grasp the economic potential and, once he had satisfied himself that Kyebambe was the legitimate heir to the Toro throne, he made the recapture of the kingdom from Kabalega a priority. The initial expeditionary force that advanced on Toro included about two hundred Batoro with bows and arrows, and Lugard's Nubian soldiers armed with guns, but as it advanced toward its first target, the salt lake in Busongora county, it mobilized more and more support.

Lugard described Toro as a land of "almost terrible beauty." He decided en route to test the people and see if they could recognize their king. So he dressed up a Toro prince called Yafete Byakuyamba and presented him to the crowds, saying, "Behold your king." The crowds looked on with contempt and then started to wander away.

"So they know their king," said Lugard, and presented Kyebambe, dressed in simple trousers, known as *Balinkekaho*, a simple cotton shirt with a piece of material tied on his shoulder like a Roman toga, and a cloth tied round his head like a turban.

"Behold your king," he said. Immediately, the crowds broke into a dance and started to play on their *Obuhulere* (seed flutes), singing, "*Niye, yenka Omwingane wa Kasagama Kajwerire Orutege*," meaning "Truly he is his father's son." From then on, Kyebambe was also known throughout Toro as Kasagama.

At a place nicknamed "*Ekyakapere*" ("of the captain"), the expeditionary force met the first resistance from Kabelega's troops, which had been strategically placed to guard the salt lake. "*Isansa*" (the nickname given to Lugard's machine gun by the Batoro because of the sound it made when operated) successfully routed Kabalega's troops, which were driven off to the mountains. The last battle was at Muhokya, on a beautiful hill where in 1944 a holiday camp was built. My parents camped here in 1945, and Patrick was conceived, hence his nickname "*Rwamuhokya*" ("of Muhokya").

However, the victory was to turn sour. Lugard drew up a treaty in which Kyebambe was forced to cede his sovereign rights to the BEAC and to agree that the company should take over the ivory and salt trades. Nonetheless, Kyebambe's return to Toro was regarded by the Batoro as nothing short of a miracle, and rejoicing accordingly, thousands thronged the streets of the capital, Kabarole.

The future of the kingdom still rested on a knife edge, but that day, the people only saw their triumph.

As I faced my own future, I envied their certainty. I had come such a long way, but I knew that there would be enormous challenges ahead.

3

At Cambridge

With Mrs. Schofield and Nanka I drove from Melksham across England to Cambridge, the city of cloistered palaces, of the Great Courts of Trinity, of glorious resonant King's, of studious St. John's, of the quiet timeless meadows, until we arrived at last at Girton, an imposing Victorian fortress of red brick, fit to imprison virgins of scholastic intent and make them into ladies if not matrons!

We went straight to the Porter's Lodge, to be directed to Mrs. Lindsay, my prospective director of studies. The porter, an elderly silver-haired man with a huge nose, spoke to us through a peephole. That afternoon and indeed for the three years I was at Girton, all I ever saw of him was his head and shoulders—perhaps that is all there was. His name was Andrews and he was a man of great character (he had to be, as the only man in our nunnery). He never turned a blind eye to anything we did, and made us sign in and out, just in case any other man tried to trespass on his charges. "Don't be late, Princess Bagaaya," he would say in stern tones as I went off to yet another social engagement.

Through the long, chilly, ill-lit corridors of learning we made our way to Mrs. Lindsay. She received us in her stern room with restrained civility. With her was my supervisor, a quiet, shy lady called Miss Chibnall. Both women had their hair brushed back and tied in buns. Mrs. Schofield read a long message from my father as to how he saw my future role in Toro and what training he wished me to receive. "The princess will be like Plato's Philosopher King" was Miss Chibnall's gaunt reply. Fortunately, I was not so lacking in feeling as the philosopher kings were expected to be and at least I existed, which they never did. But the phrase and the concept captured my imagination and inspired me. It seemed somehow to crystallize my purpose in being at Cambridge. I would be the perfect ruler. My studies of law, history, and political science were all directed to one end—to mold the power and influence I would wield as the princess royal of Toro.

When our meeting came to an end, Mrs. Lindsay presented me, as all freshwomen were, with a little book of instructions on how to be a Girtonian, one of which was "Never refuse the homage of a kiss." (I never have.) I spent the evening rearranging my room and placing my pictures and other belongings.

Three years later my godmother, Mrs. Mary Stuart, wife of the head of Uganda's Anglican church, came to visit me. She herself was an old Girtonian. She burst into my room aflame with excitement. "How most extraordinary! This was my room fifty years ago."

The academic life of the university began two days after I got there. The founders of Girton had built the college in 1873 four miles from the city center, so our happy band of first-year historians set off to our first lecture on the bus.

As I walked through the quadrangles and courts and cloisters of the ancient colleges, I felt uplifted to a higher plane of existence. This was the moment of my awakening; I now belonged to the venerable University of Cambridge, and it belonged to me. Six centuries of unbroken learning and philosophy, six centuries of protecting and nurturing freedom of action and thought: this was my inheritance. I was a child in the cradle of ideas where some of the greatest thoughts of men have been formulated since the sixteenth century, when the university was the center of the Protestant reformation, and the philosopher Erasmus, a fellow of Queen's, was burned to death on the orders of the Catholic Queen Mary. I felt that I walked with the shades of great Cambridge men such as Cromwell of Sidney Sussex, Pepys of Magdalene, the dashing, irresistibly eloquent younger Pitt of Pembroke, Milton, Wordsworth, and Tennyson, and William Wilberforce, who had emancipated the black slave and initiated the process which brought me to Cambridge. I was at the university of Francis Bacon and Bertrand Russell of Trinity, and her other sons Lords Macaulay and Acton, who made history a discipline. Alfred Marshall, the father of modern economics, was a son of St. John's, and J. M. Keynes, who had been to King's, gave the Western world the idea of economic management by government.

But Cambridge has probably contributed even more to science than to any of the great arts. Sir Isaac Newton was a fellow of Trinity in the 1660s, and two centuries later Charles Darwin, of Christ's, revolutionized the concepts of evolution and the doctrines of religion with his still controversial classic *The Origin of the Species*. More recently, the master of Trinity, J. J. Thompson, discovered the electron in his work at the Cavendish laboratory, Lord Rutherford split the atom, and Sir James Chadwick discovered the neutron. But perhaps there is one greater achievement: Cambridge is the mother of Harvard University, which was founded by John Harvard, a fellow of Emmanuel in the seventeenth century.

However, it was not just the inheritance of the creators of Western thought and energy which so moved me as an African; I was the beneficiary of contemporary genius as well—G. R. Elton, the leading authority on Tudor history, was my lecturer on constitutional history; Pevsner, the Slade professor and most distinguished art historian, lectured me on history of art; Rossiter on American history; E. M. Forster and F. R. Leavis on English; and Holland and Epstein on law and political science. Here was I, an African with such a different inheritance, privileged to share the best minds of contemporary British thought with friends who were to go so far in our own generation: David Owen, Britain's youngest foreign secretary, David Frost in television, Germaine Greer, feminist author of *The Female Eunuch*, and Leon Brittan, home secretary in Mrs. Thatcher's government, who was to handle all my ten libel actions against the international press with brilliance and success.

I soon became a member of a very lively social club with all its eccentricity and triviality. Idleness went hand in hand with the energies of rowing, theater, and elegant dinners, drinking, sophisticated coffee and tea parties, balls, debates, hunting, horse racing, dining clubs, and politics: all vied for our attention and allegiance. To make the most of Cambridge, one must sup from its *gravitas* and its *levitas* in such proportion as suits your spirit, for both are part of its special and formative experience. To overdo *gravitas*, one loses half its message; to overdo *levitas* may lead to the catastrophe of being sent down—and to disgrace and a sense of failure and, no doubt, cynical resentment as well. I enjoyed my full share of both and think I got the balance right.

I was thoroughly spoiled. In my first year I was escorted by one of Cambridge's leading socialites, Eben Hamilton, a tall, handsome, wealthy, sophisticated, and amusing Scot. He had rooms in the Great Court of Trinity where he entertained lavishly the rich and the beautiful. I was not rich. Nonetheless, my wardrobe had undergone a dramatic metamorphosis from the dull clothes befitting a missionary's daughter ordained by Mrs. Schofield to the model gowns of the great fashion houses of Paris. Eben's car would sweep into the forecourt of Girton and I would sail off on his arm to the Pitt Club or Grantchester Meadows, the envy of my fellow students.

In my second year my escort was Alistair Hamilton, who was at King's. The son of the publisher Hamish Hamilton, he was half Italian and introduced me to the wonders of Italy when we visited Rome, Florence, Venice, Pisa, and Milan.

I also had a royal escort—Prince William of Gloucester, who came up to Magdalene. Wherever we went, everyone recognized him because he looked exactly like his father and his uncles, King George VI, Windsor, and Kent, at the same age. Instead of a bicycle or car, he had a private plane. King Juan Carlos and Queen Sophie of Spain and Princess Irene of Greece came to see him at Cambridge, and we all spent an hilarious day together. We had a superb lunch in Prince William's rooms and then danced through the streets to the cinema, where Juan Carlos threw sweets from the circle to the stalls, despite pleas from Sophie not to do so. Mercifully, being a Cambridge audience, they were amused. Even more mercifully, there was no zealous journalist there to run high jinks into scandal. (I was not always so lucky.

When I attended Prince William's twenty-first birthday at St. James's Palace, the press published a photograph of me leaving—with every possible innuendo of wrong.)

When Prince William went down, he entered the diplomatic service and was posted to Nigeria, where he was able to indulge the deep interest in African culture we had so often discussed. He dedicated himself to the different cultures of other peoples and other lands, and his death later in an airplane crash deprived the Commonwealth and Africa of a valuable resource.

The highlight of my public impact at Cambridge was the visit of Jomo Kenyatta and Tom Mboya. I gave a cocktail party and a dinner in their honor in Trinity, attended to capacity by Cambridge society. I wore an Yves St. Laurent dress and led my distinguished guests into dinner. Here, with the sons of the imperial rulers of Kenya and the head of the nationalists, shortly to be president of Kenya, black and white, love and hatred, met head on. The atmosphere was tense until Kenyatta greeted the company with a wave of his fly whisk, the symbol of African monarchical authority. Then he became just another human being, and many people came forward to shake his hand. I remember Kenyatta banging on the table and saying: "We will make English in Kenya what Latin is in England," and indeed Swahili has replaced English as the national language. The will of Africa is always to reassert itself. I was thankful the evening passed without incident, because Kenyatta's presence in London for the Kenyan independence talks had provoked ugly scenes in Park Lane from those who detested the activities of Mau Mau.

But my worries were more often similar to those of the other students. The most ironic episode of all was after the May Ball at King's. I had invited our party back for breakfast in college and we all climbed in evening dress through my friend Judy's window for a hearty breakfast of bacon, eggs, and crumpets. Afterwards, I saw my guests out by the same route. Returning to my room, I found a note from my tutor asking me to report to her immediately. I went shaking and still in my evening dress, and presented myself before her. She stared at me with crushing disapproval. Eventually she spoke. "Princess Bagaaya, could you explain to me why you found it necessary to climb into college at six o'clock this morning when the gates are wide open?" I had forgotten—the May Ball is the only occasion when the college gates are open all night! I bowed my head in exhausted shame and she dismissed me with contempt.

Perhaps the greatest gift of all that Cambridge life confers is its friendships. University is a time of intense emotion and sensitivity for undergraduates, and of storms of conflict and rage. Doubts are expressed as bravado, which heightens the doubts and inadequacies of the less assertive. Without true friends, these doubts are hard to bear. I had five special friends: the exquisitely beautiful, mystical Bith-Cam Hynn, from South Vietnam, who was reading economics at Newnham; Elizabeth Cuthbert from Scotland, reading history at Girton; my brilliant Irish friend Joan O'Connell, a true-blue academic who was also reading economics at Newnham; the elegant and generous Judy Burch, reading medicine at Girton; and Sue Landon from Sweden, reading natural sciences at Girton.

Outwardly, I looked supremely self-confident, even arrogant, for I was in great demand. Inwardly, though, many battles raged. The permissive society with its "free love" was in full swing in the sixties. Was it right to indulge; was it cruel to refuse? I had to remind myself that I was in a sense public property, a symbol of my country and my culture. My life was not properly my own, so while others could afford to indulge and to let themselves go, I could not. So I stoically denied myself any sexual activity or emotional involvement with any man, leaving Cambridge a virgin, and it was to my five true friends that I turned whenever I felt the situation was getting me down.

We would spend hours together in The Whim (an eating house in Trinity Street popular with undergraduates—now a hamburger joint!) or in our rooms talking. Through hours of animated conversation and heated argument we were able to test and form our ideas and develop that great Cambridge tradition, the art of tolerance.

Years later, I was staying with Bess Cuthbert's parents at Killearn in Stirlingshire, Scotland, when we were invited to the Highland Ball in Edinburgh. As Edinburgh was a long way from Killearn, Elizabeth and I had to spend the night in the Waverley Hotel. The night porter, who had watched Bess and me come and go, and seeing how close we were to one another, said, "Excuse me, are you two sisters?" We burst out laughing and said, "Yes, we are." That is how close we all are to one another. Time and separation make no difference. I often ponder the universal paradox posed by E. M. Forster: "If I had to choose between betraying my country and betraying my friend, I hope I would have the guts to betray my country." God forbid that I ever have to make that choice.

In July 1962 my father, looking majestic in tails and a top hat, arrived in Cambridge, having traveled from Toro to see me graduate. He watched the ceremony in the Senate House and afterwards I took him and the royal entourage on a tour of Cambridge, which was looking breathtakingly beautiful in the blazing sun. My father loved the traditions and beauty of the colleges. But he took me by surprise when he not only obliged me by having coffee in The Whim, but seemed greatly amused by it. He must have been the first and last ruling monarch to do so!

After the ceremony we returned to London and went straight to the Uganda High Commission in Trafalgar Square. Andrew Adimola, then head of the mission, congratulated my father on my success. My father turned to him and pronounced: "When my daughter is called to the bar, she will be the first woman barrister not only in Uganda but in the whole of east and central Africa." The words left me aghast—it was a challenge which I had to meet, for I could not disappoint my father or betray his dream. I was called to the English bar in November 1965. This time my father was not present, but I telephoned him and he was thrilled. He advised me that before I returned to Uganda I should do a year's pupilage in the chambers of Sir Dingle Foot, whom he had already approached with success.

I decided to celebrate by throwing a gala party. On December 20, 1965, hundreds of friends and acquaintances flocked to the Royal Commonwealth Society, a private club in an old mansion in London's elegant Trafalgar Square. Dressed in a pink silk Guy Larouche gown that contrasted with my dark skin and eyes, I felt as if I were floating through the old halls. Amidst sweeping staircases and ornate crystal chandeliers, I welcomed my guests, who were announced as they stepped gingerly from their limousines and fancy cars. Waiters in tails sailed through, balancing trays of hors d'oeuvres, while champagne and chatter flowed freely. But it was after the party that the real fun began. My family and immediate circle of close friends whisked me off to a nightclub, where we danced away into the early hours of the morning. We loved to dance and take part in the London nightlife. Everywhere we went, the Beatles seemed to accompany us; "I Want to Hold Your Hand" blared from the taxi radio, and we sang backup as the city flew by us and we made our way to the nightclub.

I lived with my sisters Mabel and Gertrude and my cousin Angeline, who were studying to be secretaries. Our apartment was in Beauchamp Place in Knightsbridge, a very fashionable part of London. What it didn't have was central heating, and some mornings I woke up convinced my toes were frostbitten. Small as it was it had become a nerve center for our crowd, the place where our friends gathered, dropping in at all hours of the day and night. There was always somebody camped out on the couch, en route to Africa or the United States.

After my celebration, we finally arrived home, exhausted and happy. I got out of my party clothes and into bed, drifting off quickly. But a few hours later, at 7:00 A.M., the phone jolted me from a deep sleep. I stumbled out to the sitting room to answer it. Timothy Bazarrabusa, the Ugandan high commissioner, was brusque and brief. "Akiiki, *amata gatikire*" ("The milk is spilled"). This message could mean only one thing: my father, the king of Toro, was dead.

A king's death was so tragic, so traumatic, that historically the messenger bearing the news was sometimes killed. Luckily, as time passed, a method for passing the news with less drastic results evolved: a servant would climb on the roof of the palace's main house and spill milk over the side. While deeply saddened by the high commissioner's call, I was not surprised, as I had strongly suspected my father's death was imminent. He was not a sick man but, from 1964 on, the intrigues of party politics had so disillusioned him that he had lost the will to live. In the tradition of the Kitara kings, he resolved to die rather than acquiesce in the disrespect which arises from lack of patriotism—and to die not by poison, as ancient custom demanded, but by force of will. My primary concern was that he had gone peacefully and honorably; and the high commissioner assured me he had died quietly in his sleep.

I hung up the phone and hurried into the bedroom where my sister

Gertrude and my cousin Angeline were sleeping. "You better wake up," I said, shaking them both. "Wake up, Daddy is gone."

Angeline became uncontrollable. Gertrude just sat there on the edge of the bed. "You see, we told him. Now look what he's done to us."

My sister Mabel, who had already gone off to work, happened to call from her nearby office. When I gave her the news, the phone dropped from her hand as she collapsed to the floor. She was brought home from the office, shaking and disoriented. I knew that I couldn't fall apart like the others. My father had counted on me to make the transition as smooth as possible for Patrick, and I had to be firm. I immediately began throwing things into my suitcases, and booked myself on the next flight out of Heathrow. Gathering my luggage, I said good-bye to my sisters and cousin. As I turned to leave, Mabel stopped crying and said, "Elizabeth, *you* have to be strong."

Aboard the plane I recalled the last time I had seen my father. Fifteen months earlier, in 1964, during the hot, steamy summer, he had come to London for a medical checkup. At the time, I was studying for exams. I adored him and always looked forward to his arrival. I also enjoyed his visits because with him came the nice meals, the comfortable transport, and the days spent sight-seeing instead of studying. One afternoon we went for a walk in the garden of Beaulieu, the stately home of Lord Edward Montague. I took my father's arm as we walked in the hot sunshine and said softly, "Daddy, you know you have not much time to live?"

"How do you know?" he asked, his voice listless and remote.

"I have been too close to you not to know how you feel," I answered.

4

The Kingdom
by the Mountains
of the Moon

It is a great temptation to romanticize an earlier era of one's life, as memory is tricked by time and by the amazing twists and turns of surviving to tell the story. But the texture, the essence, remains, and is sometimes even stronger many years later.

Daily life for a royal child was governed by a strict routine. It was like an endless play, with each day having its set acts and scenes. At seven o'clock each morning, Rwaheru would sound the dawn bugle and Kisurrumi, the chief drummer, would beat his drum for reveille. As I opened my eyes, the rugged snow-capped Mountains of the Moon* greeted me majestically. But like the other princes and princesses, I needed no encouragement to meet the new day. We leapt from our beds and gathered with the whole family for morning prayers in the Court House. We took turns leading the prayers, and it was a sin of great magnitude to argue about whose turn it was.

After prayers we ran round the front veranda and down the long staircase out of the Court House to the little house where our nannies waited to wash and dress us in our clean clothes and oversee the breakfast of milk before our two-mile run to school.

At eight o'clock each morning, we would leave the Palace by way of the sacred huts and go down the steep grassy hill to the boundary of the palace grounds. Here all the royal children and their friends, about twenty-five of us, met up. If any were missing, we would leave a branch to signify our departure. On the long walk, we shared our hidden goodies of maize, cakes, even pudding, secreted away in bras, sleeves, and pockets. Gradually, the procession would wind up the hill, past Mrs. Davis's handicraft center, to the church where the boys and girls went their separate ways.

The school day would begin with the gathering of litter and leaves from the central compound. Each group of children, under a leader, would be assigned an area to clear, and then we had prayers followed by the morning's lessons. At midday in Toro the rain clouds gather, signaling the end of morning school. Often, heavy rain and hail would compel us to take shelter on our way home for lunch, but usually we sauntered back along the same two-mile route.

When the king was at home, we set off immediately to see him in the royal enclosure.

We were strictly forbidden to look through windows of the royal enclosure, so instead we had to adopt the almost equally unpleasant habit of listening at doors. Then, a timid knock—and if he murmured "Yes," we would announce our names, enter his presence, and kneel before him. If he was busy, we would wait there on our knees. As he turned, each child touched his forehead and chin with the tips of both forefingers, and bade him good morning. Afterwards, the child would retreat walking backwards and sit on the floor till all had greeted the king.

Lunch followed, under the stern command of the headwaiter and the head cook. The head cook insisted that the royal children salute him as well as kneel to greet him. Under threat that I would never leave the dining room alive if I didn't eat all the food set before me, I would sit for hours gazing at the never-diminishing mound of food, while Muniga, a nickname I gave him meaning "hangman," watched. However much I chewed, the food seemed everlasting, and however much I cried, Muniga would never relent.

The tortures of lunch were followed by the boredom of siesta—two hours of lying awake in silence and wishing we could be outside playing.

By two o'clock the sun was usually shining again and we walked back to school. The afternoon was always more fun than the morning. As Girl Scout Brownies, we fetched wood and water for the elderly, swept out their homes or did their cooking, and visited the sick—at 3:45 P.M. school ended and we walked back home. So, four times a day, we would walk the two miles to and from school. My father had issued strict orders regarding our education. Henceforth, we were not to be chaperoned to school. Only torrential rain could justify our being driven there by car. No child could feign illness or any other excuse, for absence required express permission from the king, which was hard to obtain.

However, with the sounding of the bugle in the ceremony of lowering the Toro flag at four o'clock, the fun could begin again.

The procession of the Royal Spear, *Kaitantahi*, was a magical and awesome event for us children. Kaitantahi stood by day in the courtyard of *Kyamununua*, the hut of the princes, and at night it went from the second of the seven huts of the Sacred Guild to the throne room. The procession consisted of four men led by the bearer of the Royal Spear, who recited the historical events of Toro while the chorus of three men chanted in reply. All the men who saw the great spear stood to attention in silence, and all the women knelt before this symbol of power.

After the ceremony of the Royal Spear, we were left to play. We played the sort of games that are familiar to children everywhere—board games, cards, tennis, football, high jump, hide-and-seek, skipping and hopping, sliding on banana skins.

We were called indoors at sunset, as it usually grew quite chilly in Kabarole, where the palace was situated 6,000 feet above sea level. Between play and bedtime came a spendid interlude when family, relatives, and servants gathered to trade gossip, sing songs, and tell tales of the great empire Kitara, of which Toro was once a part.

Above all, it was a time when we could be with our parents, normally so busy and distant.

Our father, George David Matthew Kamurasi Rukiidi III, had five wives but was nevertheless a Christian. King of Toro from 1924 to 1965, he was a good king to his people, who looked on him with love and reverence, for kingship in Africa is, as it once was in Europe, divine.

A giant of a man with an imposing manner which added to the sense of mystery and enchantment surrounding all royal occasions, he was also humble and generous, deeply interested in his people's traditions and concerned for each of his subjects. His sense of observation was acute and his memory meticulous. He was devoted to his children. We stood in great awe of him and were taught always to kneel before him, and even before his servants.

All my co-mothers lived in harmony and affectionate agreement, though of course each had her own home. My mother was the legal wife, and only she lived in the royal palace.

Queen Kezia Byanjeru, my mother, is a woman of great culture, with a gift for music and the recitation of poetry. Above all, she is a wonderful conversationalist, with a vast store of folk tales, riddles, and anecdotes. Every minute spent in her company was a joy— especially for those who were privileged to join in her séances.

Apart from the Court House and the seven houses of the Sacred Guild, the most important house was *Rwengo*, where my mother entertained and sometimes slept.

In Rwengo my mother would be seated on a platform made of cement and covered in the skins of lion, leopard, and white cow. Other royals would be invited to sit on the platform with her, while the most senior male royal would be offered the dignity of a chair. Lesser mortals, children and servants, would sit below the platform, in a pyramid of rank.

Sometimes she would play her harp and go on to teach the children how to play it, sometimes traditional poetry would take precedence, followed by animated conversation and much laughter. We always seemed to be laughing and happy.

Sometimes we would go on a tour of some of the many houses in the royal compound. The princes entertained in *Kacwabwemi*, and the princesses in *Kabagarama*. The lesser ladies of the royal court, the aunts and the little queen mother, entertained in the house known as *Bwikya*.

But always, with a nanny clasping one hand, the other gripping a lantern, we would set off in the dark toward the Court House to say our good-nights.

The Court House was two stories high, a very un-African structure designed for my grandfather by the Reverend Maddox. It still stands on Kabarole Hill, reduced to ruins by the tyranny of Milton Obote and Idi Amin.

In the evenings my father sat in the front room on his throne, which was placed among nine drums. It was made of a solid block of African wood, carved so that the canopy and seat were united by eight columns. It was decorated with copper and iron and covered with lion, leopard, and cow skins. The king's throne was guarded round the clock by the faithful guard, Masa Omukona, and two women. In front of the door lay a giant elephant tusk over which only the king was allowed to step.

The room was usually crowded with family members, servants, chiefs, and peasants—each having as much right as the next person to an audience with the king, regardless of rank. He sat sucking on his pipe and gazing at the ceiling, seemingly deep in thought, almost trancelike. Occasionally he would speak and someone would answer. But the atmosphere was not always tense. My father laughed often, sometimes so hard his laughter would reverberate around the compound.

As children, we were not encouraged to speak except to ask questions about the history of the tribe. Otherwise, we sat quietly next to the two lion cubs, which attended until they became too big and were removed to the national park. I hated these cats. They frightened me, but I endured them in order to remain present. I hid my fear from my father because animals were very much a part of the court, and nobody was permitted openly to abuse or even dislike them. There was an ancient Toro tradition that no one could even raise his voice at the animals, except the king when emphasizing a command.

My father's dogs, Karoo and Askari, were particularly revered. They were loyal to those who treated them well but wicked to those who crossed them. One day a wife of the king's father emptied a basin of water over the pair, earning herself perpetual harassment. They tore to shreds the frail woman's clothes that were hanging on the washing line, and, finally, the king granted her request to build a house for her outside the palace.

Our day ended when the bugle sounded at nine o'clock. The elders stayed up to listen to the BBC World Service, while one by one we solemnly knelt before our father, said good night, and then walked backwards out of the room, our backs never to the king.

I cherished these rituals. In their wisdom, the elders understood our childish comfort in strict routines and the indelible value of learning the lore of our culture by heart. I listened—and I remembered. In fact, my earliest and strongest memories are of the poetic songs that embody the history of our dynasties.

At one time, the empire had stretched beyond the boundaries of present Uganda—to Mboga and Bulega in Zaire; to Karagwe, Buziba, and Buhaya in Tanzania; Wkavirondo in Kenya; and to Ruanda and Burundi. Its people were called "Abanyakitara"—believers in *Engabu* (shield) and *Icumu* (spear).

The empire was ruled by three dynasties; first, the Abatembuzi; then, the Abacwezi, of whom the great Iron Age site of Mugenyi in Mubende district is a relic (they were of Hamitic stock, which meant their culture was centered round cattle); and last, the Babito, descendants of the Bacwezi and of whom I myself am a descendant.

In the fifteenth century the empire disintegrated as regions broke away to form separate kingdoms: Ruanda, Burundi, Buganda, Ankole, and Bunyoro—of which Toro was a part. These became independent nations—for a nation is an entity defined not so much by boundaries as by feelings and shared traditions which are built up over the years until they become living history.

The creation of Toro as an independent state came about at the end of the eighteenth century when Kaboyo, the eldest son of Kyebambe III Nyamutukura, the king of Bunyoro, led a rebellion against his father. Kaboyo was the favorite, but he had a mischievous and defiant nature and was forever tormenting his younger brothers. The *Omukama* (king) used to consult oracles on behalf of all his children to try to find out what sort of men they would become. But Kaboyo was clever and, in order to conceal his rebellious intent, he always gave a specimen of someone else's saliva, not his own, as the oracles required.

One day the children's grandmother invited them to a feast, and each of them was asked to recite a poem for her amusement. Kaboyo's poem struck her as being particularly insurrectionary, and she was so worried that she summoned Nyamutukura to hide behind a fence and listen while the princes repeated their poems. Two days later the king was concerned enough to call a meeting of elders and kinsmen to discuss the meaning of Kaboyo's poem. The general feeling was that Kaboyo was dangerous and that he would have no difficulty in disposing of his brothers if his father were to die. The king was too fond of his eldest son to arrest him, but eventually the elders convinced him that he should separate Kaboyo from his brothers to avoid confusion in the event of a controversy over the succession. It was suggested that he be declared *Omugurusi wa hairembo* ("an old man of the entrance"), which would place him above the other princes during his father's lifetime, but which would disqualify him from competing for the throne thereafter. This would secure the safety of the other princes. The king acted on the elders' advice and Kaboyo was made to grow a tuft of hair to be adorned with beads, which confirmed his exclusion from a contest for the throne. Kaboyo was very annoyed and began to plan his rebellion.

As the eldest son, the dukedoms of Mwenge and Bunyangabu were Kaboyo's and, soon after his disqualification, he was sent to these areas to collect taxes of cattle and salt. There the people gave him a rousing welcome, and he contracted with the chiefs to return and lead a rebellion against his two aunts, the Princesses Mpanja and Batebe, who ruled over the two provinces as representatives of the king. The king's sisters reported their nephew's plans, but Nyamutukura refused to believe them.

Kaboyo tried everything he could to persuade his father to let him stay in Mwenge. First, he said he wanted to be there to defend his property in the event of a Baganda invasion, but his plea was rejected because Nyamutukura said that as king he would be the first to hear of such an invasion. Next Kaboyo, who had married a woman from Mwenge, told his father that his wife had just given birth to twins and that he was anxious to go and perform the customary twin ceremony. This time permission was granted and Kaboyo left, accompanied by many personal friends and by royal trumpets and drums provided by his father. Before he went, he sent the king a puppy, asking him to select a name for it. When his father declined to do so, Kaboyo named it *"Lyabaira,"* meaning "It is time" or "Long overdue." . . .

When he arrived in Mwenge, Kaboyo found that his wife had given birth to a boy, whom he called *"Barongo,"* literally translated as "Twins," because he said, "I cannot lie to my father." Kaboyo then cut off his tuft of hair and sent it with the beads to Nyamutukura. In this way, his father and everyone else knew that Kaboyo had seceded.

When King Nyamutukura heard of his son's secession, he summoned a meeting of the chiefs, who advised him to send an army to quash the rebellion. As the king was too weak physically to lead the army, he was carried on a stretcher. A fierce battle was fought at Mandaku near Kazingo in Burahya, a county of Toro. The Toro army inflicted a heavy defeat on the Banyoro. Nyamutukura was twice injured in the arms. Many leading Banyoro did not survive, including Prince Kahaibale, Chief Igisi of Buziba, Chief Dwangu of Buyanja, and Chief Wamara of Kihukya. Mugema was injured in the eye. The Banyoro forces were dispersed, and Nyamutukura was isolated.

Though victorious, Kaboyo still loved his father and sent his ambassador Kitota to assemble together the scattered Banyoro at Kamengo. He sent a detachment of men to carry his father from Kijanju to Kamengo, and he even provided milk cows for the duration of his father's stay in Toro until Nyamutukura could be taken back, unharmed, to his palace in Bunyoro.

Meanwhile, the neighboring Baganda took advantage of Bunyoro's weakness and invaded. Nyamutukura fled to an island on Lake Albert. When Prince Mugenyi (the next in line to the throne) heard of his father's plight, he went to him and urged him to make peace with Kaboyo so that together they might drive out the Baganda. Nyamutukura accepted Mugenyi's advice, praised Kaboyo for having been a good son—even in revolt—and sent him a royal drum as a gesture of recognition, with the message: "I did not realize that all the good things you did were destined to lead to disaster."

The king grew too old to conduct affairs of state and eventually, enfeebled, was unable to drive the Baganda beyond the Kafu River. Before his death around 1800, he called upon Kaboyo to come home and succeed, but Kaboyo refused. "Let others succeed you. I am content with this kingdom," he replied.

As children, we were constantly reminded that we were heirs to the Kitara Empire. All year round, we would count the days, weeks, and months as we waited for the one event around which our lives largely revolved: the anniversary of my father's coronation on January 29, 1924. Other events such as Christmas and Easter—so important to Europeans—made only fleeting impressions on us. When the anniversary of the coronation arrived, we were released from our normal routine altogether.

The architect, and overseer of the works during my father's time, was called Rwabuhesi. He was a man of the most extraordinary energy, dashing around the palace courtyards like lightning.

January is the hottest month in Toro. Yet the workmen never seemed to be deterred by the heat and always worked at full speed. Their chattering and laughter, together with the enthusiasm of their leader, must have acted as a driving force. They normally completed their work in about three weeks, repairing the grass roofs of the sacred huts and other houses in the enclosure, cutting grass in the compounds, digging paths, and doing whatever was necessary to prepare the palace for the great occasion.

My mother, together with a large group of women including some of the princesses, members of the royal clan, and the women who attended to the throne and regalia, would gather every day to inspect and if necessary repair various items. They worked in a grass-thatched hut, built in the shape of an archway, without doors, that was specially designed for the purpose. The floor on which they sat was carpeted with *Obugara*—fresh lemon grass. We were allowed to join them to watch the work and listen to their conversation. Above all, we looked forward to joining the women on the day they aired and cleaned the royal crowns (all the royal regalia was surrounded by an aura of secrecy and mystery).

Meanwhile, the whole of Toro went on a shopping spree, and the shops in Kabarole were suddenly packed with people from near and far. The noise of the sewing machines on every veranda trebled, and the town was full of local gossip as to who was buying what, while everyone was at pains to avoid buying what another might have chosen to wear.

It was in fact easy to know what people were buying in the thirty shops of Toro's capital, all of which were owned and run by Asian traders. If you wanted a dress, you went into the shop and asked the trader, by pointing with your finger, to bring down the material you wished to inspect. With his measuring rod he would get it down from the wooden shelves, and heated and prolonged bargaining would ensue. You never bought anything straight away; you shopped around, along with everyone else. When at last you had completed a purchase, the dress would be made up that same day, on the veranda of the shop, and you sat on the cement floor or on a bench until it was ready.

Very few people could afford to patronize the shops in the capital of Uganda, Kampala, although there was far more variety. I recall that many of our relatives could not afford anything new, and indeed possessed hardly any clothes suitable for the forthcoming grand occasion. For this reason, a lot of borrowing went on. My mother always lent dresses, hats, gloves, blouses, and skirts to our relatives, and often never saw them again. Many families in Toro did the same. My father must have been just about the only person who didn't lend his clothes—not because he was the king, but because very few people could match his gigantic size and fit into his clothes!

By about January 25, the shopping sprees would have finished and the workmen would have completed their repairs. They would then return to their homes, some of them long distances away.

There would now follow a period of calm—except for my father, who would be spending longer hours in his office, working on his address to the nation. To help him there was Ezira Musozi, a man who was both court jester and a brilliant speech writer, and whose command of English has yet to be matched by any other Mutoro I know. He was brought up by my great-grandmother, Queen Mother Victoria—he belonged to her clan, the Ababopi—and later on he served as a page at my grandfather's court. He was well versed in Toro's history and, when he decided not to drink, the preparation of speeches went extremely well! But the fact that he helped my father with his annual address had to be kept secret; he had to be protected from the colonial authorities, in case any aspects of the address were controversial.

Musozi became a close companion of my brother Patrick when he became king, and he helped Patrick to write his first address to the Toro people on his coronation day in March 1966. We were deprived of this irreplaceable friend when, in 1966, a madman speared him to death. His exceptionally noble wife was narrowly saved from a like fate.

As soon as my father was ready with his speech, the prime minister, the finance minister, and the chief justice met him, and between them they agreed on the final version. Also to the palace came the Church leaders, the bishop and others, to work out how the church service should be conducted. Finally, my father had to decide whom to invite to his garden party and the banquet. These two events were the only nontraditional ones, and they were mainly for the European residents in Uganda, civil servants and professional people from the Toro hospitals and schools.

Then suddenly we knew, without anyone telling us, that it was no longer a matter of weeks or even days but only hours before we would be awakened in the early hours of the morning, not by the usual bugle but by the sound of flute players. At cock crow on January 29, these players would arouse my father with their music, the signal that the nine days' festivities had truly begun, and the cry *"Hurra Omukama, yahasuka"* ("Take heed, the king is awakening from sleep") would announce the fact to everyone.

Nothing can show more clearly the nature and role of the monarchy than the ceremonies which would now take place, each one symbolizing a function of the king and the concept of the monarchy. In these rituals were embodied the entire civilization and culture of a people.

As soon as my father was awake, an attendant led him to the royal bathroom, *Omulyambukiro*, and there was total silence everywhere.

When he had finished bathing, my mother brought the royal amulets and ornaments for his neck, wrists, and legs. A variety of barkcloths* or robes was also brought, from which the king made his choice of apparel, and he then proceeded to the milking ceremony.

The milking ceremony was such a significant ritual that it should be described in some detail. My father carried it out meticulously during the annual coronation festivities, and at certain other times throughout the year. The ceremony, known as *Enkorogi,* was based on the pastoral background of our country and formed one of the sacred duties of our kings. My father, like his immediate predecessors, kept only about twenty cows in the capital. The men who saw to them had to be prepared by purification. There were special houses for them in the kraal opposite the main entrance of the royal enclosure. They were engaged on this important duty for a month at a time, during which they had to be very particular in their speech and behavior. In all the years I knew them, I never heard them say anything profane or abusive. It was striking to see how they maintained an atmosphere of serenity and calm, so that to be in their company was like being in a world of total peace. They came on duty fasting and they had to have their faces, chests, hands, and arms whitened with clay. So rigid were the taboos they observed that they were on duty for only two days at a time, and took turns to relieve one another. Some of my father's wives and sisters, purified and whitened like the herdsmen, took part in the milking ceremony as milkmaids.

The proceedings began with the cows being driven up the hill from the kraal and into the royal enclosure, to the courtyard in front of the Court House. There had to be complete silence while this was done, the only sound you heard came from the cattle themselves. You were not allowed even to cough or to clear your throat.

The king's wives and the princesses brought the milk pots and placed them in the correct positions. My father then seated himself on the throne. A mat of newly cut grass had been spread outside and in front of the throne room doorway. The two cows which were to provide my father's meal were brought forward, and two of the ladies also came forward. One cow was led on to the grass mat and its calf,

* The making of barkcloth is a dying art. Bark is taken from a tree called *Omutoma* and is pressed and pummeled into a strong clothlike fabric.

which had been tied up in the courtyard, was encouraged to go to its mother and suck till the milk flowed freely. Then the calf was pulled away and held before the cow while one of the herdsmen cleaned the udder. The cow's legs were secured with a thong so that she couldn't whisk dust into the milk. A milkmaid poured water over the hands of the *Omukorogi*, the man who was to milk the cow, and he would hold his hands high as if in prayer. Next, he squatted at the right-hand side of the cow and one of his colleagues folded his garments under him, to get them out of his way (after the washing of his hands he was not permitted to touch anything himself), and the milkmaid placed a pot on his knees, leaning sideways as she did so, as he was not supposed to look at her. He would milk as much as he thought necessary into the pot, raise his hands again, and then the pot would be removed by the milkmaid, who lifted it over his shoulder and carried it to the dairy. The cow was released and the calf returned to it, and then the second cow was led forward and the ceremony repeated.

Meanwhile, a process called *Okwitira* had been carried out. This was the sterilizing of the milk pots for the king's meal. They had been washed, dried in the sun, and afterwards fumigated over a pottery furnace in which a particular kind of grass was burned. The milkmaids placed the king's meal on a platform, and then one of them came to him in the throne room and knelt before him to say, "*Oruhangorutabaire*" ("The royal meal is ready"). She would withdraw, and the king would get up and go to the dairy to drink, while the doorkeeper proclaimed: "*Arakakorra, Omukama atabaire*" ("Take heed and be silent, the king is drinking"). And, indeed, there would be absolute silence.

My father sat on the stool covered with nine white cow skins; the stool was called *Kaizirokwera*. He wiped first his hands and then his lips with two special sponges, handed to him by the dairymaid. Beside the stool stood *Kikago*, the small table where the milk pot had been placed. The dairymaid took off the cover, wiped the rim of the pot with a leaf sponge which had been put ready on the lid, and handed the pot to the king. While he drank, she waved a fly whisk and, when he had finished, she handed him the mouth sponge so that he could again wipe his lips before returning to the throne room. The doorkeeper would at this point announce to the expectant court:

"*Omukama Omunsiika arugiremu*" ("The king has returned from the dairy"). The rest of the cows were milked in the kraal and their milk was put aside for the use of the king's children, wives, princesses and princes, and the other people in the palace.

This ceremony was regarded with the greatest reverence and formed one of the strongest links in our country with the past. It would be repeated early in the evening on each day of the coronation festivities.

The serving of the royal meal was another ritual of immense significance, with a sacrificial meaning, so that again there had to be complete silence from everyone in the palace. About one o'clock, my father would come to the throne room, dressed in fresh robes, and when he had taken his seat on the throne, the timekeeper would inform him that the royal meal, *Oruhango*, was ready.

The king then beat once on each of the famous drums, using his special one last of all. The sound of the drums was the signal for the royal cooks, led by the head cook, to enter. Several people shared the duties attached to the office of royal cook, and they too lived in the capital for a month, with duty shifts of two days at a time. These cooks also had to have their faces, chests, arms, and hands whitened with clay.

When they were led from *Kyokya*, where the royal meal was cooked, to the king, they were not allowed to enter the royal enclosure by the main gate but went round to the gate where the sacred cows had been brought in. The head cook carried the two-pronged fork with which to feed the king, and his assistant carried a large basket, called *Kasingo*, in which there was meat and vegetables covered with plantain leaves. On top of this stood a vessel covered with a piece of barkcloth containing the boiled meat for my father. Only the head cook and his assistant could go into the throne room; the others remained outside in the courtyard.

Without any greeting, the head cook would enter and kneel before the king; his assistant took the pot from the basket, placed it beside him, and then moved out of sight (the king's ceremonial meal had to be taken in complete privacy). The cook stuck his fork down into the meat, secured a piece, and put it into my father's mouth (the king was not allowed to touch the meat with his own hands). Four times the head cook repeated this. When my father had eaten the four pieces, the cook covered the vessel and removed it. Though the large basket was uncovered in front of the king, he only looked at the food and did not eat any of it. The cook then went away by the same route he had entered.

While the royal meal was in progress, the bandsmen with drums, flutes, and other wind instruments were on the watch from the top of the mound known as *Omukaswa*, in front of the royal enclosure. People would now start to gather around this mound. Bamuroga, the principal chief and head of the Sacred Guild, would come to my father and say: "You have outlived the moon and your people are a fighting people and rejoice with you. May you conquer." Then my father would come to the door of the throne room and pronounce a blessing on the country, after which he would send word to the *Omusuna*, master of ceremonies, that the band should strike up and the festivities begin.

As soon as the trumpet sounded and drumming started, accompanied by the wind instruments, people flocked to the palace. They came running, drawn from every region of the country. The procession of the royal musicians, joined by hundreds of people, started from the mound and ended in front of the room where my father and members of the royal family were waiting. When the bandsmen were in sight, the princes and princesses would start to dance toward them. Then everyone, the musicians and the crowds, came dancing and pressing forward in front of my father, who was seated on the throne. The royal bands had to play continuously for the nine days of the festivities, except for short intervals when the milking ceremonies, the royal meals, the thanksgiving services, the garden party, and the royal bath were being celebrated. One or two players at a time would retire for food or rest, but the music went on night and day.

On the second day of the celebrations, my father wore the crown of the Sacred Guild. The day started with the royal bath and the milking ceremony, followed by thanksgiving services throughout the kingdom, in which people of all denominations joined. As soon as my father and mother returned from the service, he went to *Omwihundiro*, the room where the crowns were kept. While the crowning was being enacted, huge crowds of people would be assembling, surrounding the sacred huts and lining the route along which the procession would come. Others went to the Parliament hall where the address to the nation would be delivered, and the rest settled anywhere they could find space. Every inch of Kabarole Hill was covered with people on this day.

The gatekeepers got the royal mat ready for the king to walk on during the procession. My father wore the crown, and on his feet the royal shoes, called *Biganja*. Round his ankles there were strings of blue beads, fringed with more beads, and round his neck a string of white cord, made of the same fiber as the crown, from which hung a pair of lion's claws, forming a crescent. When the robing was complete, he left the Court House and proceeded along the strip of matting from the door of the throne room to that of the first sacred hut, *Mucwa*, the queen's reception room. No one but the king and the royal flute players might walk upon this mat, and it was rolled up again as soon as they had passed.

Preceded by the flute players, the king would go in procession from the queen's reception room through the seven sacred huts. When my mother heard the flutes and knew that my father was approaching, she rose from her throne and took her place at the head of the line of princesses and her sisters. Starting with my mother, each one of them greeted my father by placing the tips of the fingers of her right hand on his shoulder and, with a special movement of the palm, on his arm, between shoulder and elbow. This was done in silence, and my father would move on without a sign. While he was going through the huts, the crowds went round them and through the gates in the fences to join him in each courtyard. Mats like the one that had been spread from the throne room door were unrolled across each courtyard, to be rolled up again when he had passed through.

Children of the reigning monarch were not allowed inside any of the sacred huts, so we pressed forward with the crowds. I did once stealthily enter my mother's hut, but I did it so clumsily that my Aunt Geraldine saw me and ordered me out at once!

The seventh courtyard, *Omurugo*, was even more sacred than the others. Here the king would come on all special occasions. Attached to the fence of this courtyard was a canopy under which my father stood, on rugs. The chiefs, robed and crowned, stood on either side of him. They all spent ten to fifteen minutes here, the presence of the king signifying that he was accepted as king by the chiefs, as he had been accepted before by population acclamation. It was here also that my father would try a few cases, symbolically. The accused, awaiting sentence, were brought forward one by one supported by *Omwigazi*, the bearer of the king's staff. If my father let the man kiss his hands, it meant that that man was pardoned, but if my father withheld his hands, the accused man knew that judgment had been given against him, and that he might expect death—still only symbolically, of course.

At this stage, three cows were brought to the king, who stood and watched them for a short while as though he were herding them. Then he made his way to Toro Parliament, where, in the presence of the governor, Her Majesty the Queen's representative, he delivered his address to the people. He then returned to the Court House, going through the seven huts, and resting on the way in the third or fourth court, accompanied as usual by the royal musicians. After the ceremonial meal, he retired until the evening milking ceremony at about five o'clock.

At about six o'clock, when the sun was setting, music and dancing would be resumed in front of the throne room. More crowds would gather and, from time to time, my father would appear before them and sit on the throne to watch the dancing. At intervals he would go to another room to be greeted by members of the royal family. This was when my mother came to pay him an official visit. After her scepter, the symbol of her authority, had been brought in and her rug spread out, she would discuss any special business with him. About ten o'clock, my father would get up to go to the throne room, followed by my mother, who took precedence over the princes, princesses, and chiefs.

My father once more seated himself on the throne, with my mother on her throne on his left. On his right sat Musuga, the head of the princes, followed by the Batebe, head of the princesses, and some chairs were placed for the other wives of my father. The rest of the royal family sat round the king on the floor.

In front of my father, in the courtyard of the Court House, the music held the dancing crowds enthralled. But the climax was yet to come, and everyone's attention was now focused on the courtyard of the Court House. When the clock struck midnight, Kituku, the head of the royal musicians, approached and knelt before the king. He told him that the time had come for him to join and rejoice with his people. Suddenly, the whole nation would be gripped with euphoria.

My father stood up to join the line of the trumpeters and, as he did so, the crowds cried *"Omubyemu Agutamba"* ("Rise in strength"); when he stepped into the courtyard, they shouted *"Hamulyango Nzaire"* ("Go out safely"); and as he walked toward the bandsmen, they exclaimed *"Hakyaro Mbahira"* ("Go without fear, the land is yours"). My father was handed his own trumpet, which had been specially decorated by his grandmother, Queen Victoria. At this moment, nobody remained seated or stood still. Even my mother, my father's other wives, and the chiefs of the Sacred Guild were all on their feet, ready to dance.

Nine trumpeters played at a time, and one now dropped out so that my father could take the central position, flanked by four on each side. Music consisted of nine numbers. Each round started and ended with *Irambi*, the special refrain which marked both the beginning and the end of a round. The extra dimension given to the occasion as soon as the king began to play is indescribable. The women, maintaining silence, expressed their emotions with every part of their bodies, particularly in their facial expression, while the men cried *"Hangiriza Agutamba"* ("Long live the Provider") and jumped high toward the sky, with their hands stretched forward.

In the joyous procession of the days of my childhood, none were more enchanted than these.

As the plane taking me back to Toro began its descent to Entebbe Airport, I was snapped back into the present. As Patrick's Batebe, I was about to take over a position second in importance only to that of the king. I was to be Patrick's most valued adviser. I knew my father's careful orchestration of my education had been with the express purpose of grooming me for my role in the inevitable succession. I felt prepared to do my part.

TORCHBEARER

5

The Coup d'État

The king is dead. Long live the king. The new king was only seventeen years old and still at school. Inevitably, a power vaccum had been created.

On landing at Entebbe Airport, I sensed the impending political crisis that was to end in the 1966 coup d'état, the first one in my country's history.

The two antagonists in the power struggle were my uncle, the Kabaka (king of Buganda), and Milton Obote, then executive prime minister. The strategy of each was immediately discernible. Obote aimed at weakening my uncle through isolation from his fellow monarchs, and my uncle strove to maintain their support. With instructions that Patrick should be driven straight to him, both men had sent a car to the airport to fetch him. I knew Patrick was going to be pulled in all directions, and it was imperative that I warn him. At the news of my father's death, I had been so anxious to return home that I hadn't waited to see Patrick. I realized that I should wait at Entebbe for Patrick to arrive so that I could brief him.

A few hours later I watched him descend from the plane—tall and solemn, already his manner measured, as if unconsciously his body was bracing him for the throne and its immense responsibilities. I began to brief him at once because we were short on time. The high commissioner, an Obote supporter and Patrick's godfather, began immediately to gently persuade him to go to Obote. I was relieved to see that Patrick instinctively knew the right thing to do. He explained that it was unthinkable that he bypass his uncle, a fellow monarch as well as his legal guardian.

While we wanted desperately to avoid Obote, we knew we had to be careful. I emphasized that we recognized Obote's authority as the executive head of Uganda and were grateful for the support he had given us since the death of our father. We struck a compromise that my brother would see both Obote and our uncle.

Patrick and I accompanied the high commissioner to visit my uncle. We found him in mourning for my father but so enraged at the Uganda government over the simmering issue of the lost counties of Buyaga and Bugangaizi, that he would not speak to the high commissioner. The lost counties had been part of the kingdom of Bunyoro, the only state in Uganda to militarily resist the British colonial invasion. Our kingdom, Toro, and my uncle's kingdom, Buganda, had allied themselves with the British. The British had carved up Bunyoro and given Buganda the two counties in 1896. Bunyoro had waged a legal battle and in 1964 gained independence for the two counties.

Throughout the meeting my uncle ignored the high commissioner, directing his attention to Patrick, gazing into his nephew's eyes while rhythmically twisting his gold cuff links. Finally, he took Patrick to another room, excluding the high commissioner altogether.

After the meeting Patrick and I started our 200-mile journey to Toro. We rode in silence as we contemplated what awaited us. In our childhood we always started crying when we crossed the border from Toro into other kingdoms, and we always began to sing when we reentered. As we crossed the border that day, we did not sing, of course, our border crossing marked only by the sudden sullenness of the landscape, our beloved Toro rendered lifeless without its king. We traveled through Kyaka County, known for its abundant cattle, and then Mwenge, the county of rolling low hills, carpeted in green by tea plantations.

When we reached the capital, Kabarole, we drove directly to Patrick's place of seclusion, my uncle's house in suburban Rwengoma. He was to remain there until his coronation, apart from the one day he would come out to bury our father, who had used the same place in 1929 as his precoronation place of seclusion.

I left Patrick at Rwengoma and headed for the palace. Driving through the capital was like driving through a city in a blackout. Shops and houses were shut down. Bicycles and cars were strewn along the roadside, people having abandoned them to run uphill toward the palace. On the morning of my father's death, my paternal uncles were with Aunt Kabokya, my father's sister, attending the funeral of her maternal aunt at her home four miles from the palace. Suddenly, my uncle Daniel, who had strayed from the open grave to the main road, saw people running and cars speeding past him. A passerby told him the news and he ran back toward the grave. He began to throw himself to the ground, then pull himself up, only to hurl himself back to the earth, kicking and pounding his limbs on the ground. When close enough for my aunt to hear, he yelled, *"Kabokya, amahungu ga-tutera"* ("The hurricane has struck us"). Everyone, including the grave diggers, fled to the palace, leaving my distraught aunt with the unburied body.

My mother learned of her husband's death as she made her way from her house to the Court House. As she walked toward the offices, she saw one of the secretaries and an aide-de-camp off in a corner of the veranda talking. She clasped her hands to command their attention, but they turned and scurried off. Puzzled, she continued on her way. As she neared the Court House, she thought she heard the sound of a death wail. She stopped to listen, but it had ceased. The death wail was a ritual that, coming from the Court House, could signify only one tragedy. It began again, and upon hearing the unmistakable wail, she realized her husband was dead.

The king's Batebe, Princess Ruth, was in Kampala, Uganda's capital, when my father died. When she was told of his death, she cried out, "My brother, couldn't you wait for me?" His death was a terrible blow, even harder to bear because she had not been at his side.

When I arrived at the palace, thousands of people covered Kabarole Hill, and their wailing could be heard miles away. As I climbed the hill, I could see the flag was down, but it was the sight of royal spears and drums turned upside down that finally convinced me that my father was dead. Only my brother Patrick could turn them back at his coronation. I broke into a run toward the Court House, where I knew my father's body lay. When I entered the imposing hall, the wailing ceased. "Bagaaya has arrived, Bagaaya has arrived," the mourners whispered to one another. I threw myself at my father's feet, remaining there in silence. This became my spot for the nine-day mourning period. I felt the eyes of a grieving woman watching me, noticing that I wasn't wailing. "She is being brave," she cried out.

I looked around and what I saw at that moment crystallized for me the meaning of kingship. It had never occurred to me before that the man whose body lay in state was no ordinary father and that even I, his own daughter, had no better claim to him than anyone else. For he, George David Matthew Kamurasi Rukiidi III, king of Toro, was the descendant of the Bacwezi, "semi-gods," kings who were the descendants of the Abatembuzi kings, who, according to the tradition of the people of the Kitara Empire, were divine. My father, like his ancestor kings, was regarded as a deity, a priest-king whose person was so sacred that everything pertaining to it—the parts of the body, clothing, food, weapons, actions—was referred to in a special language. All his daily activities were ceremonialized and regarded with reverence. He was the chief symbol of the people's spiritual life, representing, through descent, the intangible part of the nation. He was the living embodiment of its rituals, and so his death had created a devastating spiritual void. It was evident in their faces that they felt their spirituality was endangered. The Batoro, the people of Toro, like their predecessors, the Bakitara, are a deeply religious people who believe their happiness depends on striking the right equilibrium between God and man—between the spiritual and the physical world—and the pinnacle of that equilibrium is the king.

Everyone I saw, young or old, Christian or non-Christian, was grief-stricken and stunned. In one corner I saw Nyinabarongo, Yaya, Munaku, and Nyamwoni; each, more than one hundred years old, had been carried there on a stretcher. All four had been princesses who had been taken as prisoners of war to Bunyoro kingdom during my grandfather's reign. One said to me, "Child, it is enough to see a king's death once in a lifetime, but it is a curse to see it twice." They sat on mattresses, motionless and solemn.

Nearby sat a group of three men, and right beside me sat Nyaika, one of my brothers, who leaned over and whispered, "Look at Vitali, Ikomyo, and Bakamya—what will become of them?" Vitali was the most eccentric of all the characters in my father's palace. A thinly built old man, not more than four feet tall, dressed invariably in a white tunic with a rosary hanging from his neck, Vitali spent his life cultivating his vegetable garden or wandering through the palace grounds muttering prayers and blessing palace dwellers with his rosary. When we were children, we believed passionately in his powers and welcomed his blessings. The two other men were Ikomyo, the head gatekeeper, as his father and grandfather had been before him, and Bakamya, who had herded my father's goats, as well as my grandfather's when he was king. It was clear these three had lost not only a leader but a dear friend. The king had given each individual direct access to him, as well as a sense of belonging and a place in society. The king symbolized the unifying force of the nation, and the 150 clans that comprise the Batoro tribe had come together to pay their last respects.

In the old days the king's death was known only to close attendants, whose duty it was to see that the news did not get abroad or even spread outside the house in which it had occurred, for reasons of national security. It was concealed even from his wives until all the precautions had been taken. Not until the servant spilled the milk from the roof did the death wail of the palace women begin. Wailing is an art form in which everyone participates; those more skillful recount the ancestry of the deceased as well as the achievements of his life while the rest of the wailers form the chorus. Wealth in Africa is measured not by your purse but by the people in your life, your relatives. When an African dies, his wealth can be measured by the manner in which he is mourned.

On several occasions I had to leave my place among the mourners to attend to problems while Patrick was kept safely in seclusion. I gathered a group of advisers: Princess Ruth, my cousin Katama, my uncle Dr. Byaruhanga, and Toro Cabinet ministers. During one meeting, the question arose as to whether the Ugandan Parliament should announce its formal recognition of Patrick as the heir to the Toro throne. Some believed that this was unnecessary, since under the independence constitutions of Uganda and Toro, and under my father's will, Patrick's succession was automatic. I reminded everyone that two precedents had historically been set in support of recognition: both my grandfather and father had been recognized. Therefore, I felt the Ugandan Parliament would only be taking legal notice of the law and of a fait accompli. The central government was in no way going to encroach on the prerogative of the kings and Parliament of Toro.

Recognition was simultaneously announced by the parliaments of Uganda and Toro.

One day, during a precoronation meeting, a guard burst in and asked me to hurry outside. Following him, I discovered that he had rescued my father's parrot just in the nick of time from the grip of the palace leopard. My mother had told me about this creature, "*Engo Engaragara*," "The Leopard who is the King's servant," who would occasionally roam around the hill at dusk. It had not been seen for years, appearing only now, during the mourning period.

The leopard attacked the parrot in its cage, trying to snatch it through the small metal grill. But the bird dodged it by springing from one spot to the next, shaking the cage so violently that the leopard failed to grab it. The leopard decided to take the parrot, cage and all, and started to drag it away. The shrieking parrot attracted the guard, who forced the leopard to drop its prey. The guard had come to ask for a car to take the bird for emergency medical treatment. When I saw the scratches the leopard had inflicted, I burst into tears, for this parrot could imitate my father's voice exactly.

At last the nine days of mourning came to an end. On the ninth day we waited for Patrick to come to the palace, from which he had been barred up to now, and fetch the king's body to take it for burial. In the old days a prince hardly ever succeeded to the throne without having to go to war. Each contender sought to secure possession of the body. But Patrick came in peace, thanks to two factors. First, under the independence Constitution of Uganda incorporating the Toro Constitution, the king's sons by his legal wife take precedence over his other sons in succession to the throne. Second, in his will, my father had made Patrick his heir. No one knew of the will's existence except for my aunt, Princess Ruth. His succession had not been entirely smooth, and he wanted to ensure that Patrick would have an easier time. So he had sealed and deposited the will with the governor of Uganda, to be opened only upon his death. The permanent secretary to the prime minister of Uganda flew the document to Toro in a specially chartered plane for my aunt to identify my father's signature.

When the mourners saw Patrick, their wailing reached a crescendo. With Patrick leading, the funeral procession set off on the five-mile route to Karambi, the royal tombs, leaving behind us a totally deserted palace.

We went first to Kabarole Cathedral for the service. Then solemnly we moved on to Karambi, where we removed our shoes and entered the shrine. This did not appear to be a place for the dead. The shrine had its own two queens, its cattle, and its regalia. No wailing was permitted, and as we performed the funeral rites, it occurred to me that we were treating my father as if he were still alive. Outside the grave, symbols of his reign were placed. After completing these rites, we visited my grandfather's tomb next to my father's, and we sat in silence for a while. As I sat there, I noted that my father was taking his place among the immortals—and that he had taken with him an unblemished record.

After Karambi my brother returned to his place of seclusion. He complained of aching joints due to the sudden change from a daily game of squash to an imposed sedentary life-style. The Toro elders didn't understand my brother's need for physical activity. They were more concerned with the spiritual preparation of the future king of Toro than his muscles and intended to guard him closely until his safe installation on the throne. Finally, they gave in, allowing him to exercise at the Toro sports club, where he established new friendships and contacts.

As the elders had feared, we found ourselves amidst political tensions threatening to explode at any moment. One week before the scheduled coronation, Toro's prime minister learned that Milton Obote had arrested five of his cabinet ministers and Colonel Opolot, the head of the Ugandan Army, replacing him with Idi Amin. In addition, Kwame Nkrumah, the president of Ghana, had been overthrown. Ghana had been the first African state to gain independence from Britain.

The coronation day arrived, but before Patrick could be crowned, he had to go through rituals symbolizing the death of his old personality and the acquisition of a new one by purification. The rituals began with a procession from Rwengoma—the place of his seclusion—to the palace. At 3:00 A.M. my brother, surrounded by princes, chiefs, elders, and crowds of men carrying spears, sticks, and firebrands, started walking the four miles to the palace. No women were allowed in the procession. They had to stop nine times on the way, and each time the flames were snuffed out and kindled afresh. The number nine recurs in Toro traditions, as it is considered a lucky number.

Upon arriving at the gates, Patrick fought a mock battle against a pretender and then entered the palace to cheers. I watched from the roof of the Court House, as women were not allowed even to be seen, but hearing the cheers propelled me forward, and I flew down the stairs toward the scene. The palace gatekeeper reminded me that if I went any further the crowds would beat me with their sticks. Frustrated, I returned to my rooftop perch, where I observed the purification rite.

A woman of the princely clan, Babito, dipped two bunches of sacred herbs into water from the royal well that had been mixed with clay, and sprinkled Patrick. Then Patrick proceeded to the throne, where he was crowned. The crowds surged forward and hailed my brother with *"Zona Okali"* ("All there is is yours"). Other rites followed, and then he was instructed on the milking ceremonies by two women.

The following morning we attended another service and then we drove in procession to the first Toro Parliament of Patrick's reign. Patrick, being so young, had worried many people about how he would perform. Composed, and with great humility, he delivered a moving speech. In his majestic blue and gold robes he so resembled my father that many in the crowd began to sob.

He told his people that he had been named Kaboyo Olimi after the

Kaboyo Olimi during whose reign Toro first obtained its independent status, and like his namesake he would work to create a renaissance of Toro. The procession made its way back to the Court House and everyone danced and celebrated while Patrick looked on from the throne.

I danced too, thoroughly enjoying myself, until someone leaned over and whispered to me that there had been a coup in Kampala.

Obote had abrogated the independence Constitution of Uganda, deposed the president, my uncle, and made himself president. I left the dance floor and told Patrick what had transpired. He didn't want to draw attention by leaving the throne, so he asked me to call my uncle. I was only able to get through to a private secretary, who told me the Kabaka was all right, although there was much commotion and confusion in Kampala. I reported back to Patrick and we continued celebrating into the night as though nothing had occurred. At midnight it was time for Patrick to join the drummers and trumpeters. He rose and the crowds called out, "Long live the king!" When he drummed and played on his gourd trumpet, the crowd went wild and danced through the night, which they were to do for the next nine days. Toro, at least for the time being, had a king, and that was all that mattered.

The elders warned us that there was always an earthquake as a good omen for the new king. I dismissed their warning as mere superstition.

The earthquake came in the middle of the night. Most people had gone to sleep in single-story houses so that they could easily run outside when the earthquake arrived. Only Patrick, an aunt, a servant, and I were in the two-story Court House. I woke up to find the whole house shaking like a piece of paper. My bed was trembling. I didn't know what to do, so I remained there and prayed. Meanwhile, Gwayaka, the servant guarding Patrick's room, noticed that the king's spear, propped up in a corner, was shaking violently and about to fall on Patrick. Gwayaka leapt toward it, catching it just as it was about to fall on the king. He woke Patrick up, and my brother, realizing that the building was about to collapse, opened his window to jump out. Just then, the earthquake stopped.

An excited crowd had surrounded the Court House, shouting for us to come out. This new, all-concrete, earthquake-proof dwelling was more damaged than the old mud-and-wattle buildings of the village. The earthquake was more than a gentle reminder that even the forces of nature regard true kings as more than ordinary men. The heavens, the earth, and the gods had confirmed the departure of my father from this world and his arrival to the other world, and now ushered in the new king.

I had witnessed the transformation of my little brother into someone more than ordinary through the rituals. My uncle Switzer told me, "My child, when your father died, I refused to believe it was possible for Patrick to replace him. But that night as we walked to the palace, I looked at him and saw that he had been transformed, and I said to myself, 'Yes, he is the king.'" My aunt also told me that when her father died she refused to recognize my father as the king, and refused to use the title queen mother for her mother. But she said that after the coronation ceremonies she found herself accepting him as king.

Even my father had had difficulty with the transformation and when he was crowned, the thing he dreaded most was the royal salute, *"Zona Okali"* ("All there is is yours"). Whenever someone shouted this out, he would inwardly shrink, trying to become as inconspicuous as possible.

Patrick was not the only one dealing with a new role. I, too, had to ease into my new position as the Batebe. My father's Batebe, Princess Ruth, insisted that I completely assume all her duties. I had taken over my responsibilities in terms of advising Patrick, but I did not officially want to strip my aunt of her title, Batebe, which signified her status as First Sister. She wanted to fade into the background. "You cannot change history," she said. My aunt was determined to follow tradition and step down from her position upon my father's death. I, however, knew times were changing. My brother and I were young, and knew we needed her voice.

"In law, yes, I am now the king's Batebe," I told her. "But you should retain some control." I refused to take her title. For many years she was addressed as Batebe, keeping her title until the very day she died.

*   *   *

Shortly after the coronation, I parted company with my brother. I went to Kampala, two hundred miles away, and joined Kazzorra and Co., a firm of lawyers, and did six-months' pupilage before being called to the Ugandan bar. I became the first African woman to do so, and to mark the occasion the then attorney general, Godfrey Binaisa, who later briefly became the president, came to court unexpectedly and introduced me himself to the bar.

Patrick, meanwhile, embarked on a tour of his kingdom, accompanied by the Toro prime minister, members of his Cabinet, my aunt, Princess Ruth, princes and princesses, several of the elders, and three English school friends from Sherborne School for Boys. Whenever he addressed the village crowds, his English buddies addressed them also. Wherever he went, a celebration of dancing and rejoicing followed.

Then Obote decided to strike. On May 23 he ordered his crack force and some Ugandan troops under Amin to surround the Kabaka's palace in Buganda. Fighting ensued, the palace was sacked, and many people were killed. Obote declared a state of emergency and arrested all the Baganda chiefs. The news reached my brother on tour. As a sign of mourning, he ordered the music and dancing to stop, although he continued his tour. He sent my aunt by plane to Kampala to find out if the Kabaka had been killed; she returned with the good news that the Kabaka had escaped safely to London. This was some consolation, but my brother's Sherborne friends left the country immediately at Patrick's insistence.

At the tour's completion my brother had to decide whether to go to Sandhurst in England or to stay in Uganda to attend Makerere University, the foremost university in East Africa. If he were to go away to England, he would be removed from an extremely dangerous political and military arena. It was thought better to appoint a regency and let Patrick go abroad. However, the thought of Patrick's absence from Toro, at a time when the kingdom was divided by party loyalties and threatened with secession by the Rwenzururu movement, two tribes in the Mountains of the Moon, was troublesome. Also, Obote could more easily abolish the monarchy in the king's absence. Needless to say, Obote preferred the Sandhurst plan.

Patrick opted for the Makerere plan, preferring to stay in Uganda, where he could nurture his relationship with the people and provide spiritual and moral leadership for his subjects.

Makerere was a great success for Patrick. The only problem was that Obote had surrounded Patrick with his spies, having infiltrated the university with his General Service Unit, the Gestapo's equivalent. But outside Makerere, throughout the country, Patrick filled a void. The kings of Bunyoro and Ankole were old men, and the king of Buganda had been banished, and so it was the Toro monarchy that gave Uganda the boost it needed. With his youth, good looks, gentle yet strong presence, and international exposure, Patrick's appeal to the country was unrivaled.

The new king's popularity soared. Even in urban Kampala, the cry *"Zona Okali"* ("All there is is yours") was heard from passing cars as we zipped around the city with the Toro pennant flapping in the breeze from our antenna.

Obote's government was trying to dominate the media: it controlled all broadcasting, and even privately owned newspapers had to watch their every step, but even so, the Toro monarchy managed to get considerable coverage. Obote was alarmed, particularly by Patrick's appeal to the younger generation, and so he decided to strike the final blow. On September 7, two days before Patrick's eighteenth birthday, he surrounded the Ugandan Parliament with troops and addressed the members as "citizens" (rather than the usual "honorable members") and went on to say, "I give you a constitution, which you will find in your pigeon holes." They were forced to vote on a constitution they hadn't had a chance to see. The kingships of Toro, Bunyoro, Buganda, and Ankole were abolished forthwith. The Honorable Obwangoro, who dared to suggest amendments, was sacked. Needless to say, the Constitution was passed. This was only the beginning.

Patrick, my mother, and everyone else in the palace were evicted. When Patrick asked where they were to go, an official told him, "That's no concern of ours." They were instructed to pack only their personal belongings. My mother explained that after having lived there for more than thirty years it was hard to distinguish what was hers and what wasn't. She was told to hurry up and hand over her keys.

Before we left the palace, a government newspaper, *The People*, called Patrick and asked him what he thought about Obote abolishing the monarchy. Patrick asked me to respond and I told the reporter, "If that is the wish of the people, so be it." The newspaper turned my quote into a banner front-page headline the following morning. Then Obote's people started a rumor twisting my words around to say that if the people did not agree to the abolition of the monarchy, then the palace would not accept it.

A loyal Mutoro, Mr. Mwirumubi, hearing that the king had no roof over his head, lent him his house about six miles from the palace. Patrick was warmly welcomed in the village there. But government helicopters circled the house constantly, and the General Service Unit kept calling to harass him and circulated rumors that soldiers surrounded the residence, intending to frighten off loyal subjects. This was just as well, as Patrick did not want crowds of people visiting. They would have only fueled Obote's paranoia. But he had many individual visitors and it was obvious Toro was on his side, despite his being powerless in the face of Obote's Army, Special Force, and General Service Unit, which from 1966 until 1971 created a police state in Uganda.

The rest of the palace residents were scattered in different homes. A physically handicapped aunt and her elderly mother went to my uncle Fred's home. Rachel, my little sister, went to an aunt. The palace staff had homes to go to but were left jobless. The parrot, dogs, and cat were kept by my brother and mother. But the cat kept returning to the abandoned palace and eventually was hit by a car during one of its trips back. Obote's people confiscated all the regalia, the crowns, the robes; even the king's bed was taken for personal use by Obote's Toro representative.

I wanted to remain at my brother's side. But Aunt Ruth urged me to leave Uganda. She told us that she had been told, in strict confidence, that two government ministers had been overheard to say, "She has always been too proud. Now she will see." For my safety, Patrick and my aunt begged me to go into exile. I acknowledged that I was in danger, but I knew my exit had to be carefully planned. Meanwhile, I would return to Kampala and my work at Kazzorra and Co.

With only one car remaining at my brother's disposal, I had to hitch a lift to Kampala. Fortunately, as the result of an inquiry I had made at the Mountains of the Moon Hotel, the friendly English manager and his wife, who had helped me organize the coronation banquet, arranged for a German tourist couple to take me to Kampala with their teenage daughter.

Once they arrived at the palace in their Mercedes-Benz, Patrick and my aunt walked with me to the car. I knelt down on the earth and said good-bye, first to my brother and then to Aunt Ruth. Each one touched me on the shoulder and bade me farewell. We drove off, leaving behind us their two lonely figures against the backdrop of the deserted palace.

6

"A Message from Home"

Halfway to Kampala, we came to the town of Mubende and pulled in at a gas station. From inside the car we had a magnificent view of the surrounding hills, and the teenage daughter could not resist the temptation to take a snapshot while her father was busy at the pump. As she got out of the car, I cautioned her not to photograph the army barracks next to the station. I watched her focus on the hills and heard the click of her camera. But she did not have time to return to the car because a Ugandan soldier pounced on her, demanding in Swahili that she hand over her "pistol."

There was a violent scuffle. But all the soldier's strength failed to tear that camera from its strap round the girl's shoulder. Her father rushed to her aid, which saved us from an ugly scene. By this time her mother and I had got out of the car. I tried to explain to the soldier and to the crowd of people which had now gathered that it was a camera and not a pistol.

There was a total impasse. The soldier didn't understand English and we didn't understand Swahili. The only word we recognized was "pistol." He demanded that we follow him to the police station. When we got there he alleged that the girl had photographed the barracks, which showed that his supposed ignorance in mistaking the camera for a pistol was only tactics aimed at confiscating the camera. After the girl and her father had made statements to the police I took the girl to a nearby hospital so that the bleeding scratches the soldier had inflicted on her face and arms could be treated. We drove the rest of the way in utter bewilderment.

I, however, unlike my German friends, had just had a taste of things to come.

Within a day or two a police officer arrived at my desk in the chambers of Kazzorra and Co., and told me that the minister of internal affairs required me to make a statement to the police about the Mubende incident. I had intended to keep a low profile in the matter, but I went to the central police station and made my short and carefully worded statement.

Shortly afterwards, the minister made a vague reference on the radio about an incident at Mubende and issued a warning about certain individuals who falsely accused members of the security forces of misbehavior. Very few people would have had the slightest inkling of what he was talking about. But I knew. I carried on working, but I prayed for a miraculous deliverance from my predicament.

Patrick had remained in Toro until he felt that his people were settled after the abolition of the monarchy. He drove to Kampala to ask for permission to continue his studies abroad, but the trip was a big disappointment. Obote refused to see him or grant permission.

Eventually he was granted permission to leave, and so he went to Kenya, where he started a new career in the tea industry. Patrick had inherited tea plantations in Toro from our father and he had some knowledge of how the industry worked.

I continued working at the law firm, although my family was still urging me to flee the country.

At last the safe exit presented itself in the form of an invitation from HRH Princess Margaret and her husband Lord Snowdon, to model in a fashion show at Marlborough House in London. The idea of a Commonwealth fashion show grew out of a state visit to Uganda by the princess and Lord Snowdon in 1965, at the end of which they gave a pledge that they would set about raising funds for the eradication of polio in the Commonwealth.

There was immediate opposition from the Obote government to my representing Uganda. It thought that a republic should not be represented by a royal princess. Princess Margaret did not agree. She felt that the Commonwealth had in me a well-known personality who should be used, and, in any case, the invitation was a personal one. Since the idea had been conceived in Uganda, it would have been difficult for the government to be seen to frustrate such a humanitarian enterprise.

The organizers of the show invited Philippa Todd to design the Ugandan collection which, for me, turned out to be a fortuitous choice. Mrs. Todd and her husband were prominent figures in Makerere University's art department. At that time, in 1967, there were no fashion designers as such in Kampala. The public relations firm which had been designated in London to organize the event got in touch with Mrs. Todd, who relayed the invitation from London to me.

Secretly we prepared for the show in the secluded atmosphere of the university, where I was measured and fitted for the collection. When the time came for me to leave, Attorney General Binaisa advised me, "Just go. Don't say good-bye to anybody." Just as the plane was taking off from Entebbe Airport, the police arrived. Mrs. Todd told them I had gone. As the jet lifted itself into the clouds, I watched my country fade, and worried what would happen to my brother Patrick.

In London the British press gave the show prominent coverage. Marlborough House was usually the setting for important conferences between heads of state; for the first time it was to be the setting for a fashion show sponsored by royalty. I didn't know what to expect, but the organizers predicted that I would draw a great deal of attention.

The Ugandan government's last-minute attempt to enter a rival candidate did not work, as the organizers insisted that, with the exception of myself, all the models in the show were to be professionals. In other words, they were not asking countries to send representatives.

Marlborough House glittered for the occasion. The complete Commonwealth collection by designers from all over the world had been assembled hours before the show's opening. When all ten models were present, the allocation of clothes began. The scramble that followed was like a bargain basement sale at Macy's; the other models pulled and grabbed clothes. This was a world in which each person had to fight for what she wanted, and I found the language and manners alien. I assumed that eventually the organizers would help me. By the time they did, it was too late; all the best clothes had been taken. Each model was now busy with makeup, hair, and trying on clothes. Guests were beginning to stream in, and soon it would be time for Princess Margaret and Lord Snowdon to arrive. I panicked and grabbed whatever clothes were passed on to me. At least I had priority for the best of the Ugandan collection.

As the royals arrived, all the models pressed forward to catch a glimpse from the stage wings.

Music played and as each model walked on stage, the announcer called out her name and the country from which the dress came. For maximum effect, the organizers had ruled that I, unlike the other models, should make only a few carefully select appearances. The first of these came almost halfway through the show. The announcer said, "And from Uganda, the Princess Elizabeth of Toro models a dress designed by Philippa Todd." Princess Margaret looked pleased and led the applause as I strode onto the stage, feeling proud and animated by the spirits of my ancestors.

Soon after, top British modeling agencies and fashion magazines bombarded me with modeling offers. I now had to choose between a career at the English bar and modeling, which could lead to an acting career. A major consideration in making this decision was which career would be the most effective way of symbolizing, projecting, and preserving the torch of my black culture. Modeling was considered rather a frivolous thing to do, and I had a hard time convincing my friends and advisers that it would help me achieve my goals. Modeling was a means to an end for me, enabling me to make an important point regarding my beloved country. Beauty is not one's own but rather a reflection of one's people, one's country. It is an asset one holds in trust. At that time, a black model appearing in top magazines was rare.

I wanted to destroy the myth of white superiority in terms of beauty and sophistication.

Obote had done his utmost to erase the monarchy in Uganda from the national consciousness. The monarchy was virtually extinct. It was not my aim to revive it, but, in adopting my new and unexpected role, I hoped to bring attention to my heritage, to emphasize my ancestral identity, which, Obote believed, could be eradicated with one brash sweep of his pen. Obote was depicting royalty as though we were traitors to the people, ignoring all the contributions that we had rendered. The language of clothes, of fashion and its attendant publicity, is a significant one. And I was determined to utilize such a powerful weapon to remind everyone that Uganda's culture was still a force with which to be reckoned. If I couldn't do it politically, I would do it with haute couture. I felt that somehow the torch of our culture had to continue.

I signed up with the Peter Lumley Agency, at the time the top agency in London. And I was also to start work at top rates. Jill Rushton, the manager of Lumley's, was married to a judge, so we had something in common. She invited me to dinner at her home, and whatever lingering doubts I had about deciding not to join the English bar were dispelled that evening by her husband. He inquired as to whether I had any private income and I admitted that I didn't have a penny to my name. The Ugandan monarchs, being the patriots that they were, never kept Swiss bank accounts. He pointed out that at the bar I wouldn't be earning any money for the first year or two. In addition, there were other factors such as discrimination against women and blacks, and having to start at the bottom, which meant that a legal career would not start to take off for six years or more.

At this point, Jill interrupted. "Elizabeth, we have never had a model with a degree, let alone a law degree from Cambridge! With no trouble at all, we will launch you not from the bottom but from the top. From modeling, you will go on the stage. In other words, your dream target is New York."

It was true that I had some distinct advantages, not least of which was being black—black models, successful ones at least—were unusual in those days. I was also already something of a personality in my own right, thanks to ample press coverage in my undergraduate days and afterwards. My brother's coronation ceremony in 1966 had been featured in the *Sunday Telegraph* color supplement and a year later I had appeared on British television as the first black judge in the Miss World Contest.

And so I was launched by Lumley's. Every morning for two weeks, Sarah Dawson, a top model, drilled me in modeling techniques. I acquired the model walk, the model language, the model dress sense, the model bearing, and the model size. I had to diet severely in order to attain the skinny model "look." African women are by and large not slenderly built, at least not from the hips down. I can't say, in retrospect, that I looked all that well on my meager diet of fruit and black coffee. One advantage I had was that I didn't smoke or drink, so I didn't have to give either up for my career. When I went out to clubs, I was forever annoying waiters by asking for fresh-squeezed orange juice or tea, as well as my companions who wanted me to join in the drinking. I suppose my aversion to drinking stemmed from my fear of losing control. I didn't want anything to get out of place. The only cigarette I ever smoked was when I graduated from Cambridge, and then my friends laughed at my inability to hold it correctly.

Everywhere I went, I carried my portfolio. My early photos showed a somber woman. I was very sad, and I couldn't hide it from the camera. I remember one session when the photographer said, "Elizabeth, can't you think of something happy? Think of your boyfriend."

"What boyfriend?" I thought to myself. It was a lonely period in my life, and that was coming through on camera. Not only had I no boyfriend; I had no country, no home.

I started off living in an apartment in Westminster Gardens owned by Baroness Joan Vickers, a former Conservative M.P. and now in the House of Lords. I was fortunate in that I had so many friends to champion me in those early days. Hugh Fraser, formerly Lady Antonia Fraser's husband, and a good friend of my father's with an abiding interest in Africa and things African, introduced me to Lord Harlech. Aidan Crawley and his American wife, Virginia, were instrumental in getting me acquainted with David Bruce, the American ambassador to London then. His wife Evangeline and I became good friends, and she accompanied me to places like Thea Porter's and

Zandra Rhodes's, and to fashion shows in Paris. It was through Evangeline that I came to know Marietta Tree, Mary Warburg, and Felicity Sarnoff, all great hostesses on the New York social scene.

From being penniless and roofless, I came to have a choice of three homes apart from Joan Vickers's spacious flat adjoining the Houses of Parliament. Peter Tapsell gave me his children's former nanny's room in Albany; a French count lent me a flat in Paris; and later I was to rent my own flat on the King's Road, Chelsea. Altogether, I spent about one year in London. David Bailey photographed me as Queen of Sheba for British *Vogue*, Patrick Lichfield, a British earl and cousin to Queen Elizabeth, photographed me for American *Vogue*, and I modeled in fashion shows at Norman Hartnell's, Thea Porter's, and Annabel's, while other photographs of me appeared in *Harper's Bazaar* and *Queen* magazines. I joined the Paris Planning Agency, where I found myself at my first session in the company of Picasso's daughter. Alexander, then the top hairdresser in Paris, did our hair. A photograph of me appeared on the front cover of a Swiss magazine called *Ambiance*. Advertising photography took me all over Europe. On one occasion, I had to advertise German beer in the snow-covered mountains at a ski resort in Switzerland. My colleagues were running around having fun and I was in tears, my hands freezing. "Be a sport," they scolded me. I wasn't used to the cold and so I had to pretend to smile and look cheerful while I desperately wanted to be indoors.

But there was definitely a payoff for all the running around. If I had chosen the path of law, I never would have been exposed to the people I met through modeling. One day I was introduced backstage at Covent Garden to Dame Margot Fonteyn and Rudolf Nureyev. Margot and her husband Tito had an elegant flat at 1 Princes Court in Knightsbridge, and we became very close.

I also became friendly with Lord and Lady Hartwell, the *Daily Telegraph* owners. All these friends helped in ensuring my success, but it was Margot who introduced me to Jacqueline Kennedy when she was in London, and it was she who set the next step of my career in motion.

Between them, Jacqueline Kennedy and Lord Harlech were to make my New York dream a reality. One morning, Lord Harlech had walked into the Lexington Avenue offices of American *Vogue*, much to the astonishment of its editor in chief, Diana Vreeland. Harlech's standing in America in the sixties was second only to Churchill's. He was the link between British Prime Minister Harold Macmillan and President John F. Kennedy, and during his tenure as British ambassador (1961–1965), relations between the United States and the United Kingdom were extraordinarily close. It was Jacqueline who had arranged the interview between Lord Harlech and Diana Vreeland. He told her, "America loves beauty and the princess cannot fail." Diana formally invited me to come to the states and model for *Vogue*. It was not the first time I would be photographed for American *Vogue*, but this invitation turned out to be pivotal to my modeling career. *Vogue* paid the least, but no one minded because to appear between the pages of *Vogue* is a terrific coup.

Vogue was not long in telephoning me with a booking. The photographer for my session was an Italian named Penati, ranked among the best America had to offer. When I arrived at Penati's studio, I was overwhelmed. Two elegantly dressed *Vogue* editors welcomed me and ushered me to a well-lit dressing table. I was presented with a menu from which I ordered my breakfast, which was brought in from a restaurant around the corner. After I had eaten, the beauty editor supervised my making up from an extensive selection of makeup. A fashion editor helped me into my costume, chosen from an amazing array of clothes from different designers and boutiques. The hairdresser created a lovely hair style for me. Finally, the fashion editor adorned me with jewelry and matching accessories.

All this time Penati had been studying me intensely from a distant corner. *Vogue* had chosen him because they hoped his Italian temperament would loosen me up. He led me from the dressing room to a floodlit spot in front of the camera. Then he started shooting; from time to time I altered positions and the editors rearranged my costume. After about an hour, Penati walked out.

Soon he returned, carrying a pair of scissors, and began ripping at my costume. Horrified, the editors whisked me off to redress me. When I returned, the studio was reverberating with African music and drums! Penati, from behind the camera, shouted, "A message from home."

Everybody screamed with laughter, but his strategy worked. The music, the drumbeat, seduced me, and slowly I began to sway and dance. Penati shot relentlessly for hours, breaking only for a brief lunch.

As I returned home, I replayed the session in my mind. I had never experienced anything like it before. But the afternoon left me with more than memories: soon after, the Elizabeth of Toro hairstyle, born during the Penati shoot, spread in the black American community. Shortly afterwards, *Vogue* devoted a layout to me in their 1968 summer issue. It was the first time that such an honor had been accorded to a black model. The leading agency in New York, Ford, signed me on, and suddenly I was in great demand, doing features for magazines including *Harper's, Look, Life,* and *Ebony.*

One afternoon the agency called. "Will you do a nude?"

"I don't think I can."

"Think about it. It's a lot of money." We hung up.

A few minutes later I phoned back. "I will not do a nude."

"Are you a model or are you not?" The agency representative was clearly puzzled.

"Yes, I am a model. But one day I will go back home." I stood my ground firmly.

Even though I turned down the lucrative nude modeling, soon I was able to afford to rent an apartment in Sutton Place. I was invited all over the city and met many people. But I realized quickly that members of the New York social scene appeared and disappeared seasonally, and it wasn't safe to rely on anyone. After having already adjusted to the differences between Uganda and Britain, it took a big effort to become accustomed to the American sense of humor and casualness, such as when someone caught me with the end of his cigarette and didn't apologize.

But I was lucky enough to find people whose loyalties and concerns were ordered not by the seasons but by their hearts. One such friend was top model and actress Lauren Hutton, who was living in the village with her boyfriend, where they had very small dinner parties in their small, cozy hideout away from the public. I met her modeling and I found her honesty and warmth refreshing in an otherwise aggressive atmosphere. I knew I was resented for coming in at the top and with a royal title. But Lauren wasn't fazed by any of it. All she saw was someone new on the scene who could use a little help. And help she did, giving me tips on makeup, on how to carry myself in front of the camera, and on how to get across what I wanted to express, which was that a black person can hold her own, that we have our own standing and don't have to be depicted as others would like.

While I did have my problems and frustrations with the city, I appreciated the informality and professionalism of New York, and one of its bonuses was that it was relatively easy to get into acting. The Ford Agency advised me to take acting classes and, heeding their advice, I enrolled at the American Place Theater. The classes provided me with great relief after a day of tromping in and out of studios, and served as a sort of therapy. While I was enjoying great commercial success, I still felt unsettled and ill at ease. I would walk from Sutton Place up Fifty-seventh Street to the modest studio on Seventh Avenue to join my class of twenty. We worked on plays or improvised in small groups, becoming comfortable with each other. Wynn Handman was a charismatic teacher, breaking down our inhibitions and showing us how to express a slew of emotions. As an African who had been brought up never to make an exhibition of my sexual feelings, this was a new experience for me, and for the first time in my life, I began to see myself as an individual rather than a symbol of my country.

I also discovered a Ugandan community in New York which helped me feel more at home. I spent nearly every weekend in Harlem with Israel and Regina Mayengo, my first Ugandan friends in New York. Then a cousin came to live in the city, and I wasn't lonely anymore.

The peak moment of my modeling career came during this time. Bill King, a well-known English photographer based in New York, booked me to do some photographs but refrained from telling me they were for the cover of *Harper's Bazaar*. A few weeks later, I was walking along Fifth Avenue and stopped to buy the latest issues of *Vogue* and *Harper's Bazaar*. My heart missed a beat as I stared down at the magazine in my hand and my face stared back up at me. Dumb-foundedly I handed the vendor some money, and as he handed me change, he said, "Congratulations!" Dazed, I headed home. My phone had begun to ring incessantly with friends and colleagues who had seen the issue. It was the first time a top fashion magazine had featured a black model on its cover.

The echoes of congratulations had not died down when Ford's telephoned me with my first film offer. Two film producers, Edward Mosk, an American, and Hans Schmidt, a German, had spotted me and wanted me to audition for the female lead in a film called *Things Fall Apart.* The film was based on *Things Fall Apart* and *No Longer at Ease,* two books by Nigerian author Chinua Achebe, which are now taught in schools throughout Africa. Their theme is the impact of Western civilization on Africa. Johnny Sekka, a Senegalese actor and one of the leading black actors on the international scene, played the male lead. I was given a copy of the script and was asked to report back in two weeks' time when I had read it.

I took the script to Wynn Handman and under his direction we acted some scenes out of it over the next month. "Take it, Elizabeth," he said. "You have the part within you." Indeed, I found I could relate easily to the theme. The story begins in London where two Ibos, from eastern Nigeria, one a girl called Clara Okeke, the other a man named Obi, meet and fall in love. Clara, although a qualified nurse, is also an Osu, or untouchable, thus socially inferior to Obi. Obi is working as a journalist. Everything goes well until they return to Nigeria, where Obi is reunited at the airport with members of his clan—who make it clear that Clara is not welcome. The hapless lovers are plunged into a conflict, in which the old way of life and looking at things meets the modern, Europeanized way in a painful head-on collision. On her deathbed, Obi's mother implores her son not to bring down a curse on the family by marrying an "Osu," and Clara, despairing, leaves and tries to submerge herself in her work. She discovers that she is expecting Obi's baby, and the film ends on a sad note when Obi finds out about the child, but too late.

Africa is trapped in a similar conflict; like the titles of the two books from which the idea of the film had sprung, our old world has fallen apart, yet we are no longer at ease in the new one. So I threw myself into the part of Clara with genuine empathy and shortly afterwards, in the summer of 1970, flew to Lagos in Nigeria to do the filming.

Lagos was a revelation to me. I had been so used to seeing Asians and Europeans in Kampala and Nairobi running virtually everything that it impressed me to see Africans for once in control. Lagos was very hot and I missed fresh milk, but I was enjoying myself—until I was suddenly informed that the police wanted to see me. We were shooting the first scene at the airport when I was summoned to the immigration building and told that I had to leave Nigeria immediately. Nobody seemed inclined to offer an explanation, and the film people were in a panic at having to give up shooting.

Was it political? Had the Ugandan government managed to get at me through a back door, as it were? The police asked to see a copy of the film script—so it could not be me specifically they were worried about. However, if they wanted to put a stop to the film's being made, the most effective way of doing it was to get rid of the leading actress or actor. Chinua Achebe was an Ibo from eastern Nigeria, which had tried to secede from the rest of the country, culminating in the civil (Biafran) war, still a sore point in 1970. The script was not only about eastern Nigeria and the Ibo culture—it went far beyond that—the last scene was set during the civil war. That was the problem.

Our lawyer Babs Williams's heroic efforts on our behalf succeeded in persuading the authorities to change their minds about the film being made in Nigeria, but we were compelled to delete the last scene, and we were not allowed to film in the east.

We went instead to Ibadan. I was up at six each morning to have my hair plaited in the marketplace by the local women. When it came to the love scenes, I was still self-conscious and inhibited and at one stage Johnny Sekka slapped me, and filming was interrupted for days. However, Chinua Achebe was delighted with the standard of the acting, and it was great fun making it, in spite of the small budget and the production problems we had. The film was shown in the United States, Nigeria, England, and West Germany. But fairly soon it was to be the last thing on my mind.

"A Message from Home"

The next part of my life was to be very different, and to have a very different director on a much larger stage. I was given the part of roving ambassador and then foreign minister to Idi Amin's government.

7

"Give Him the Decorations to Play With"

The sun was barely up on the wintry morning when Dan, the husband of my South Vietnamese friend (from Cambridge days) Bith-Cam, knocked on my bedroom door and urged me to wake up. He was a press attaché at the South Vietnamese Embassy in Paris, and according to the latest news reports, there was trouble in Uganda. At first, I didn't want to hear the details, fearing as I did that something might have happened to some of my relatives. But Dan hastened to reassure me. Apparently, there was rejoicing in the streets in Kampala, which I knew could mean only one thing: that Obote had been overthrown.

I was astonished. On January 25, 1971, another coup d'état had taken place in Uganda and General Idi Amin was the new president.

Almost immediately, I rang the Ugandan ambassador to France to find out what was happening. He was surprised to learn that I was in Paris (I had refrained deliberately before from contacting him, in case it got him into trouble), and asked me to go and see him at once. He confirmed that Obote had indeed been overthrown. Shortly afterwards, I flew to England, where I was met at the airport by reporters and cameramen. They bombarded me with questions about the situation in my country and about Amin, but there was very little I could tell them. I had never met Amin and from hearsay and discussion I could hardly believe that he was the central figure in the takeover.

In London, I got a message through my sister Mabel that Amin's foreign minister and brother-in-law wanted to speak to me. He told me over the telephone that "they" would very much like me to come home, and that he had something to discuss with me. I assured him that I had every intention of returning, whether he wanted to talk to me or not, and I flew back to Uganda immediately, without ever returning to New York. I have no idea what happened to my Sutton Place apartment, or my belongings there.

In Kampala, the prevailing mood was one of sheer euphoria. Amin had lifted press restrictions. When I arrived my photograph appeared on the front page of the *Uganda Argus* showing me mini-skirted, with shimmery tights and gold-colored shoes. The new president had invited all the hereditary rulers back, and I embraced my family and friends joyfully. A first cousin of mine, John Kabeba, murmured that Amin was "all right" but, poor man, was incapable of uttering a word of English! An uncle butted in, jokingly describing Amin as a "gorilla." The general feeling was that it didn't really matter who replaced Obote; the Ugandan people had suffered so much under Obote's regime that any change of leader and of government was viewed as good cause for hope.

The conditions for Amin's rise to power had been set in the previous century, during my grandfather's reign, when Captain Lugard on behalf of the Imperial British East Africa Company had recruited a mercenary army to combat the defiant King Kabalega. This army was composed largely of Nubians from the south of Sudan, and for a long time it had terrorized the civilian population of Uganda. They were known as the Uganda Rifles, and in each kingdom clearly defined Nubian settlements formed. Before 1914, the Uganda Rifles had become the King's African Rifles (KAR), covering Uganda, Kenya, Tanzania, and Nyasaland (Malawi). In 1931 the KAR was reorganized so that the appointment of African officers was abolished, with the exception of certain honorary commissions which were conferred on princes such as Daudi Chwa, the king of Buganda, and my father. Otherwise, the officers were all from the United Kingdom, until 1961, a year before independence. At independence there was no officer corps and the security forces were dominated by tribes from the north.

Amin joined the KAR in 1946, formerly as a cook to a European. By 1962, he was second in command to Colonel Opolot, who was from Teso in eastern Uganda. At Independence, Britain favored the Protestant Uganda People's Congress (UPC), led by Milton Obote. It is generally understood that the elections which accompanied independence were rigged in favor of the UPC, and even though the other main party, the Democratic Party, had appeared to enjoy the support of the majority of the civilian population, it was Obote's UPC which achieved power.

Under Obote, Uganda was run by the Army and the General Service, amounting to a police state. As a northerner and a republican, Obote was supported by and favored the Army, which was made up chiefly of northerners. To start with, he was obliged to use delaying tactics, as the political setup was controlled in the main by intellectuals from the more fertile and wealthier south of Uganda. Obote's strategy was to operate by divide and rule, which involved expelling the more populist and nationalistic elements in his own party, the UPC, and wooing members of the Opposition party, the DP, to win their allegiance. Thus a one-party state gradually evolved, culminating in Obote's first coup of 1966. Shortly before the coup, Obote, Amin, the minister of tourism, and the minister of internal affairs had been accused in Parliament of having accepted huge amounts of gold in exchange for supplying arms to rebels in eastern Zaire, which bordered on Ugandan territory. The result was a motion of no confidence carried against Obote. Obote denied the allegations and abrogated the Constitution, replacing it with a new one which Members of Parliament were to vote on under pressure. He arrested Opolot, the head of the Army, and five Cabinet ministers, who were detained for five years without trial. Amin, whose suspension had been recommended by Parliament for his involvement in the gold scandal, was promoted by Obote to overall commander of the Army, which was then brought in to subdue the civilian population.

Obote also brought into being the General Service, a secret police force headed by his cousin, Akena Adoko, who came to be feared and hated more than any other individual. The GS's headquarters was at Nakassero, to which Obote's residence was connected by a secret tunnel, and people were hauled off there to be interrogated and tortured, as well as to the Parliament building itself, where passers-by in the street below could often hear the screams of the victims. The GS infiltrated everywhere; into the civil service departments, the judiciary, Makerere University, even into the family structure itself. Unless one was affiliated to the GS, it was difficult to land a job or to gain a scholarship. The kingdom governments were put under "secretary generals," some recruited from the GS. Obote created his own political army—the Special Force. Vicious gangs roamed the countryside indulging in armed robbery, and there was a sharp decline in moral standards—and where Obote and his cronies drank, the president was worshipped by his entourage, even called such names as Jesus.

Two of the first actions that Amin took after he had snatched power from Obote were to release all the political prisoners, including Opolot, the former Army commander, whom Amin made his ambassador to Ghana and treated with generosity right up to Opolot's retirement, and to disband the GS. He formed instead the Public Safety Unit, which quickly set about checking armed robbery and restoring the peace. Life seemed to be getting back to normal. In Entebbe at State House, a beautiful building set in sumptuous grounds overlooking Lake Victoria, formerly the governor of Uganda's residence and now the official residence of the president, Amin held "open house." All kinds of people, religious leaders, tribal representatives, civil servants, businessmen, flocked there to shake his hand and to pour into his willing ears their congratulations, their troubles, and their advice on how he should conduct his policies. There was also an open telephone line to him personally.

In the eyes of the rest of the world, however, Amin's image was not quite so unblemished. From his place of exile in Tanzania, Obote was declaiming that Israel had engineered Amin's successful coup, and that Britain, the former colonial power, had also had a hand in it. Obote's accusation meant that, even though Amin himself was a Muslim, the entire Arab world was against him. Even the black African states in the Organizaton of African Unity refused to recognize Amin at first. On the other hand, Britain was the first to recognize him, even inviting him to London to dine with the queen at Buckingham Palace. Amin was several hours late in arriving at Downing Street, where he was to meet Prime Minister Edward Heath and his cabinet ministers—he had stopped over in Tel Aviv without warning the British government. He also stopped there on his way back to Uganda.

There is circumstantial evidence to support Obote's charge that foreign intelligence agencies played a part in Amin's ascension. Some former CIA officials admitted in the *Washington Post* of February 24, 1978, that the intelligence agencies of Britain, the United States, and Israel plotted Obote's overthrow and assisted Amin to power. In sections of the British press, at the time, Amin was hailed as "our man," and the British high commissioner in Kampala had direct access to the president. (Later Amin was to embarrass a Ugandan delegation to the UN, of which I was a member, when he said in Kampala that Uganda would support dialogue with South Africa, an obviously pro-British stance, at the same time as his foreign minister, Wanume Kibedi, was stoutly denying at the United Nations conference that Amin was a British "stooge.")

As for the Israeli involvement, there was a large Israeli presence in Uganda after the coup and, later, the former head of the Israeli military mission, Colonel Baruch Bar-Lev, admitted in the *New York Times* of July 17, 1976, that he had assisted Amin to overthrow Obote. It transpired that he had been seen the day before the coup with Amin at Entebbe Airport. Amin, of course, had always had close relations with the Israelis, ever since he had assisted them, on Obote's orders, in the north of Uganda in their operations against Sudan.

Obote's alliance with the Israelis had been a strategic one. Israel had been very popular with the Third World in the late sixties. After independence, in spite of their acquiescence in his rise to power, Obote had been suspicious of the British because he said that they supported the Establishment. He had brought in the Israelis to train the Army, the Air Force, and the intelligence services, and in return for their help, militarily as well as in many other spheres, he allowed them to use Uganda as a springboard into the south of Sudan, where a Christian secessionist movement was under way against the Arabs in the north.

Obote started to find himself in trouble when certain contradictions in his policies became apparent. Although he was a tyrant at home, he tried to be something of a missionary abroad. He saw himself as a Pan-Africanist, a champion of anti-colonialism, and entertained an ambition to become a great world leader like Nkrumah, the former president of Ghana, which had been the first African country to gain its independence from Britain. However, he could not be pro-Israel *and* become a hero within the OAU. So his loyalties started to shift. He ordered the Israelis to stop their operations in northern Uganda, and he took steps to nationalize British interests when Britain continued to sell arms to South Africa.

Meanwhile, rival factions were beginning to emerge within the Army, and there was a division between the West Nile tribes and Obote's tribal group, the Acholis and Langis. Obote attempted to obtain domination by removing Amin as head of the Army. Amin, who is half Kakwa, half Nubian, with Sudanese blood, retaliated by inciting the West Nile tribes to revolt.

Amin's coup was executed while Obote was out of the country attending a Commonwealth conference for heads of state. Obote was informed in mid-flight. He wanted to go to Kenya, but Kenyatta refused to have him and he ended up in Tanzania, where he was joined by many of his supporters in exile, and was to make strenuous efforts to undermine the new régime in Uganda.

The professional way in which the coup was carried out signified that there had been a sophisticated military hand behind it. Even more significant was the way in which Amin's new Cabinet was composed. It was fairly obvious that someone was advising Amin when it came to appointing his ministers, most of whom were promoted from the civil service. People were appointed over their own heads, such as Professor Banage, a professor of zoology at Makerere University, who first learned of his appointment as minister of animal resources from a radio broadcast. A former ambassador to the United Nations, Apollo

Kironde, was also brought in as minister of planning and economic development, and it was he who proposed that I should be made Uganda's first roving ambassador.

Apollo Kironde, had a great deal of international experience, had lived in America for a long time, and was married to a black American. His suggestion that I be made a roving ambassador was consistent with the American concept of "ambassador at large." It was Kironde's considered opinion that, in the face of so much international skepticism regarding Amin, the country was sorely in need of someone who could travel around and rally support. When I told him that I had never met the general, as he always referred to Amin, he said that he would arrange a meeting.

Soon after, I was invited to a luncheon at State House. I was one of hundreds milling about, all pressing to be introduced to the president, who at that time was accessible to everyone, as well as always appearing on television and speaking on the radio. Apollo made a path for us to Amin, who was standing, dressed in military uniform, in the middle of the huge banqueting hall, talking quietly and slowly.

Apollo had briefed him on what to say to me because Amin's English and his ideas were not well-developed at that stage. He assured me "You have been a very good 'ambassador' for Uganda abroad." Our conversation was limited. He struck me as an unsophisticated man, whom people evidently felt they could influence.

Kironde kept in constant touch, urging me to think further about the roving ambassador idea. About this time I went to a government coffee party and was approached by the Israeli ambassador in Kampala, who asked me what position I would like in the new government. I was surprised that an ambassador should talk in this way and, even more, I was impressed by the implication that Amin was being "shepherded." I replied that I was not really interested in a government appointment, although I didn't mind doing some public relations work for Uganda abroad. The truth was that I was reluctant to completely renounce my acting career.

Meanwhile, my brother had returned from Nairobi, and with other royal *retournés* from the former kingdoms of Buganda, Bunyoro, Toro, and Ankole, was entertained lavishly on February 22 at State House by Amin, who was making an overt display of reconciliation. Amin also embarked on a tour of the country, taking in Toro where Patrick and I organized a celebration dinner and dance. Amin was very friendly and asked Patrick to accompany him everywhere he went in the kingdom, producing him before the enthusiastic crowds and proclaimng that here was their former king returned to them.

However, it is unlikely that Amin ever seriously considered reinstating my brother and the other kings on their thrones. He knew what the feelings of the people were regarding Obote's summary abolition of the monarchy. These were made abundantly clear at the various public gatherings he was holding at this time, during which everyone was encouraged to speak his mind. At one conference in the new conference center in Kampala at which I was present, it was expressed quite openly that the greatest gift Amin could confer on the civilian population was the restoration of the monarchy. But he was strongly aware of the Obote elements in the Army which were terrified of just such an eventuality, knowing perfectly well that if Amin were to reinstate the kings, he would rule Uganda forever. At this stage Amin could not afford to do anything actively to upset these elements. The truth was that most of the soldiers in the Army were from the northern and eastern areas of Uganda, and republican. This was brought home forcibly to me when later Amin spoke privately to me, advising me to warn Patrick that it would be dangerous for him to meddle in this matter. It was so unusual for Amin to utter an "opinion" in private that I knew it was a genuine warning. Neither Patrick nor I was particularly surprised.

By way of compensation, Amin offered Patrick a position as an ambassador. At this time, I had also been approached to participate in some way in the government. We held long consultations with trusted men from Toro and came to the conclusion that my brother should not at this stage enter service with the government, as it would look like total acquiescence by the monarchy. However, it was important that one of us should show willingness, so we both went to State House and informed the president of our decision.

Amin seemed pleased enough that I should accept, and in July of that year I was summoned unexpectedly by Jonathan Ekochu, one of Amin's two principal private secretaries, to State House, where I joined a line of people in a waiting room to see Amin.

When I walked into Amin's office on July 22, 1971, he told me that he was appointing me roving ambassador, with all its attendant privileges, and a Ministry of Information spokesman who was present in the room was dispatched outside to inform the waiting reporters. I was amused to see Wanume Kibedi, Amin's foreign minister, dash out after him to ensure that the news was given out correctly as "Miss Elizabeth Bagaaya has been appointed by His Excellency as the roving ambassador for Uganda," not "Princess Elizabeth," as it almost certainly would have been otherwise. Kibedi, a fellow lawyer, was to become a good friend of mine, but he was a republican and was anxious to make it clear how matters stood.

I learned later from my sister-in-law, who was then Kibedi's secretary, that that morning, only hours before my appointment, Amin had rung through to Kibedi to ask him what a roving ambassador actually did. The foreign minister explained that a roving ambassador was a kind of troubleshooter, who would act as a presidential envoy in times of crisis, conveying messages directly from one head of state to another, and being able to cut right across red tape because it was not required for a roving ambassador to go through the foreign minister of each country.

My next task was to work out the terms of my contract with Mr. Bigirwenkya, Amin's Permanent Secretary. Initially, there were problems as I had never imagined. I had thought to continue my acting career in New York, and only take on specific missions for the Ugandan government when it was deemed necessary. Amin was agreeable to begin with, but half the Cabinet objected vehemently; there was in fact some opposition to my appointment, chiefly because I was a royal. Amin was bombarded with telephone calls and called me in to assess my reaction to certain cabinet papers relating to the matter. These papers were normally confidential, and I was not a member of the Cabinet so actually I should not have been allowed to read them. But Amin seemed, as ever in those days, concerned to hear all sides of a question before committing himself. I said I would reconsider and, after discussions with Apollo Kironde and other ministers, I agreed to become roving ambassador full-time, and to reside in the country. Amin was pleased, as he had been receiving a lot of flack from all sections of the government, including the religious leaders.

I could now go ahead and sign my three-year contract granting me an ambassadorial house in Kampala, my own office and staff, and a ministerial car flying the Ugandan flag. My first and most urgent task was to go out to the Muslim world—Sudan, Senegal, Gambia, Morocco, Guinea, Niger, and Tunisia—to try to convince the governments there that Amin was better for Uganda than Obote, one of whose victims I had been. It was imperative that I manage to mobilize foreign support for the new regime, particularly as some African states had agreed to supply planes to Obote in Tanzania to invade Uganda.

8

The Dismantling
of a Civilization

Contrary to the impression given by the international press, the appearance of Idi Amin in the Ugandan political arena was no mystery. He might have been a phenomenon who rose and then disappeared without a trace if the British invasion of Uganda led by Captain Lugard of the British East Africa Company had not resulted in the dismantling of a civilization.

At first, it seemed as if the Batoro would be able to prevail. After years of internal struggle, they had at last defeated the armies of Kabalega. They threw all their energies into restoring their nation to its former glory, beginning with building their king a new palace on Kabarole Hill. It was covered with rocks and undergrowth, but the people slashed and hacked away with enthusiasm until they had cleared the area.

The spiritual and moral strength of the people during my grandfather Kyebambe's reign has never since been surpassed. It seemed that all individual interest had been submerged into the interest of the nation as a whole as the Batoro set about rebuilding their country.

Eseri Nyakabwa, who was trained and groomed by Kyebambe and his queen, Damali, in the palace from the age of nine to become one of the first twelve female preachers in Toro, was over a hundred years old when she told me, "I who saw the glory of Kabarole and Toro, I thank God I am blind now not to see Kabarole and Toro in their present state."

Such tribal solidarity ran against the imperial interests of the British Empire, for it was now a matter of imperial interest, not just the interest of a British trading company, that was at stake. By 1893 the BEAC was on the verge of collapse and had been replaced by the colonial state, which was far better placed to force the population into submission. The mercenary colonial army made up of Sudanese Nubians terrorized the population, dressed in skins and proudly proclaimed, *"Nyowe mwana wa mujungu"* ("I am the child of the white man"). They looted and robbed the population of its food, cattle, goats and hens, and even killed people.

Kyebambe's efforts to build up an indigenous army of Batoro were thwarted partly because only a handful of the Batoro and a small unit of his bodyguards were given licenses to possess guns and partly because of the colonial control of the purse, which meant that he possessed no means to finance the building of a native army. Kyebambe's constant protests about the colonial army, which he submitted to the colonial fort and abundantly recorded in his diaries, led to nowhere.

While the population was being victimized, divide and rule was the weapon that fragmented the united leadership of Toro. The question here was whether the king, the *Rukurato* (Parliament), and the chiefs were responsible to the people, or whether they were agents of the colonial state. In precolonial times, the monarchical concept was that the king ruled with his people. As the elders said, "A king who did not abide by the advice of his people was no king. Where else would he get subjects to rule?"

The king's powers were exercised through a well-organized traditional, hierarchical structure, stretching from the king at the top, to the *Rukurato*, down to the county chiefs, then to the sub-county chiefs, the parish chiefs, and finally the sub-parish chiefs. In most cases, all the affairs of state and matters affecting the subjects—be they administrative, political, judicial, or social—were dealt with through this reasonably democratic network, which ensured that the leaders were responsible to the people.

But the new colonial order demanded that my grandfather and his chiefs take and implement orders handed down through a distant and centralized bureaucracy, stretching from the British queen, to the Secretary for the Colonies in London, to the colonial governor and the provincial commissioner, and to the district commissioner at the bottom of the scale in the colony.

Wednesday was Parliament day in Toro. Every Wednesday morning my grandfather, accompanied by the full ceremonial splendor of the band of the royal trumpeters, flute players, and drummers, and by Toro councillors, rode on his white horse (the only one in the kingdom and an acquisition in trade exchanges between himself and King Kalugi of Kiziba, Tanzania) through the capital to the fort, where he met the provincial and district commissioners, the representatives of the British queen, to thrash out constitutional, political, and administrative problems. These sessions were sometimes held out in the open air before the crowds and sometimes behind closed doors. Kyebambe kept detailed diaries of these, more often than not, stormy exchanges. The picture that emerges from them is a desolate tale of vanishing expectations and cries of anguish.

Kyebambe records in his diaries: "Even when I appealed to the PC [provincial commissioner] and the DC [district commissioner] that elephants were killing my people, they told me that they would refer the matter to *Barozi* [the local word for the governor.]" In fact, "We will refer the matter to the Barozi," like *mañana* in Spanish, became the standard response to practically every action my grandfather and his government attempted to take for the well-being and advancement of their people. Through such tactics, the colonial state blocked the king's attempt to enlarge the *Rukurato* so that it could be made more representative.

As a young girl, I used to hear—as every Mutoro gets to hear at some time or another—references to chiefs who betrayed the king and the country to the English. However, whenever I sought further information, people were reluctant to elaborate. So I was grateful that such a sensitive subject is covered in great detail in my grandfather's diaries. In them, he records his distress over the PC's and the DC's arbitrary dismissals of chiefs without good cause or on trumped-up charges. He failed entirely to get the commissioners to abide by the age-old convention that a chief should be tried first by the king and the Rukurato, and only dismissed if the charge had been established. Not only did the colonial authorities ignore his pleas, but they usurped his power to appoint, transfer, and dismiss chiefs. Once a chief's tenure and personal protection depended on the PC and DC, he could be successfully manipulated.

The chiefs divided themselves between those who were loyal to the king and the country, and those who were loyal to the colonial state. The pro-colonial chiefs displayed open defiance and disrespect toward their king and the Rukurato. The Toro leadership was thus thrown into disarray and my grandfather could no longer hold it together, let alone exercise any authority. The colonial authorities had achieved their objective. A united resistance to colonialism had been broken, and the ensuing confusion was used as an excuse to bring in chiefs from outside Toro.

Contrary to a popular myth, the diaries show that it was the PC and DC, against my grandfather's wishes, who brought in the Baganda chiefs and installed them in the positions of prime minister, county chiefs, sub-county, parish, and sub-parish chiefs, right down to office clerks. "*Toro Yazikwa*" ("Toro was buried"), Mr. Rwakabuguli, an expert on the history of Toro, said to me, "Our chiefs were not allowed even to smoke pipes. A Muganda prime minister brought in a law so that people were beaten, fined, or imprisoned for being seen smoking pipes in public. It became so scandalous that the prime minister was beaten and thrown off his bicycle by a defiant Prince Paul Byembwa in a street encounter. But, you must distinguish between the Baganda chiefs brought in by the colonial authorities and the Baganda who came back with Kyebambe on his first return to Toro; men like Paul Zirimugwira and Eriya Rutaro who came as private individuals and were made chiefs by the king. Paul Zirimugwira was greatly loved by the Batoro; indeed, when he died he left King Rukiidi as heir to all his wealth and on his deathbed ordered his son Yowasi Kironde to take the key of the store to the king."

With the leadership of the country effectively divided, it was upon the control of the purse that the authorities relied to perfect total dependence of the king and his people on the colonial state. By virtue of the treaties of 1885, 1894, 1900, and 1906, together with later decrees, the natural wealth of Toro, including land, minerals, ivory, and salt, was acquired for the British Crown.

My grandfather at first refused to sign the 1894 treaty in which he was referred to as "chief" of Toro instead of "*Omukama*" ("supreme ruler"). "Where are my countries of Busongora bwa Makara, Bulega, and Mboga?" he demanded. The explanation for the reduced size of Toro was that at the Berlin Conference of 1885, when the Western European powers arbitrarily divided up Africa, Busongora bwa Makara went to the Belgians, and later, at the conference of Brussels, Britain gave Mboga and Bulega to the Belgium Congo in exchange for Arua, which became part of northern Uganda.

Kyebambe again refused at first to sign the 1900 and 1906 treaties because of the erosion of his own and the people's rights. He was warned that if he didn't sign, he would be king no longer. As the people attached great importance to the legitimacy of the throne, his survival was seen as synonymous with the survival of Toro as a kingdom. The Batoro pleaded with him to sign for Toro's sake, which he eventually did. He did try to press the colonial authorities to grant freehold land under the treaties to as many of the people as possible (the rest was the property of the Crown), but only he and a handful of Batoro were allotted any. It is important to note that for the first time in our history a landed gentry was created in a country where land and the natural wealth of the countryside had, from time immemorial, belonged to the community as a whole.

Kyebambe and his subjects were described as rebels by the colonial authorities, who outlawed the useful precolonial trade between Toro and Tanganyika, where there had been barter exchanges in ivory, clothes, iron tools, and beads, for fear of contact between the Germans in Tanganyika (now Tanzania) and the population of Uganda. Nevertheless, my grandfather and his friend, King Kalugi of Buhaya (western Tanganyika), carried on a clandestine trade through agents who stayed in Toro or vice versa, sometimes for as long as a year or more.

The colonial decree forbidding mining and processing on the part of the Batoro did irretrievable damage to our self-reliance and inventive ability. For centuries the empire of Kitara had been renowned for its iron tools and weapons, and blacksmiths had played a vital role in the community. Now the new decree put an end forever to the accumulated experience and expertise of many generations.

Another tragedy that befell the Batoro was the killing *en masse* of their cattle, which had always constituted our main wealth and means of self-sufficiency. From the beginning of time, the cow had been a holy animal around which our civilization and culture—language, poetry, religious belief, rituals, and customs—had grown up. The cow had provided nearly everything: milk, frozen blood and meat for food, skin for clothing and floor carpets, urine as medicine for skin care, horns for glue and utensils, dung for manure.

The colonial authorities knew that cultural, economic, and therefore political domination of the Batoro would have been impossible to achieve had the cattle remained abundant, and so they took a cruel shortcut and slaughtered the cattle with foreign vaccines they introduced by the planting of the eggs of tsetse flies from Botswana and Gambia. The tsetse ("biting insect") flies from Botswana brought sleeping sickness (*Mongota*). Eyewitnesses, such as my maternal uncle Ezekyeri Rukuba, who saw cattle dying in their millions, are still alive. He told me recently, pointing to an area in Kyaka country, "Our family lost thousands and thousands of cattle over there—just like that."

In no time at all, a new colonial order to serve the interests of metropolitan Britain had been brought into existence. Just as in any other colony the role of the kingdom in the new order became a source of raw materials for British industry, and the role of its citizens to provide cheap labor, by force initially and then through the tax laws—the logic of which was that since people were not allowed to pay taxes in kind, they were obliged to work to earn money to pay the taxes. In this way there was a permanent supply of cheap labor. The precolonial, traditional currency, *Ensimbi*, was withdrawn from circulation and replaced by silver money bearing the portrait of Queen Victoria (not my great-grandmother, but the British queen!)

Toro has the most fertile land in Uganda and a temperate climate which is suited to Europeans. Not surprisingly, a community of white settlers, similar to the ones in Kenya and South Africa, had soon formed. For these new European arrivals, the colonial state provided large tracts of land and cheap labor to grow coffee, rubber, and cocoa, the intention being to develop a plantation economy on similar lines to that in the West Indies, Assam, and Burma. It was not until the First World War and the collapse of commodity prices in the 1920s, which led to the collapse of the rubber trade altogether, that the colonial state fell back on a peasant economy with coffee and cotton being grown on small, scattered plots. Even then the cotton and coffee production remained in eastern and central Uganda, and did not reach Toro until the latter half of my father's reign.

Implementation of the new order caused untold suffering to Toro. Africa was not as fortunate as India in the caliber of the colonial officials it got. The provincial and district commissioners in my grandfather's time were mostly military men and were simply instruments of oppression. The repression reached such a pitch that my grandfather once demanded of the PC and DC, during one of his daily confrontations with them: "What is the meaning of protectorate?" In other words, had the treaties of protection, professing to create Uganda as a protectorate, been a farce, a deceitful and immoral method of securing the subjugation of a free people of an independent kingdom? In effect, had they created a colony?

The truth is given by Lugard himself, who describes these treaties as "the farce of acquiring jurisdiction by treaties. It was surely more justifiable for the European powers frankly to found their title of intervention upon force instead of assuming they themselves derived the right of intervention through cessation of sovereignty, under the guise of "treaties" which weren't understood and which rarely provided an adequate legal sanction for the powers assumed" (*The Rise of Our East African Empire*).

However, the entry in my grandfather's diary shows that he and the Batoro understood perfectly well the importance of the treaties—in particular, the difference between a protectorate and a colony. The only difference was that military force had rendered them powerless to resist the creation of a colony.

As far as the colonial officials were concerned, the object was to implement a grand British design. Just as the British had created an Anglo-Egyptian Sudan by annexing Sudan to Egypt, so they intended to create an Egyptian-Uganda union by annexing Uganda to Egypt. The three most notorious colonial administrators in all of Toro's colonial history are Provincial Commissioner Cooper, Captain Ashburnham, and Captain Rally.

A song I learned to play on the guitar as a young girl dramatizes the tragedies that Ashburnham (given the derogatory name of *Rutabisunga*, "The most notorious of them all") inflicted on the Batoro. The words go: *"Okanyita Rutabisunga Okanyita"* ("You have slain me, Rutabisunga, you have slain me"); *"Wantemaho Omukono Gwange Ogwobulyo"* ("You cut off my right hand"). Captains Ashburnham and Rally made several raids on the palace and on ordinary homes, using searches for guns and ivory as pretexts. Among the many innocent victims who were arrested, beaten, and tortured as a result of the raids was Michael Rusoke, my grandfather's treasurer and a brother of my maternal grandfather, his assistant treasurer, Nyakusara, and Nekemiya Bafuma, my great-grandmother Queen Victoria's treasurer. Nyakusara was tortured to death because he refused to implicate the king or anyone else.

Toro had become a police state. The population, in particular Batoro women who were sleeping with colonial administrators, was made to spy on each other. Even children were not spared. The Reverend Mr. Lloyd habitually invited children to tea, only to ask sly questions such as "I have a gun. Is there one at home?" Once Girigi Winyi, a grandson of Queen Victoria, innocently answered "yes." Fortunately, it was licensed.

My grandfather records how he was fined for every wrong his subjects were said to have committed. He was in an impossible position. Constitutionally, he was bound to accept Her Majesty's "advice," which to all intents and purposes meant "command." To refuse to do so would have meant the British government's withdrawal of recognition, and exile. In other words, he was required to be a mere agent of the colonial state, implementing its interests, in effect, a traitor to his people. The pressure exerted on him became so intolerable that, according to an entry in his diaries, on October 25, 1910, he once proposed his abdication.

Although his opponents in the British Protestant administration were formidable, Kyebambe found that he had two advantages that would help Toro make a great leap forward. The first was that there were many good people in the Church whom he could trust. The missionaries—men and women such as the Reverend H. E. Maddox, Père Achete, Edith Pike, Ruth Hurditch, Dr. and Mrs. Schofield, the Reverend G. E. Blackledge, and Commander Caldwell—were not interested in European domination over Africans. However, in order to get a grip on the population they needed the king, who was a stabilizing influence and whom the people trusted. At first, before it perfected its control over the country for lack of a state apparatus and infrastructure, the Church was the intermediary through which the colonial authorities obtained the people's obedience. This meant that there was less interference by the state in the relationship between the Church and the people, and the Church was a restraining factor in the harassment of the king and the Batoro. Because his colonial oppressors were the British Protestant administrators, Kyebambe's natural allies, despite his own Protestant faith, became the French Catholic missionaries, two of whom, Père Achete and Père Bosa, became extremely close friends of his. This was Kyebambe's second advantage.

The celebrated legacy that Toro has inherited from my grandfather is the absence of the religious animosity which has left permanent scars on other parts of Uganda. He was aware of the religious wars in Buganda and Ankole and was determined to avert them in Toro. His "plan" for doing this involved him taking practical, visible measures to demonstrate that the monarchy belonged not only to the Protestant religion but was also associated with the Roman Catholic religion.

Bishop Magambo, the incumbent head of the Roman Catholic Church in Toro once told me: "Your grandfather was very Mutoro and very human, and because of that he never discriminated against his people on the grounds of religion. The land on which our mission is built originally belonged to your great-grandmother, Queen Victoria, and was given to Père Achete by your grandfather. Not only that but the king generously donated cattle, sheep, and plantains toward the building of our cathedral, and the cathedral was called 'Nyinabarongo' after the Roman Catholic sister of the king. And he went further than that. As a result of the consultations he held with

Père Bosa, he had two of his own children, Prince J. Rwakatale and Princess Agnes Kakoko, baptized in the Roman Catholic Church and later his two cousins, Sister Pauline and Princess Antoneti Kabahindi, the mother of Father Kisembo, the incumbent Vicar General of Toro who is deputy head of the Roman Catholic Church here."

The colonial government found the Batoro's progress in education through the Church so alarming that they tried to call a halt to it because it was undermining its authority. It ordered the missionaries to put the brakes on the education of Africans, which led to a decline in the independence of the Church and consequently its influence. Such a decline meant there was a change in the content of and attitudes toward education, and there was a gradual shift away from community education, where the aim was to develop the individual's social conscience and awareness of his or her duty to the community, toward classroom education, where the aim has become the means to secure a social status in society. In the long term, this shift in emphasis has contributed to the present discord in Africa, in so far as it contributed to the creation of a self-centered leadership without a social conscience and alienated from the community.

Government interference in the Church jeopardized earlier gains and future development. The first Rutoro Grammar was written by the Reverend Mr. Maddox for the Protestant schools in 1902; and Caumartin, a French Canadian priest, did the same for the Catholic schools. Both had been published and were in use, but the colonial government ordered their withdrawal. I am not aware that any single Rutoro Grammar exists today. The colonial administrators also deprived Toro of its two most formidable instigators of progress in the persons of Edith Pike and the Reverend Mr. Maddox. Miss Pike had introduced education for women in Toro, and her one wish was to work, die, and be buried amongst the Batoro. But the government forced her to retire and insisted that she return to England. They did not even have the courtesy to provide her with transport and she had to travel over two hundred miles by bus. Needless to say, she was heartbroken.

As for the Reverend Mr. Maddox, no European single-handedly has ever surpassed the value of his contributions to Toro. Within a very short space of time he had built my grandfather's official palace, Queen Victoria's residence, Toro Hospital, the school and the palace workshop for the Toro youth, translated the Bible into Rutoro and written the first Rutoro Grammar. The crisis that led to his enforced exit was cleverly engineered by the colonial officials so that the Batoro were obliged to choose between him and the Reverend Mr. Fisher. Innocently unaware that they were being used as pawns in a highly sophisticated game of intrigue, they foolishly chose the Reverend Mr. Fisher, who had done nothing to prove himself. The Reverend Mr. Maddox was so hurt that after leaving Uganda he never again set eyes on a Mutoro. Almost fifty years later, my parents visited the United Kingdom and tried to get to see him, but he declined. Ever after, any misfortune that befell the country was often explained away as the Maddox Curse.

In political terms, the decline in Church influence meant that it could no longer exercise a restraining effect on the colonial state and there was an escalation of political oppression.

The raids for ivory and guns, which were pretexts for harassment, intensified. During one of these raids, Captains Rally and Ashburnham arrested my grandfather for two days. When they released him he took refuge in the Mountains of the Moon amongst the Bakonjo and Bamba tribes. His friend Père Achete sought him out at his hiding place and advised him, "You must not allow Captain Rally and Captain Ashburnham to humiliate you in this manner. You should appeal to the governor."

Before the two captains knew of it, the king had traveled over two hundred miles to see the governor, and as a consequence they were summoned to Entebbe. Fortunately, my grandfather was exonerated, but he persisted in his opposition to the colonial state until what had always been dreaded by the Batoro, happened. The king was exiled.

Provincial Commissioner Cooper was going on leave and as acting PC the government appointed Sullivan, a European settler. My grandfather objected on the grounds that Sullivan had a notorious record of beating and insulting his Batoro laborers. He followed up his objection with a letter expressing his grave concern about Sullivan's appointment. During the heated exchange that ensued, Cooper threatened the king with reprisals. The king replied, "Don't think you'll succeed in setting Toro ablaze as you did with Sese Islands"—referring to some of Cooper's dubious activities as an administrator in Buganda. Cooper accused the king of being anti-European and reported him to the governor. My grandfather was called to Entebbe, where the governor accused him of having once said, "One day you Europeans will have to go and we will be independent." He informed my grandfather that HM's government was withdrawing its recognition of him and accordingly he was no longer king of Toro. He was placed under house arrest and imprisoned at a place called Kitara, near Entebbe, until the place of his permanent exile could be decided on.

News of Kyebambe's exile cast the kingdom into deep gloom. Thousands of Batoro amassed on Kabarole Hill, where they stayed put, day and night, for almost two months, refusing to work or to do anything; in short, the first general strike happened, without anyone organizing one or declaring one.

Queen Victoria left her palace and moved to the king's palace. Queen Damali refused to follow my grandfather into exile. A campaign for the king's release began, and a flood of telegrams and letters began pouring into the governor's office.

Georgina Armitage, later Mrs. Schofield (my English guardian), went to PC Cooper and demanded, "What have you done with the Omukama?" On being informed that he was no longer *Omukama* and had been exiled, she replied, "Very well then. My father will raise the matter in the British Parliament." Mr. Armitage, MP (member of Parliament) for Leeds, Bishop Willis, who was the head of the Protestant Church in Uganda, and the Reverend Mr. Blackledge and many other missionaries worked hard for his release, as did his brother king, the king of Buganda, who also appealed to London.

After two months, my grandfather was reinstated as *Omukama* and returned to Toro. But he told many people, "I will not tolerate a second exile. I will not suffer the same fate as Kabalega. There are many ways I can end my life. And it will be done."

Uneasy peace prevailed, but now the fragile harmony between the Church and the people began to be upset. The specific arguments centered around the coronation rites, polygamy, the Rutoro language, and drinking, among other things. But the overall trend led to a grudging realization among the Batoro that the colonial government was not alone in undermining the culture and attempting to dominate it.

9

The Roots
of Resistance

The chief exponent of resistance to cultural domination was Akiiki Mukakijabara Bagaaya Rwigirwa (after whom I am named), the princess royal—the Batebe—to King Kyebambe. Her personal experience with Europeans had made her exceedingly cautious about their intentions.

As a young girl, she had been given in marriage by her father, King Nyaika of Toro, to Kabalega, king of Bunyoro, to secure the peace between their kingdoms. When the British arrested her husband and sent him into exile, she escaped with his mother to Buganda.

Kyebambe sent for her. She expected to be taken directly to her brother, but, instead, she was taken to a palace at Kamengo that had been built specially for her. Finally, the day arrived that she was to be brought to Kyebambe's palace, and she prepared to leave with her possessions.

To her surprise, the messenger who had come to fetch her said, "Stop. You cannot take those satanic things with you, for your brother is now a Christian."

Reluctantly she left her belongings behind.

Her encounter with Kyebambe was no less dramatic. As she entered his reception room, everyone gathered there sang a hymn and then knelt down to pray. Bagaaya hesitated, but seeing that even the king was on his knees, she followed suit. Everyone had their eyes closed, but she was determined to see the strange things that were going on. She covered her face with her hands but watched everything through the spaces between her fingers.

In time her brother would convert her to Christianity and she would be baptized Maliza (Martha). But she never lost sight of her people's ancient traditions.

When she returned to Toro, she found that the European missionaries had decided which rituals pertaining to the monarchy were to remain and which were "satanic" and had to be discarded. Incredibly, most of them had been labeled "satanic" and abolished, destroying much of the mystery surrounding the Toro monarchy. Among the most important rituals to be done away with was the official greeting called out by male citizens the first time they saw the king each day: *"Ngundu Zona Okali,"* which means "All there is is yours." The British objected to *"Okali"* because, they argued, it conflicted with the Bible by equating the king with God. Since no man could be given the ritual greeting unless he had been crowned, the British forbade Kyebambe to have a coronation ceremony for thirty-three years, from 1885 to 1919.

Bagaaya, however, said to the king, "This book you swear by, the Bible—it is not in conflict with Toro culture. The Bible recognizes the necessity of a crown for every king. Oh no! it is your European missionaries who are against Toro culture. They are using the Bible to undermine your authority."

Through her insistence, and with the help of the missionaries, my grandfather was duly crowned in 1919, and for the first time he was greeted with *"Okali"* and officially assumed the kingly name of Kyebambe. The governor, Sir Henry H. Bell, gave him the gift of an umbrella to use on coronation anniversaries.

Bagaaya struggled on with her efforts to uphold our ancient traditions and customs. This time she argued in favor of polygamy. Following his baptism, the missionaries had insisted that the king select one queen out of the fifty-two in the palace. For as soon as the new king was old enough to marry, the Batoro had brought him their best daughters. (Most of them had never reached the royal bed.) The king chose Tibaitwa, who was later baptized with the name Damali. Tragically, the queen had about ten miscarriages, which meant there was no heir to the throne. There were rumors of witchcraft, and the murmurings developed into a furor of criticism against Christianity, which had forbidden their king to have more than one wife.

Meanwhile, the colonial government pressured my grandfather into naming an heir presumptive from among his nephews, which was bitterly resented by the Batoro. On the other side, Bagaaya kept reminding the king that he had a duty to present Toro with a child of his own as an heir. She managed to convince him that the Queen should undergo traditional treatment, called "*Omuhinga.*" So my grandmother was taken to the village of Kitumba, where a wide, deep pit (*Endeba*) had been dug. The bottom, which had been leveled out, was covered with banana leaves that had been softened over a fire, with care being taken to ensure that there were no torn leaves. The pit was then filled with cold water and a wooden wall was built across the middle so that it was divided into two equal halves. One half was filled with stones which had been heated until the water reached boiling point. My grandmother was massaged with perfumed traditional oil, dipped into the hot water, and rhythmically turned from side to side till she was dripping with sweat. The temperature of the water was kept hot. Periodically, she would be taken out so that more heated stones could be put in to reheat the water. The process was repeated until she could bear it no longer and then she was removed and made to rest in the cold water in the other half of the pit. Meanwhile, a goat had been killed and cooked, and after a while the queen was fed with hot soup and goat's meat. She received this treatment for several months.

Miraculously, the treatment worked and she gave birth to a baby girl who was baptized Ruth Komuntale. She was also called "*Kabwimukya,*" which means "reminder of past grief." However, as far as the Batoro were concerned the birth of the princess was only a limited success. There was still no heir. The country had to wait for four years, until, on March 6, 1904, my father was born. The nation rejoiced and the royal musicians played day and night for nine days. Asanasiyo Byairungu, my father's tutor, remembers the day the young heir was baptized. Everyone had gathered in the capital to await the arrival of the king. Unknown to the crowds, Kyebambe had received news from the PC that the governor would be passing through Toro that morning on his way from one part of Uganda to another. He required the king to be there when the governor crossed Toro, at a point some fifty miles away. A message was sent to the crowds waiting at the church in Kabarole to tell them what had happened. To everyone's relief, my grandfather managed to make it back in time. The Reverend Mr. Kitchener lifted the baby prince up toward the crowds, and said, "At last Toro has a king." The crowds responded with death wails, happy, but fearful that so much rested on this slender life.

It was true that there were grave fears for the little prince, especially as he was attacked by cough after cough, so much so that my father was nicknamed "*Bakoko*" ("of coughs") and a special wing was added to the hospital so that he could be quickly attended to on his frequent visits there.

It soon became clear that the queen was unlikely to have any more children and, with the dubious health of the young prince to bear in mind, the king was once again under pressure to ensure continuation of his line. Bagaaya argued that the Bible was not against polygamy but against adultery, and she quoted the examples of Kings David and Solomon, both of whom had hundreds of wives and were still God's favorites. She pointed out that the Bible also spoke well of Abraham, who had two wives, and of Jacob, who was the father of twelve tribes.

Finally, my grandfather was persuaded by Bagaaya. He informed the Churches that henceforth he was going to base his faith and the practice of it on the Bible itself and not on the interpretation of the European missionaries, who, after all, were influenced by their own culture and social backgrounds. He took more wives and had twelve children.

However, by this time Kyebambe had both the colonial government and the Church against him. According to his diaries, the Reverend Mr. Lloyd forbade him to partake in Holy Communion and turned him away each time he turned up for it. For my grandfather, it was the last straw. He left the capital and went to live in the village of Kyangabukama, in the county of Mwenge. There he saw hardly anyone, ate little and went into a state of physical decline. He died on December 29, 1928.

Unfortunately, my grandfather had one very serious disability: he was not only a king but, like his ancestors, he was a priest-king—otherwise he would have been canonized by the Christian Church. The African concept of the priest-king, worshiped as a deity, has been one of the chief obstacles to the Europeans in their endeavors to dominate the African mind and heart. A reign which had started with so much tribal unity and spiritual togetherness had ended in conflict.

When my father succeeded Kyebambe in 1929, he found himself faced with the grave task of effecting a rapprochement between the Batoro on one hand and the colonial government, and the Church on the other. Secondly, he had to secure a place for Toro in a new Uganda. Fortunately, he was capable of handling even the toughest problems because he had two unique assets: an appealing nature and broad exposure.

His tutor once told me, "He was a wonderful child. Never a nasty word left his lips. The secret of his success was that up to the day he departed from this life, he never caused the slightest grief to a single citizen of the kingdom."

He received the widest possible exposure in schools outside his own tribe, in the Ugandan Army and the police force, which took him to the remotest parts of Uganda. He went to England to study in 1924, the first time a Toro ruler had ever left Uganda to study abroad. In the United Kingdom and in his travels throughout the world, he came to see that education was the key to the future. He also understood that the economy was vital to the survival and advancement of the kingdom and of the other three monarchies in Uganda.

The first act of his reign was to remove the Baganda and to replace them by Batoro chiefs. He had been educated and brought up partly among the Baganda, so he comprehended their mentality extremely well. The king of Buganda, Daudi Chwa II, was not only his cousin but his guardian and close friend, which meant that the gradual removal of the Baganda chiefs was achieved without undue animosity. My father used this opportunity to appoint chiefs from every class of people, the Bahuma or cattle class, the Abairu or agricultural class, and the mountain tribes of Bakonjo and Bamba.

Under his leadership, Toro's economy expanded. He promoted a project to mine and purify salt (even though it was later blocked by the colonial officials), instigated the fish and copper industries, began to set out the national parks for animal protection and the tourist industry, and extended the railway, which he baptized "Batoro," from Mombasa and Kampala to Toro. He also campaigned to convince the Batoro to welcome these new employment opportunities. He never saw the educated Batoro as a threat to the monarchy and labored to ensure that as many of his people as possible were educated or got scholarships to be educated abroad. He worked too for their participation in Toro government, and managed to win important concessions from the colonial administrators. By the end of his reign he was to have gained a good measure of regional autonomy for the kingdom. He won back the people's right to royalties from minerals, fish, salt, and the national parks, and to the office of prime minister of Toro he had added the offices of finance and justice ministers. When Kabarole Hospital was threatened with closure, he headed the campaign to save it, and when the building of the Cathedral was halted through lack of funds, he gave money from his private purse and made sure it was completed, which it was in 1937. He crowned the achievement with the presentation of an organ, built in memory of his mother, Queen Damali, which he selected in the United Kingdom. Above all, he earned from the Batoro the same love and faithfulness which they had accorded to Kyebambe at the beginning of his reign. His motto was "God and the Batoro."

It is impossible to assess how the conflict between the Batoro and the colonial state would have been resolved, because it was superseded by the impending independence. Suddenly, a twofold world force reversed the colonials' policies. To begin with, the national liberation movements based on mass mobilization and armed struggle flared up—as in Kenya, Algeria, and Vietnam—and were threatening the stability of the colonial order. Then the Second World

War came about and resulted in the decline of the British and French empires and the emergence of the supremacy of the United States of America, which supported the independence of the colonies.

In this way, worldwide dismantling of the colonial system became inevitable, and in Uganda as elsewhere the question was no longer whether independence would ever be granted, but to whom the colonial state would be handed over. The British decision, which was designed to perpetuate British influence and its economic exploitation of the country, was to implant the British political system, handing over state power to hurriedly formed political parties and bypassing the age-old and well-organized indigenous systems.

The first ever general election during sixty-eight years of British colonial rule took place in 1961, only one year before independence was granted in 1962. Up until 1958, Africans had been deliberately excluded from participating in the central legislature (the embryo sovereign parliament), but in that year they were permitted to elect ten members to a still nonrepresentative legislature. It was not until May 1962, five months before independence, that they were allowed to exercise executive powers at the central level. The first generation of the educated elite had been absorbed mainly into the civil service, which robbed the political leadership of any caliber, and the principal organs of the state, namely the Army, the judiciary, the legislature, and the executive were all headed by expatriates. (The political consciousness of the nation had, in any case, been blocked through all the oppression we had suffered.)

In contrast to the center, the principal organs of the kingdoms and other regions, judiciary, legislature, executive, and the civil service (the kingdoms were forbidden to have armies or police), were all African-manned and -run, with age-old ability and experience in governing and in the exercise of power.

The consequences of imposing an alien system on Uganda were catastrophic, both politically and socially. The fundamental conflict between the central government—the successor of the colonial state— and the monarchies came to a head: in a conflict between dictatorship and democracy. The monarchies and the regions were crushed in 1966 and 1967 by Obote's *coups d'état*. The policy of the British to build a state of Uganda based on force and deception was continued by the African political leadership under Obote and Amin, which led inevitably to the state itself disintegrating and to our whole civilization and culture being dismantled. Defiantly, I resolved that if I could play a part in saving our civilization from within Uganda, I would try. My name was a daily reminder of my responsibility.

10

Through
the Landscape
of Amin

During the two and a half years I worked for President Amin as his roving ambassador, I came to admire the way he grappled with the complex lexicon of politics. When he came to power, he was almost illiterate, but he seemed to have a gift for languages (unlike Obote and most Ugandan politicians, he was able to speak several tribal languages, including Lugbara and Kakwa, Luganda, Lusoga, Langi, Acholi, and Swahili), and he quickly became proficient in English. Whenever I returned from a mission abroad, I would compile my report, then make an appointment to brief the president. Afterwards, he would call in the press and reproduce what I had told him almost word for word.

Unfortunately, Amin was not as competent at procedures of government—Cabinet and other essential meetings—because, in typical soldier-fashion, he was never content to remain for long in one place but would jump about from one place to another, with an entourage of secretaries, civil servants, and government ministers trailing in his wake.

It is doubtful whether Amin ever grasped some of the more difficult concepts of government, although, in a way, his inability to fully comprehend the consequences of his actions was part of his strength—in that he and his government never became crippled through inaction. But such a limitation was also his weakness, because it meant he could be easily led.

Once, for instance, his finance minister, Mr. Kiyingi, was anxious to finalize the budget. He asked for an appointment to see the president, who was about to dash off to Somalia on a state visit. Amin scribbled his signature on the Finance Bill and departed to catch his plane. Kiyingi went ahead and announced the budget, but some elements in the Cabinet and Army objected and tried to make it look as though the minister was personally responsible for what was at that time an almost impossible economic situation. Kiyingi was in fact a brilliant man, who had been a governor of the Bank of Uganda and had served with the International Monetary Fund. Amin came back to find himself in the middle of a staged outcry, and complained to me, as one of the first ministers he saw on his return, that Kiyingi, in creating such discontent in the Army and elsewhere, was plotting to overthrow him. Concerned for Kiyingi's safety, I took him to one side before a Cabinet meeting and warned him to be prepared for an outburst. Sure enough, Amin stalked in and began hurling accusations at Kiyingi, who was not given a chance to say anything in his own defense.

Amin simply did not understand that the apparent chaos could not have been created by one man alone. I was so frustrated by his inability to perceive the deception going on under his nose, that at a Cabinet meeting following, I burst into tears, and afterwards implored him to see that Kiyingi was innocent of any misdealings, and that he had only been doing his best. Amin laughed, even though he was still angry, and merely replied that he didn't want ministers coming to Cabinet meetings and breaking down. Later, at a public meeting in the Conference Center, Amin openely denied that he'd been a party to the budget, in spite of having put his signature to it, in the presence of the minister of justice, and Kiyingi was shifted out of the Ministry of Finance. But Kiyingi was convinced that I had saved his life, for a personal accusation from Amin could easily mean the death sentence.

This incident is a prime example of Amin being skillfully maneuvered by his own enemies. He did have good ideas, but somehow the implementation of them was always being frustrated and those who meant well ended up with the blame. Inevitably, given Amin's character, the country as a whole and many blameless individuals were eventually to suffer.

At the beginning, Amin was pretty firmly entrenched as president. In its early stages, at least, his coup had been bloodless; what fighting there was was confined to Army barracks, and he was greeted with relief and gratitude by the civilian population. He was protected by sophisticated security methods, such as his personal telephone number. To get through to the president, you had only to dial one number (Entebbe 2241) and you could be put through to him wherever he was, even if he was hundreds of miles away in the bush. This elaborate security precaution meant that nobody could ever be certain where Amin might be.

Above all, however, Amin at the time of the coup had the Army behind him, and provided he was able to maintain that unity among the West Nilers, he was practically invincible. So anybody who wanted to get rid of Amin knew that he had to start with the Army, and that is exactly what happened.

In late 1971 or early 1972, Amin started to turn against the Lugbaras, a tribe from the West Nile region who constituted a powerful faction within the Army. The first victim was Ovudria, a signal man in intelligence, a sensitive position to hold and which Amin felt he had abused. Ovudria's car was stopped by a Nubian at a traffic circle in Kampala outside the Parliament building, and he was taken away and quietly executed. Nevertheless, everyone heard about it. Then Obitregama, the minister of internal affairs, and Colonel Wilson Toko, the head of the Air Force, both Lugbaras and highly intelligent and capable men, lost their positions. There was another man, Wasswa, who had been the first to anounce the news of the coup on Ugandan television and whose face was therefore quite well known, and who managed to escape to Kenya. Amin requested his extradition, and he was brought back to Uganda and killed. Amin was indulging in a purge, but unwittingly he was weakening his own position because he was removing his best men and replacing them with ignorant people.

The real trouble, however, started in 1972 with the expulsion of the Israelis and the British Asians. It was at this time also that Amin began to swing toward Islam and the Arab world.

One day I had just finished briefing the president after a mission when I was told point-blank by Amin that if the British were not careful he was going to send all the British Asians in Uganda to England, just as Libya had expelled the Italians. Amin had asked the British government for a loan to finance his projects, but he did not understand that a government loan would take some time to process, and he was growing impatient.

A short while before, while on a state visit to West Germany, whose government he had also approached for a loan, Amin had received a message that Libya would be pleased to help him with the finances he needed, and that he would be welcome there. Now, up until that time, relations between anti-Israeli Libya and pro-Israeli Uganda had been very bad. Britain and Israel were strong allies. It was during my mission to the UN with the Ugandan delegation that Amin spoke out for dialogue with South Africa, in defiance of the OAU. While we were there, a PLO representative came up to me and pointed out that our pro-Israeli policy was all very well, but was I aware that, under British Prime Minister Arthur James Balfour, the British had offered Uganda to the Jews as a place of settlement, and asked me what I thought we would have done if the Jews had not said they preferred to go back to Palestine instead.

Now while he was still in Germany, Amin announced to his horrified ministers and other members of his delegation that he was going at once to Libya. Everyone was convinced that he would be assassinated and refused to accompany him. Amin thanked them and said that, in that case, he would fly his plane himself. Eventually, Colonel Toko, who had not at that time been dismissed as head of the Air Force, agreed to accompany him.

They arrived in Libya to red-carpet treatment, being met at the airport by Colonel Gaddafi himself. Amin was immensely impressed by Gaddafi, and picked up the information about the expulsion of the Italians; hence his threat to expel the Asians from our own country.

Concerned about the implications of such a move on Amin's part, I mentioned to Judith Hart—then a junior minister in the Labour

Government—on my way through London that the British loan ought to be finalized as soon as possible. When I returned to Kampala, I also saw the British high commissioner, Mr. Slater, who assured me that the loan was going through. But lately relations between him and Amin had started to cool—it had become much more difficult for Slater to gain access to the president.

There were other indications that Amin was beginning to change camps. Arabic was introduced on the radio, and suddenly he ordered all the Israelis in the country to pack up and leave, even their embassy staff. Shortly afterwards, Amin expelled the British Asians and nationalized British interests.

The Asian community had dominated the commercial sector ever since the late 1800s, and its integration in the African community, and the Africanization of commerce and industry had long been a problem. Initially, Asians had been brought by the British from the Indian subcontinent to help construct the railway from Mombasa to Uganda, and the colonial state encouraged them to settle and develop the country's commerce and trade. At the same time, it directed its administrative machinery toward the repression of African traders. As an alien community, the Asians were a safe bet politically, segregated as they were from the indigenous peoples of Uganda. From starting as commercial workers, the Asians progressed to being independent small traders but eventually, with the arrival of big capital from Bombay, their control went beyond the retail to the wholesale trade and processing industries. While they were under colonial protection, the Asian community thrived, trading largely in British manufactured goods and coming to control more than 80 percent of Uganda's commerce and trade.

However, they shared no common cultural heritage with the Africans, and there was naturally considerable resentment among the majority of Ugandans that their wealth should be controlled by a small immigrant community. African traders came late to the commercial sector, and they had to wage political struggles to create room for their own expansion. Their grievances over prohibitive license fees and the centralized, hierarchical nature of trade turned into a national grievance, whereby Asian shops and businesses were boycotted and racial conflict came to the fore. In the 1950s, before independence, such boycotts were suppressed. At independence, the African leadership broadened the Africans' economic base by nationalizing certain industries with the help of individual corporations, using multinational and individual capital which meant that the state was still a junior partner. The Asians were offered an opportunity to adopt Ugandan citizenship, but most of them chose to remain of British nationality.

When Amin embarked on the first phase of his "economic war," the British Asians were given a rigid deadline of three months to leave the country. Uganda was by no means the first country to expel large numbers of foreign nationals (it had been done in Sri Lanka), and it was a move which made Amin immediately popular with the African population. However, disillusionment was to descend with Amin's realization that it was British banking capital which had been the guiding force behind the Asian assets. This led him into the second phase of the economic war, which was to nationalize British interests (even though one of his first acts when he came to power was to reverse Obote's nationalization measures), while distributing smaller businesses to individual Africans, many of whom were not professional entrepreneurs.

Amin's civilian advisers did their best to ensure that the exercises of expulsion and nationalization of property were carried out fairly and with promises of adequate compensation. They also exerted pressure to make it untenable for Amin to expel Asians who were Ugandan citizens, insisting that these should remain and be accorded all the rights of Ugandan nationals. However, Amin went on to expel them as well, thereby rendering many of his country's own citizens stateless. Such inhumantiy was compounded by feelings of envy and outright anger as the experts who had been given the task of allocating businesses to nationals were replaced by corrupt army officers. Many benefited falsely, acquiring vast riches practically overnight by selling off all the goods in their businesses and then shutting them down. Shops became empty as their new owners had no idea where their stock came from, or how to replace it, and no proper records were being kept. The production and distribution of essential goods fell into disarray, and there was an accompanying breakdown in social services and the professions. Because the Army was demanding a greater share of the handouts, and Amin knew it was imperative for his survival to keep the troops loyal, he formed new committees composed mostly of soldiers to see to the allocation of business enterprises, and shortages of basic commodities and foreign exchange followed.

Amin's actions caused chaos. However, a substantial group of African entrepreneurs did develop which had never been there in the sixty-eight years of colonial rule and the nine years of Obote's rule. The tragedy was that Amin's inhumanity to the Ugandan Asians, and his lack of effective contingency plans for running the economy after the professionals had been forced to leave the country, meant that both the economy and his government were weakened. The president had started something which could have worked, but had himself moved in a direction which was self-defeating. In the end, his actions were to seem to prove that Africans were incapable of managing their own economy, and only succeeded further in isolating the Ugandan community from the rest of the world.

Internally, in spite of the financial chaos, Amin's position had been temporarily strengthened because certain important sectors of the community were benefiting from his latest actions. But the popular support he had enjoyed when he first came to power, and even the general approval he had gained when he expelled the Asians, was being dissipated by the effects on the civilian population of his security network.

When he deposed Obote, Amin had formed the Public Safety Unit (PSU), which initially did a good job of dealing with the internal security of the country. But its leaders, drawn mainly from the police force, were mostly uneducated and, instead of firing them, Amin made the mistake of giving them free rein. The intelligence network, the State Research, later came to be headed by equally uneducated men. The president dispatched some of them to the Soviet Union and other countries for training, but they were rapidly returned as "untrainable." Amin was sensitive to the feelings and opinions of his "bully boys," who were themselves open to unprincipled and brainwashing influences, so there was a network of corruption extending from the bottom to the top. Amin had created the system, but now the system was being exploited by individuals and small groups for their own personal motives, and it was slipping from his control. Even guiltless people who were pro-Amin were being disposed of, in other words, murdered.

By now, most of the vital security forces were headed by Nubians from Sudan. The PSU was headed by a Nubian called Ali Toweri, the State Research by a Nubian named Farouk Minawa, and the military police at Makindye by another Nubian, Malera—and nearly all the Army officers were Nubians. They were also in the Cabinet. Only the police force was not headed by a Nubian, but it could be discounted as a factor in maintaining order, as whoever was in overall charge was changed every other day.

The civilian population was effectively paralyzed, and I don't think it was ever at any stage capable of a cohesive rebellion. In any case, there were so many groups who were actually benefiting from the system by this time. There were plenty of people who were amassing personal fortunes, particularly as a result of the thriving black market, known as *Magendo*. After the Israelis and the Asians had been expelled and Amin had confiscated British property, there was a concerted effort to organize some sort of international boycott. Certainly Uganda's reputation with the World Bank and the International Monetary Fund was near rock bottom, and no credit facilities were allowed anywhere. Coffee smuggling was booming, which meant that the government was losing the proceeds from its legitimate sale, but certain individuals inside and outside the government, including Amin, were profiting, so nothing was done. There was an acute shortage of medicines and other supplies, and people were actually dying from lack of proper medical care. But the Army was receiving priority treatment with its own "Army Shops," and with his ill-gotten coffee gains, Amin was able to pay for arms that Libya, the Soviet Union, France, and Britain were more than willing to provide him.

In 1972, there had been an invasion from Tanzania by two groups of exiles, one led by Oyite Ojok—Obote's group—the other by Yoweri Museveni, attempting to take advantage of Amin's preoccupation with the expulsion of the Asians. It failed because the invading forces were so disorganized, and Amin was able to repel them. But Obote, on the whole, would not cooperate with any other exile groups and even kept Amin informed, in a roundabout way, of invasion and guerrilla activities, until such time as he was ready to recapture power himself. Amin was constantly going on the radio to warn about possible threats from Tanzania, but by this time he had lost credibility and was not always believed, even if they were true. Obote's strategy was that Amin should survive until he himself captured Uganda.

Kenya, a neighboring country, was the landlocked Uganda's lifeline, as goods and smuggled coffee had to pass through it to get to Mombasa and the sea. But Amin was never in any danger from Kenya, because from a currency point of view, that country was benefiting. For one hundred Ugandan shillings, you could get something like twenty Kenyan shillings (the two currencies used to be on a par). Libya and Saudi Arabia, meanwhile, anxious to keep Amin within the Muslim axis and under control, were busy injecting cash aids into Uganda.

Plots to overthrow Amin abounded, but only one ever came near to being successful, and that occurred in early 1974. It was organized by Colonel Charles Arube, an efficient and well-respected officer, but he made one crucial mistake. The last stage of the plot involved a contingent of men, supported by one or two tanks, being sent to arrest Amin at State House. Unfortunately, the officers Arube chose to perform this task were of junior rank, and Amin managed to hoodwink them into giving him time to make a quick telephone call and summon his own troops. The troops arrived in force and arrested all the men who had been sent to arrest Amin, and Arube himself was picked up and murdered.

Western countries, especially those whom Amin had offended, could have done something to overthrow him, but for their own reasons they chose not to. He was certainly vulnerable to external action, as the famous Entebbe raid demonstrated. The Israelis had been itching to get back at Amin ever since they had been humiliated by Uganda's expelling them (particularly as Uganda's action had triggered off a chain reaction in which Israel was expelled from all member countries of the OAU) and turning what used to be the Israeli Embassy in Kampala into the embassy of the PLO, with whom Amin was on friendly terms.

When the plane containing the Israeli hostages landed in Entebbe,

Amin saw his chance to grab world attention. He did not realize that the PLO were taking the matter very seriously and hoping to get some of their people freed. He made daily drives to the airport, enjoying all the drama and publicity, teasing the hostages and flaunting himself in front of the cameras. The Israelis, meanwhile, installed Barlev, the former military attaché who had by his own confession helped Amin come to power and who understood the president's psychology, to be their contact with him, talking to him on the telephone, flattering him and keeping him occupied while the Israelis got on with planning their daring raid. Finally, of course, they succeeded in snatching the hostages and scoring a point over Amin, who once again became a laughingstock in the eyes of the world.

The Israelis could have gone further and toppled Amin, but as it happened they did not. In common with other countries, they had their own reasons for not minding if and how Amin survived. In putting across a certain image of black Africa to liberal Western minds, governments have often found buffoons and crooks like Amin useful to prove the thesis that black countries are incapable of governing themselves.

There were numerous reasons, of course, why Amin's regime was able to survive for so long, not least the president's sheer brute force and ability to ride roughshod over convention and protocol. For him, no rules or laws existed, either domestic or international, except those that coincided with his own whims.

As far as internal politics were concerned, Amin had made a gross error of judgment in disposing of his more enlightened leaders. The people he replaced them with were illiterate, and the machinery of government suffered. His intelligence network, in particular, could be infiltrated by enemies. When the president had first attained economic power, he had succeeded in "commercializing" the Ugandan mentality—something which the former colonial power had always blocked—but, by 1977, the economy was on the brink of collapse. In his anxiety to pander to the demands of his troops, Amin had neglected government aid for development projects in favor of a high defense budget and the buying of useless military hardware. Because of factional splits—exacerbated by Amin himself—within the Army,

Elizabeth's father, King Rukiidi.

Elizabeth (left) with her mother, Queen Kezia, one of her uncles, and two sisters, Mabel and Gertrude.

The four kings of Uganda during the early colonial era. Left to right: *King Andereya Duhaga of Bunyoro; King Daudi Chwa of Buganda; King Kahaya of Ankole; and King Daudi Kyebambe of Toro.*

The baptism of King Kyebambe (center) *on March 20, 1896, by Bishop Tucker* (center, right).

Early missionaries, including Miss Edith Pike (standing), *Miss Fisher* (seated, right), *and Bishop Tucker* (seated, center).

Miss Pike's first reading class in 1901, which included male and female pupils of all ages.

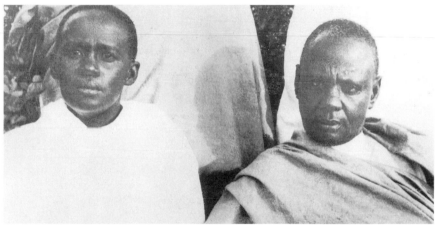

Queen Damali (left) and Queen Victoria (right), Elizabeth's grandmother and great-grandmother—the roots of national resistance to colonialism.

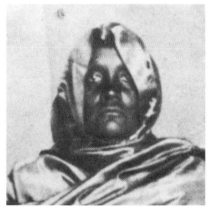

Akiiki Mukakijabara Bagaaya Rwigirwa, Batebe to King Kyebambe.

Princess Ruth Komuntale, Batebe to King Rukiidi.

During the Moon Ceremonies, King Rukiidi wears the Toro crown and begins the procession from karuzika (the courthouse) to the Rukurato (Parliament).

Amakondere (the trumpets) of the royal band.

Return to karuzika through nyaruzigati (the courtyard) after ceremonial procession through the sacred houses.

The regalia, including ekondo (the crown), enkwanzi za maguru (anklets), amawino (necklaces), ebitega (bracelets).

Mugalihya, the throne for daily reception.

During the milking ceremony, enkorogi (the royal cows) are led to the fire and brushed down. Abakorogi (the royal herdsmen) remove flies and ticks.

King Rukiidi receiving Queen Elizabeth II.

The kings of Uganda. Left to right: *The Omugabe of Ankole; The Omukama of Bunyoro; The Omukama of Toro; The Kabaka of Buganda.*

Karuzika (colonial architecture).

Karuzika (modern architecture).

Patrick is crowned King of Toro, March 1966, the last time a king is crowned in Uganda before Milton Obote abolished the Uganda monarchies in September 1967.

Prince Patrick burying his father at egasani (the shrine) of Karambi, December 30, 1965.

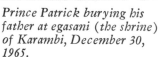

Elizabeth, beginning her duties as Batebe to King Patrick, leaves Kabarole Cathedral during the coronation ceremonies for King Patrick.

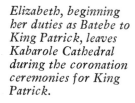

At the palace, King Patrick, with the royal servants, sits for a farewell picture spanning three generations. He holds the child of one of the servants.

Elizabeth is called to the English bar, 1965.

Norman Parkinson photographs Elizabeth for British Vogue. *(Courtesy* Vogue, © *The Condé Nast Publications Ltd.)*

Penati photographs her for American Vogue. *(Courtesy* Vogue, © *The Condé Nast Publications Ltd.)*

Elizabeth is sworn in as Minister of Foreign Affairs before President Idi Amin.

Elizabeth at the United Nations.

Elizabeth's official visit to the Federal Republic of Germany, when Foreign Minister Hans-Dietrich Genscher approved funds for building the salt plant at Lake Katwe in Uganda.

Mrs. Malyamu Amin, one of the four wives of President Amin, chatting with the Begum (wife of the Aga Kahn) and Elizabeth during a reception in Kampala.

Jomo Kenyatta, President of Kenya, with his daughter Margaret, who gave Elizabeth asylum after she fled from Amin.

Wilbur and Elizabeth as guests of honor at a charity benefit in Gloucestershire, England.

Wilbur's father, Leo Sharp Ochaki.

Wilbur and his mother, Salai Mbabi.

Young Wilbur with a school friend at Nyakasura School, Toro.

Wilbur at Kyambogo Technical College, Uganda, where he qualified as an engineer.

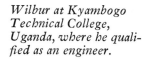

At Oxford Air Training School at Kidlington, Wilbur attains his Commercial Pilots License with Instrument Rating.

Museveni pays tribute to Nyabongo

A final tribute from the President of Uganda.

Late Wilbur Nyabongo with wife Princess Elizabeth . . .

Wilberforce Nyabongo, the late husband of Princess Elizabeth Bagaya, Uganda's Ambassador to Washington, was described as having been a useful and trustworthy person who together with his wife had worked tirelessly for the NRM,

acting as a bridge between Uganda and countries abroad during the war.

In his message of condolence to the bereaved family, delivered by the Vice Chairman of NRM, Haji Moses Kigongo, at the burial service, President Yoweri Museveni said that people at only 30 years of age have a lot to claim as their first priority, but the late Nyabongo had chosen working for peace in Uganda.

President Museveni called on all Ugandans to emulate the example of the late Nyabongo, and work hard to maintain peace for the rest of their lives.

The President thanked Chief Abiola, the proprietor of the Radio Communication Aircraft Company in Nigeria, for his assistance in bringing the body back home. Nyabongo worked for the company as a pilot, and at the time of his death, with six other people, he was a co-pilot. Investigations are still being carried out to establish the cause of the air crash.

The President's message was accompanied by a contribution of two million shillings from the government to assist the bereaved family. Haji Moses Kigongo was among other people who laid wreaths on the coffin before it was taken to the family graveyard near the deceased's home.

The grave marker says, "Akiiki Wilbur Nyabongo. 22/9/1956–15/12/1986. I am eternally grateful for your love, beauty, and civility. Your servant, Akiiki Elizabeth Nyabongo."

Wilbur is laid next to his father, grandfather, and great-grandfather at Ibonde in Toro.

The presentation of credentials to President Ronald Reagan by the Ambassador Extraordinary and Plenipotentiary of the Republic of Uganda to the United States.

President George Bush with President Yoweri Museveni.

The first Ugandan president to be received by a United States president, President Yoweri Museveni, during his official visit to the White House. Chester Crocker, Assistant Secretary of State for African Affairs stands at rear.

Elizabeth with Dorothy Height (left), *president of the National Council of Negro Women, and entertainer Melba Moore, at the NCNW's Salute to Black Women.* (Kenneth L. Byrd)

Elizabeth (center) *with her cousins in Washington, D.C., in 1986.*

Henry Kalemera (Wilbur's heir), President and Mrs. Ronald Reagan, and Elizabeth at the President's farewell to ambassadors accredited to the United States.

Elizabeth photographed in 1988 by Francesco Scavullo (© 1988 Francesco Scavullo.)

no unified command structure or any single unified nationalist movement emerged which might have helped to curb the president's excesses.

Even Amin's enemies had assisted and enabled Amin to survive by their reluctance—again on account of personal motivation—to present a united resistance. It was Amin's fault that he had alienated his former friends, without thought for their retaliatory capabilities. In everything, he suffered from a false perception that blinded him to the long-term consequences of his apparently decisive actions. The United Kingdom and Israel had helped him come to power, and he had been dependent on them for modernizing development; after he turned against them, they and other Western countries adopted an undeclared commitment to crippling his regime's economy, though by covert means. Even the United States, the first country to close its embassy in Kampala and cease its aid to Uganda, never openly imposed economic sanctions until August 1978, just months before Amin's fall. Up till then, business relations between the regime and the West had continued pretty much as before, even though in diplomatic terms the regime had been denounced, and the Western news media held Amin up to open contempt.

Amin's own erratic temperament made his propaganda value high. Initially encouraged by the powers-that-be, who professed to find Obote unacceptable but Amin quite so, the president of Uganda came to serve a sinister purpose—as a yardstick for black rule in Africa, at a time when a struggle for independence was going on in South Africa and other Third World countries. Because of his bombastic utterances, his futile attempts to compensate for his own inadequacies, and his inability to understand what was going on behind his back, Amin proved an invaluable gift to white racists—to the extent that black incompetence became stamped on the white consciousness. Even as it indulged in high-sounding rhetoric and denunciation of Amin's excesses, the West found that it could misdirect, by misinformation and the highlighting of Amin's negative qualities, more enlightened Western opinion, and by maintaining the status quo in Uganda, and by purely cosmetic political, economic, and diplomatic moves, seek to justify its own excesses in other parts of the world. Amin was no more and no less than a paper tiger—to be manipulated to serve the self-interest of others. His regime became a matter of survival, at almost any cost, and it did survive, coming to an end by accident. Amin foolishly invaded Tanzania, forcing that country into a war with Uganda. This pointless aggression exposed the dictator's back and his regime collapsed.

11

The Clouds
Gather

A Nubian minister, Juma Oris, once whispered to me at a Cabinet meeting, "No one can really ever say he is a friend of Amin because, sooner or later, he will discover that he was not an exception." My own relationship with Amin was purely formal. Apollo Kironde had warned me, before I took up my appointment as roving ambassador, never to get too close to the president, and I always bore his advice in mind.

There was no ulterior motive on Amin's part in appointing me to the post of roving ambassador. He needed the support of someone who was held in high esteem by the civilian population and international community, and he was persuaded by diplomats that I would lend respectability to the new regime abroad. By the time he had made up his mind to appoint me, it was too late for the rabidly republican elements in the government to do anything about it, but I did discover later that he was motivated slightly by the politician's game of divide and rule when he came to decide which ministerial privileges should go with my position. He had not consulted even the foreign minister, Wanume Kibedi, about which these should be.

My office and secretary were situated quite rightly in the presidential office rather than in the Ministry of Foreign Affairs, but I had to be careful when it came to deciding who was my immediate superior. There were no guidelines to say whether it should be the foreign minister, as it would certainly have been had I been an ordinary ambassador, or the president himself. It was worked out that I would be called in by the president and, very often in the presence of the foreign minister as well, given a message to carry to another head of state; then on my return I would compile my report and make an appointment through the principal private secretary and the permanent secretary to go and brief the president. I had to make it clear, however, that I was answerable to the foreign minister as well.

I believe Amin quickly came to admire me for the way I applied myself to my job, and to appreciate that I had genuine concern for my country, and as long as I could convince him that this was so, I was able up to a point to be taken into his confidence and to sway his opinions.

The first indication that Amin might have a personal interest in me came about a year after my appointment, in June or July 1972. I was sitting in my office one day when Peter Uchanda, secretary to the Cabinet, walked in and started to brief me on my impending trip to the International Labour Organisation (ILO) in Geneva. Peter Uchanda was the brother of Lt. Col. Ochima who had been the first high-ranking army officer to be killed when Amin decided to oust important representatives of the Alur tribe from commanding positions. So Peter Uchanda had good reason to detest Amin, and I admired his courage in continuing in his position.

We had been chatting for some time when, suddenly, Amin strode in unannounced, accompanied by four security men. Ignoring Uchanda, he said to me that I would be going to Geneva to attend a conference. I don't think he mentioned the ILO; in all probability he would not have been able to remember which particular conference it was. He said I would be going with Abu Mayanja, the minister of education. A minute or so later, he left as abruptly as he had entered. I was completely mystified, as normally the president would not have come into my office himself to tell me about attending a conference; this was done through a secretary to the Cabinet like Uchanda, and the minister of education would have had ample time in which to get in touch with me.

The question uppermost in my mind was, was Amin's unusual behavior directed at Peter Uchanda, or at me? Was Uchanda being "followed" for other reasons, or was the president starting to take an interest in me? The mystery took on another ominous undertone when the head of the Special Branch, Ayisu, went to Peter Uchanda and warned him to keep away from me. When Peter told me about this, I thought he was joking.

I began to wonder whether my own movements were being snooped on when Farouk Minawa—a security man—was included in the delegation to the ILO conference. Minawa's father, Ibraham Minawa, happened to be an old friend of my father's, so his son and I got on very well together, and he could only have passed on a good report of me to Amin. Security men were always included on delegations, not for our protection but to spy on us. They were easily identifiable, as they were uneducated and could not have made any useful contribution, but they entered the countries concerned as members of the delegations, not as security men.

Minawa's inclusion in the ILO delegation is interesting, as he was a Nubian and, in July 1972, we were not aware of the relationship between Amin and the Nubian factor.

The second indication that Amin might have a personal interest in me came at the end of 1972, after I had been away from Uganda at the ILO conference in Geneva for several months. Because of my prolonged absence, rumors had started to circulate in Uganda that I had disappeared. Somehow, the British press picked these up and reported that I was missing. These reports played right into Amin's hands, as people *were* disappearing at that time, but he was able to produce me before press conferences and prove that such reports were unfounded. And it was to contradict these same press reports that he included me on his delegation to Burundi and to Kenya.

On the helicopter flight to Burundi, I had to sit uncomfortably close to Amin. The visit was particularly haunting because of the connection between the president of Burundi, Micombero, and Amin. In 1966 the Burundi Army under Micombero had staged a coup against the king. Fortunately, the king was out of the country at the time, and never returned, spending the rest of his life in Switzerland. But his son and heir was not so lucky. Micombero persuaded him to assume the throne in the old king's stead, and his coronation took place shortly after my brother's. In fact, Patrick and I had both been invited, but we declined to go as we did not feel it was appropriate to attend the coronation of a king who had been elevated to that position by the very people who had deposed his father. However, it was not long before the young king was deposed as well, and the monarchy abolished altogether. Like his father before him, he was out of the country, but for some reason he accepted an invitation from Amin to come to Uganda. I remember seeing him on television being welcomed by Amin.

Shortly afterwards, Amin said he was arranging a trip to Toro for him, as Toro was such a beautiful part of Uganda, and because the president had been so kind and hospitable, the young king agreed to go. He was put into a helicopter, but instead of being taken to Toro, he was flown to Burundi, where he was handed over to the authorities and murdered. In Burundi, I was invited to lunch with other members of the delegation at the palace where Amin was staying as a state guest, the very place where the young king had lived and been flown to when he left Uganda. It made me very unhappy to think I was in the actual house and grounds where he had died.

The third intimation that Amin had an interest in me came at the beginning of 1973. By then, I had been working for the government for two years almost without a break, and I was exhausted from all the traveling. Because of my exhaustion, I started to skip certain government functions that I normally would have been expected to attend. Somebody started spreading rumors that I was becoming disenchanted with the regime, was planning to defect, and was even smuggling relatives out of the country before I left myself. Once again, the British press reported this. One afternoon, I got a phone call from Ismali Sebi, Amin's deputy principal private secretary and a Nubian, asking me on behalf of the president why I was boycotting government functions. Angrily, I told him to tell the president that I was not immune from sickness—that I, like normal people, occasionally fell ill. Sebi laughed, and relayed this to Amin, who sent back a message to say that he should be the *first* person to be told if I was unwell. I grasped the implication, but I laughed it off and, taking advantage of the president's humorous mood, went to see him to ask if I could take some leave, to which I was in any case now entitled under government law. At first, Amin refused to let me go. I sent him a reminder later through his permanent secretary, Mr. Shekanabo, and fortunately the president decided to grant permission. I left for Kenya.

However, the rumors that I had run away or was missing intensified. Apparently someone from the London *Observer* rang through to the Uganda High Commission in London to ask what had happened to Princess Elizabeth of Toro, but the person who answered the query must have been a resentful anti-monarchist, for he or she replied that there was no such person as Princess of Toro—Toro was a place.

After my leave, I returned to my desk, where I received an angry call from Amin, demanding to know where I had been. He instructed me to come and see him with a full account of all my movements to date. Puzzled, I went to see him. Suddenly more affable, he told me not to worry about my movements but to tell him about Kenya instead. He listened attentively while I gave him my assessment of the situation in Kenya; then he said to me, "You've been doing your work well and I have nothing against you, but there are so many rumors about you. Many people, including some in very high positions, have come to me to tell me about rumors concerning you and me. I said to them, am I not a man, and is Bagaaya not a woman, what is wrong with it?" I was astonished. In the same breath, he went on, "I'm flying by special military plane to the Middle East, to Iraq, Iran, and so on. Would you like to come with me?" Taken aback, I said, "Oh no, Your Excellency, I'm sorry, but I don't want to come." He replied hastily, "Yes, yes, yes, you are right, it would be very risky," and much to my relief dropped the subject.

Then he added, "By the way, I no longer need a roving ambassador, our position abroad is now secure. I want you to organize all the women's organizations into one national organization. That will be your job."

I found myself appointed "chairman" with the task of convening a conference of all the women's organizations in Uganda. I had to liaise with Henry Kyemba, the minister of culture and community development, and with Mary Astles, an Oxford graduate and an extremely capable woman. Her husband Bob worked in the Ministry of Information and was very close to Amin.

At the conference on January 5, 1973, I put forward three proposals for everyone to consider and vote on. Did they want a dissolution of all the women's organizations and then to form one body? Did they want all the organizations to be retained but be affiliated under an umbrella organization? And lastly, did they want all the organizations dissolved and then to form themselves into one organization with a department of religious affairs, which would be divided into three sub-departments: Catholic, Protestant, and Muslim.

After we'd been debating for about a fortnight there was a majority vote to accept the third proposal; the differences we had had to overcome were not tribal but religious. I drew up a constitution and presented it to the president, requesting that there should be a debate in the Cabinet about it. However, there was no debate, as certain religious leaders were against the proposal and it also had a formidable opponent in the person of Oboth Ofumbi, the minister of internal affairs, who managed to convince Amin that his original idea was mistaken.

Our objective—to form a single women's organization with a Department of Religious Affairs—was not therefore pursued to its conclusion; nevertheless, the conference was important for two reasons. First, it marked a turning point in my career, and second, it was an indication of the overall situation in the country. By this time, Amin had fallen out with Israel and Britain, the Asians had been expelled, important people were defecting, and he was moving against the West Nilers in the Army, so the president was anxious to close all the loopholes through which opposition might come, in particular external opposition. Like Obote before him, Amin suspected that the way such opposition could infiltrate the country was through the Church and women's organizations, which had definite links with the outside world—and which is why he thought one united organization would be easier to control. But Amin was also motivated by his desire to be a father figure, a champion of women's rights, that would cast him in a different role to that of villain. Nowhere was this more obvious than at the closing of the conference, which received a lot of media coverage.

The Conference Center was packed to capacity, with all the notables, including ambassadors, religious leaders, top Army officers, and government ministers, whom Amin had directed to attend. With the national anthem playing, I preceded Amin, Mary Astles, and others to the stage, where Amin sat among the women, looking proudly out at the men as though to say, "Here am I, fighting on the side of the women." In my address I said that we were lucky to have President Amin behind us and encouraging us. I genuinely believed this, for in a particularly male-dominated society it was no small advantage to have the country's leader on our side. It was the first time in my career that I had addressed the nation, for the event was being televised live and my speech was heard on the radio. I had not written down in advance what I had to say, so it was pretty much off the cuff. As we were walking out of the conference, Mr. Nkambo Mugerwa, a Cambridge graduate and the minister of justice and attorney-general, turned to me and said, "I take my hat off to Cambridge," and Mrs. Banage, the wife of Professor Banage, the minister of animal resources, said to me in Rutoro, words to the effect that "out of Toro always comes excellence." During that closing session, it was clear to me that we as women were being taken seriously for the first time, and I think Amin had come to recognize quite forcefully that a woman could perform as well as a man.

As a result of the conference, and on my recommendation, Mary Astles was made the first female permanent secretary, which was the highest post in the civil service, and I became a patron of, and in some cases a director on the boards of, certain projects connected with the YWCA, Sanyu Babies' Home, the National Society for the Blind, and Toro Babies' Home. I gained special satisfaction from my link with Toro Babies' Home, which was to become part of the hospital where my father, Patrick, and I had all been born, and I was guest of honor at its opening.

Soon after the conference, Amin put me at the head of a delegation to the Central African Republic that consisted also of some top-ranking Army officers, including Colonel Mondo, the Quarter-Master

General, and Lt. Col. Malera, who was at that time head of the military police. It was significant that I should be the one to lead this delegation, when one considers that the Army was a strictly male preserve—but, as with everything to do with Amin, the motives behind his action were complex and not without sinister implications. Was he plotting something in the absences of Mondo and Malera? To add to the complexity, Amin phoned me on the day of our departure to inform me that a certain captain would be piloting us in a Ugandan Air Force plane to Bangui, the capital of the Central African Republic. The telephone almost fell out of my hand, because the captain had been a boyfriend of mine for the past two years. I was not sure whether Amin was aware of this or, if he was, whether my boyfriend's life was being put in danger, but I was too excited to dwell on such misgivings in any depth. I had always teased my boyfriend about his flying, and sworn that I would never fly in any plane that he was piloting, but when he sent a message for me to go forward to the cockpit, I went willingly, and was treated to a glorious panoramic view of Toro, the Mountains of the Moon, Zaire, and the CAR, all the way to Bangui.

None of us had ever been to the CAR, and we were full of anticipation, but with the exception of myself everyone was disappointed with Bangui, which they pronounced a dusty, underdeveloped town with few real attractions. As a student of history and politics, I was also fascinated by the differences between Franco-Africans and Anglo-Africans, and Bangui offered me an opportunity to study these in greater detail. The little I found out about the historical role of France in the CAR, and about current Franco-CAR bilateral relations, was disturbing. The CAR's economy and currency were very much tied to those of France, which had a free license to export and import anything into and from the CAR, and vice versa. But France was obviously the chief beneficiary of such an arrangement. It had been writing off the CAR's budget for years as the CAR was not self-supporting, and it had kept Bokasa in power by virtue of a mutual defense pact, which meant that if ever Bokasa's own position was threatened, he could call in French troops. I was keen also to observe Bokasa himself at closer quarters, ever since Bith-Cam in Paris had told me about the fiasco of Bokasa's "daughter": Bokasa had served with French forces in Vietnam. When he became President of the CAR, he ordered a search to be made for a child he had allegedly fathered in Vietnam. Dozens of "daughters" came forward, some of whom Bokasa married. Also, Bith-Cam told me he had broken down at De Gaulle's state funeral, in front of all the other world leaders, crying, "Papa, papa!"

This was also the president who, on a recent state visit to Uganda, had paid me the surprising honor of rising to reply to Amin's speech at a state banquet, and addressing both Amin *and* myself. I had been sitting amongst the audience, not at the high table as I was not of cabinet rank, and when Bokasa said, "Your Excellency . . . Madame Ambassadrice . . . ," everyone had turned round to stare at me. On the evening before our departure, we attended a dinner given by Bokasa, after which he sent to see me. Hurriedly, I gathered together members of my delegation and took them to greet the president. We conversed pleasantly for some time, until after midnight, when Bokasa said good night to the other members of the delegation, but asked me to stay behind, saying he wanted to talk further with me. I politely declined, and we left for Uganda the next day.

As was the usual practice, I and members of the delegation went to brief Amin on our mission. He listened with intense interest, and laughed heartily when we came to describe "Operation Bokasa." When we first arrived in the CAR, we had all been utterly baffled by this "Operation Bokasa," references to which we heard every time we tuned into the radio. We begged whomever we came into contact with to explain what it was, but partly because of the language problem (they spoke French, while we spoke English), we still failed to grasp its meaning. Our hosts therefore offered to take us round and *show* us what "Operation Bokasa" was. We were taken to a furniture shop; our guide pointed to the furniture in the shop and said, "That is Operation Bokasa." Outside in the street again, he pointed to a pregnant woman and told us, "That's Operation Bokasa." We walked on and came to a church. Pointing to the congregation in prayer, the guide said, "*That* is Operation Bokasa." On our way back to our hotel, I spotted a barber at his task, and said to our guide, "Operation Bokasa?" Everyone had laughed. It seemed that every activity in the CAR, whether private or official, was "Operation Bokasa."

When it came to describing the internal politics of the CAR, I did not realize the bizarre effects my words would have on our own president. I told him that Bokasa had made himself a life president and had become a dictator who ruled by fear. That fear had been brought home to me most vividly by one example—if you asked anybody in the CAR how many presidents they had had before Bokasa, they would name all of them except President Boganda. He had been ousted by Bokasa, and no one dared even mention his name. In other words, history was being distorted to suit Bokasa. I also could not fail to describe to Amin the legion of military medals that Bokasa wore on his uniform, stretching from his shoulders right down to the bottom hem of his jacket.

Within days, everything on Ugandan radio and throughout Uganda, was being described as "Operation Amin"! Amin had placed an order with a London firm for a legion of military medals and had started moves to make himself life president. All in all, however, the trip to CAR had been, for all its curious experiences, a beautiful one, and no harm had come to my boyfriend, whom I believe Amin had selected for my own protection, he being a Mutoro.

Shortly after this mission, in February 1974, Amin summoned me to State House and announced that he was making me ambassador to Egypt. He said, "I really want to send you to London, but relations are still bad so you'd better go to Cairo until I decide to appoint an ambassador to the UK." I told Amin that I was thrilled to be going to Egypt because of my ancestral affinity with that country, but he said that, before I took up my post there, I was to lead a women's delegation to the All Africa Women's Conference in Conakry, Guinea.

As a rule, the composition of a delegation was a pointer to something going on in Amin's mind, although it was not always possible to disentangle what it was. The Guinea delegation was no exception. At the last minute, he sprang on us a male addition. "But, Your Excellency, it's a women's delegation, to a women's conference," I pleaded. "Won't he be embarrassed to be the only man there?" "It doesn't matter, this is a military government and I want Professor Mohamed Mohandine to go with you," Amin replied. Only Amin knew why he wanted the Makerere professor of economics to be part of my delegation—but the professor was nice enough.

I was looking forward to going to Guinea. Since my student days, Sekou Tourre, Guinea's president, had been a controversial figure, and it was in Guinea that Nkrumah, the former president of Ghana, had spent his last years in exile. The Guinea experience was to be a turning point as far as many of the assumptions I had held for so long were concerned; it was to sharpen my political and spiritual awareness. Above all, Guinea was to raise for me fundamental questions about the direction of Africa's development. For the first time, I learned to separate spiritual from physical development, and to recognize the dilemma of deciding which of the two should have priority. I now believe that the cornerstone and the aim of political independence and development should be spiritual freedom, and it was seeing Guinea which made me start to think in this way.

In comparison with its neighbors, Liberia, Senegal, and the Ivory Coast, and certainly with my own Uganda, Guinea lags far behind in physical or economic development. The standards at our hotel were extremely poor. Water was scarce, it had to be carried in buckets and, when you found some, you were forced to economize and lock the rest away in a cupboard in your room. We had plenty to eat, but the standard of cooking was atrocious; the hotel building, even though it was the top hotel in Conakry, was badly in need of repair. There were no skyscrapers in the city. Many of the delegates were to express disillusionment; but I was to be bowled over by the evidence all around me of the strength of the spiritual awareness of the people of Guinea.

At the gala performance that Sekou Tourre held in honor of the visiting delegations, we were entertained by music, song, poetry, story telling, and dance, whose emotional impact on me was such that, when it was my turn to address the Guinea nation, my speech was impassioned and sincere. The gist of my speech was that, in spite of Guinea's poor economic and physical development, Sekou Tourre's process of politicization meant that the country's spiritual life had been revived. The people of Guinea might have to be practicing self-denial, but the quality of life was being preserved, and that was what really mattered. The other delegates, one each to represent north, west, and south Africa, also spoke, but my speech was the only one to be broadcast on the radio.

We toured the country, sleeping at village centers up country, and being entertained everywhere we went by schoolchildren and youth groups, singing African songs and reciting poetry they had composed themselves. President Sekou Tourre had ordered that I should be allowed to sleep in the presidential lodges wherever there were any. On our return to Conakry each delegation paid a courtesy call on the president. A special honor was extended to ours. Escorted by palace officials, we entered the palace to be welcomed by the majestic figure of Sekou Tourre, dressed in the national costume of Guinea. He fell on his knees in greeting; before he had time to get up, I fell down on my knees in front of him—much to everyone's amusement. He took my hand, and we stood up together.

"I am not totally ignorant of who you are," he said. "I know that in Toro people greet royalty on their knees."

Sekou Tourre took us into his library, where, sitting round a vast table, we held a serious and fascinating discussion about the Guinea "experience." "It is not an experiment," he corrected me when I referred to it as such, "because an experiment can fail. It is the Guinea experience." After our discussion, he took us to lunch, and as a farewell present he gave me a record called *"Regard sur le passé,"* by Bembeya Jazz National, which was the Guinea entry in the first Pan-African Cultural Festival held in Algiers. For many years after I'd fled Amin's Uganda, it was the only record I owned, and whenever I played it, it brought back memories of Guinea and helped to revive my wavering spirits.

As soon as we arrived back in Uganda, on February 20, President Amin summoned us and, before any of us could utter a word, congratulated us on a successful mission. "I have received good reports of your work in Guinea," he said, and, just as we were leaving his office, he added casually to me, "You'd better go to that meeting at Makerere, it begins at four o'clock."

I was very tired and had been in two minds whether to attend the meeting, but I thought to myself, "You never know with Amin. Since he's mentioned it, I really ought to go. If I don't turn up, it could spell trouble." I arrived at Makerere University at 4:30 P.M.—just before Amin himself got there—and took a seat behind the group of Cabinet ministers. Several of them welcomed me home and asked me to sit in front with them, but I was neither a Cabinet minister nor of Cabinet rank, so I declined. Lt. Col. Ondonga, the foreign minister, was one of those who turned round to greet me; I noticed that he was unusually subdued and not his usual self, but I forgot about it as the president walked in to the national anthem played by a police band.

The president stood at the front of the meeting and called out in a sonorous voice: "Miss Bagaaya, come to the platform." After I had done so, Amin said, "I have consulted with members of the defense council, and they have agreed with me to appoint Miss Bagaaya as minister of foreign affairs."

There was deafening applause, then the president told me to go back to my seat. I hurried back, glancing at Ondonga as I passed him; he looked absolutely shattered, which of course was what Amin had intended.

The president continued with the meeting as if nothing out of the ordinary had happened. While the meeting was in progress, the news of my appointment was announced on the five o'clock news over the radio. My cousin Selvano Katama and a friend of his came looking for me at my house. When they broke the news to my mother, she told them, "That's impossible, Bagaaya has just left to attend a meeting at Makerere. We've started packing her things for her to go to Cairo!" Katama was still trying to convince her of the veracity of the news when a stream of relatives and friends began to arrive at the house to offer me their congratulations. When I got back, I exchanged puzzled looks with my mother, and locked myself in my room. I tuned into Radio Uganda and the BBC World Service news, and listened to the president's astounding announcement. The telephone wouldn't stop ringing and I had to take it off the hook.

I could not get to sleep that night.

As minister of foreign affairs, I had come as close to the seat of power as it was possible for anyone to come. It was a singular honor for the monarchy—the highest position a member of the Uganda royal families had ever held at the Uganda level, apart from the kings. Since the monarchy had been abolished by Obote, there had been a deliberate policy to discredit it, in spite of Amin's initial overtures, but my appointment was a clear recognition of the fact that there is ability and merit in the royals. It was also a landmark, as I was the first woman to hold that glamorous and prestigious position.

But a foreign minister attracts a lot of envy as well as attention. On the very day I was appointed, certain friends and members of my family, with inside knowledge of the Ministry of Foreign Affairs, issued warnings to me about the network of intrigue within the ministry. As early as the sixties, apparently, a report by a Foreign Ministry official had falsely alleged that the ministry was dominated by princes and people from the tribes in the kingdom areas. My sister Gertrude advised me to get a kettle of my own and have my secretary make my tea and coffee. I was therefore fully alert to the internal struggles I was somehow to cope with, as I turned up at my new office in the Parliament building itself.

Lt. Col. Ondonga was waiting to hand over the keys to me. When I offered him my sympathies, he said, "Don't worry, Elizabeth, you had nothing to do with it." I kept on his personal assistant, Emmanuel Gasana, and his private secretary, Elizabeth Bamuturaki. I noticed that the photos of Ondonga had already been removed from the walls, and gave strict instructions that no photos of me should be put up. Meanwhile, congratulatory messages poured in, directed sometimes to Amin and sometimes to me, nearly all of them affirming that the president had made a clever move in appointing me. One person who did not send me a message of congratulations was our ambassador to Ethiopia, Matiya Lubega, who explained later, "You were so much at the center of attention that I feared for you."

However, no amount of excitement and speculation about my appointment as foreign minister could disguise the fact that President Amin was beginning to lose his grip on the regime. The numerous defections by high-ranking personalities in the government rendered him a psychological blow, not least the defections of his own brother-in-law and former foreign minister, Wanume Kibedi. The ministers of finance and of education, and the ambassador to France fled.

Amin was infuriated and made jittery by these defections. It was obvious to me that unless something was said or done to appease him, he would become uncontrollable in his rage. Surprisingly, he accepted my advice as to the best policy to adopt toward such desertion. I told him that perhaps if he ignored what had happened it would die a natural death. He would not impress anyone by hitting out at Kibedi or at the international press, and I begged him not to embark on a witch-hunt against the defectors' relatives, as they were not to blame.

As well as the defectors, Amin had the Lugbaras and the Alur in the Army and elsewhere to worry about. Externally, pressure was also mounting against the president. The Human Rights Commission report on Uganda was about to come out, and he feared being isolated in international forums. He desperately needed the right foreign minister, and it had become more and more difficult to find one. The vital personal qualities of a foreign minister are international experience, equanimity in the face of pressure, and a certain breadth of vision. Amin's policies, however, constituted a perfect recipe for a disastrous foreign policy. As his foreign minister, I was soon reduced to steering him and the country out of crisis after crisis, each one engineered by Amin himself. Certainly, I could never be sure what the president was going to do next, but I was determined to brave it out and to do the best I could for Uganda and my people, taking advantage of the reservoir of goodwill extended to me by the international community, and by the country itself.

My first public function was to address the new Foreign Service officials at the Institute of Public Administration. In my speech, which was printed on the front page of the leading newspaper the following morning, I advised them to adopt as their guiding principle the political maxim: "In politics there are no permanent friends or permanent enemies. The only thing that is permanent is interest." Whereas it had been standard practice to use such occasions for the expression of simple pleasantries, of no serious consequence, it became my practice to use them to introduce political and philosophical ideas.

Shortly after this engagement, I was asked to represent Amin at the independence anniversary celebrations of Czechoslovakia. I was still feeling my way in my new job, but in Czechoslovakia I nearly put my foot in it. The invasion of Czechoslovakia had taken place while I was modeling in London, and I had followed the course of the revolution religiously; the revolution left a permanent mark on me. In my speech at the anniversary celebrations, I went on and on about the heroism of the Czech people, carefully omitting to mention the invasion, or the revolution, or Dubcek (at least by name)—but I referred to

President Svobda as towering like a rock of strength for the Czech people.

The Soviet ambassador had meanwhile been gradually inching toward me, but the Czech ambassador, his wife and other embassy officials, had formed a sort of line of defense around me. No one before in Ugandan-Czech relations had dared to blunder about in the above manner, thereby risking incurring Soviet displeasure, and the Czechs were never to forget my tribute. The reception was televised and Amin ordered it to be screened three times. He told me he was glad I had praised Czechoslovakia, as we had received a lot of arms and military hardware from them.

The Soviet Ambassador complained to Colonel Jack Bunyenyezi about Amin having appointed a pro-British minister of foreign affairs, and Bunyenyezi in my presence reported the complaint to the president. However, I made it up with the Soviet ambassador, and accepted and invitation to a dinner he gave in my honor at the Soviet Embassy in Kampala, at which I toasted the special relationship between Uganda and the Soviet Union.

Within weeks of my taking office, a railway crisis broke out between Uganda and Kenya. Kenya had confiscated our railway wagons, demanding that we pay a long-standing debt we owed them, and all transportation between landlocked Uganda and the port of Mombasa was frozen. Amin sent me to see Jomo Kenyatta. I had for years nursed a secret anger about allegations by the international press of nepotism and corruption where Kenyatta was concerned, which was threatening to undermine the legend that had grown up around him. He was a man whom I had much admired, and it hurt me to think that he might be capable of destroying my belief. "You do not belong to Kenya, you belong to Africa, to all of us," I told him, in audience. "How long does it take to create a legend? . . . It takes generations, a lifetime, and when that legend is destroyed, what exactly do you intend to leave your children, and Africa? Money?" "No, not money," he replied. I spoke to him frankly about the accusations that were upsetting me, and asked him to put an end to them if they were true, and to do something to help Uganda. He called in his permanent secretary and said, "Karithi, I am granting all her requests. I want

Uganda's wagons freed immediately so that trade can resume." His minister of state, M. Koinange, had been present throughout the meeting, and when we left Kenyatta, he shook his head in disbelief. "It was a very effective mission," he said to me.

I had to see my Kenyan counterpart, Njoroge Mungai, before I left. As he was seeing me off, Ngithi, the editor of the *Daily Nation*, Kenya's largest newspaper, turned up and said to me, "Your predecessor has just been murdered." I was stunned. "Are you absolutely sure?" I asked him. "Absolutely," he assured me. "Someone in Kampala has just given me the news over the phone."

In a state of shock, I returned to Uganda. No one believed Amin when he said that he had had no part in Lt. Col. Ondonga's murder. He explained to a gathering including ambassadors, ministers, Army officers, and civil servants that Ondonga was related to his wife, Kay—which was true—and that since he, Amin, was related to his own wife, that meant he was related to Ondonga, and therefore he had not killed him, as the newspapers were alleging. He told us that Ondonga's body had been found floating near the dam at Jinja, and that he was making arrangements for it to be taken to West Nile for burial.

However, the truth was blatantly otherwise. Lt. Col. Ondonga and a fellow Lugbara officer, Lt. Col. Ombiya, had been removed from their posts in the Army and made ambassadors at the time Amin had been indulging in a purge of senior Lugbara officers. Ondonga became Uganda's ambassador to the Soviet Union until he was appointed minister of foreign affairs. After his hostile dismissal as foreign minister, he had been warned to leave Kampala and return to his native village in West Nile, where Amin was unlikely to risk a direct confrontation with the Lugbara tribe.

Unfortunately, Ondonga hung around in the capital, where he was being guarded by security men loyal to him in the minister of foreign affairs' residence, not far from Amin's own residence. On the day of his murder, Ondonga went just after midday to collect his little girl from kindergarten. As he was arriving at the school, a car with four assassins from Amin's murder squad inside turned up. They hauled Ondonga screaming from his car and, in front of the assembled children, pushed him into the other car and drove off. A teacher rang Mrs. Kay Amin, who drove to the school herself and took Ondonga's weeping daughter back home with her.

That same day, in the evening, Lt. Col. Toko, the former Air Force commander and then a director in the East African community, called me from Nairobi where he was living and working. He was also a Lugbara, and he was also related to Ondonga and to Kay Amin. He said to me, "I am phoning to assure you that we know you've had nothing to do with all this, and you should not be made to feel bad by anyone."

Nevertheless, I couldn't move into Ondonga's former residence, knowing that I would always be haunted by what had happened, and I remained in the roving ambassador's house.

Meanwhile, the machinations in my ministry continued. Apart from the minister of Foreign Affairs, Amin had appointed a minister of state for foreign affairs, who was responsible for matters arising over the OAU. His office was situated in the presidential office, and he was a member of the Cabinet, but it was clear that he came under my own ministry. Since Amin did not possess the clarity of mind to operate a strict demarcation of duties, the situation was open to misinterpretation and delay. To say to an African foreign minister that she will not be responsible for OAU matters is like telling a British foreign secretary that his jurisdiction does not extend to Wales and Scotland. When Kibedi was foreign minister, there was no such minister of state for foreign affairs, so the same confusion had not arisen. Ondonga had dealt with it militarily—once, Amin, trying to play the divide and rule game again, had included Ondonga and the minister of state for foreign affairs on the same delegation to an OAU conference at Addis Ababa. Ondonga was in charge of the delegation, and when they reached Addis Ababa and arguments arose as to who was to do what, he merely ordered the minister to stay in his room for the duration of the conference; however, I was no soldier and soon became a victim of the confusion.

Matters in my ministry were not attended to because files were with the minister of state for foreign affairs. One day, an important cable arrived at the communication room in my ministry; I never saw it, and no action was taken. Amin phoned and angrily demanded to know the name of the person who worked in the communication room. I gave him the name and he hung up. The purpose of his call was to establish whether I knew the identity of every employee in the ministry; if I had failed to give him the name, he could have accused me of inefficiency and negligence.

The muddle reached its peak at the OAU conference for ministers of foreign affairs which was held in Kampala in March 1974, preceding the OAU meeting of heads of state to be held in June in Mogadishu. Since the OAU was the minister of state for foreign affairs' responsibility, he was going to chair the meeting. It was most embarrassing for me, especially as many more ministers than usual were turning up at the conference because they thought I would be chairing. Fortunately, there was to be a Law of the Sea conference at the same time, in Nairobi, and as I had chaired the conference of the landlocked states earlier in the year, in March, in Kampala, I was eager to pursue this. The president gave me permission to go.

During the night before my departure, there was the sound of heavy gunfire in Kampala, very close to my house near the command post. This was the night of Charles Arube's failed coup. I remember my mother and an aunt by marriage, Mrs. Rwakatale, running panic-stricken into my room. Things quieted down, and in the morning, I sent my driver to check if the roads were clear, and also rang the airport to see if it was closed. I knew that I ought to call the president to ascertain that it was still all right for me to leave for Nairobi. I managed to get through and offered my sympathies for Arube's attempted coup. Amin was keen to restore normality as fast as possible because of the OAU conference, so he agreed that I should proceed to Nairobi.

The question of access to the sea was a matter of life and death for landlocked Uganda—even Amin appreciated this. The Law of the Sea conference was a follow-up to the earlier meeting in Kampala, which had issued the Kampala Declaration, but the landlocked states were in the minority and did not have the benefit of having either of the two super powers on their side. The issues the conference had to deal with included the jurisdiction of the coastal states, territorial waters, the continental shelf, the high seas, and the right of access of landlocked states. We maintained that the wealth of the sea was not a monopoly of the coastal states but belonged to humanity. Our broad strategy was that unless the coastal states agreed to an equitable sharing of the sea's wealth and to reasonable access for the landlocked states as part of a new economic order in the world, there was not going to be a Nairobi Declaration. You could say we succeeded, for there was no Nairobi Declaration.

When I returned to Uganda, I found that Amin was still reacting to the coup, and wanted me to implement certain misconceived moves which were intended to close all possible loopholes through which threats to him might come. One of these involved his decision to post two Nubian security men as diplomats to each of our embassies abroad. The president rang me and told me curtly that he wanted these men, twenty-six in all, to report to the embassies at once. Two days later, he came on the line again, wanting to know why the men had not yet left. I told him that if I were to dispatch them without their having received their inoculations, they would be held in quarantine at the airports. Furthermore, after vaccination they were supposed to wait for a certain period before they could leave the country. "This is a military government. You must send off those men in two days' time," Amin barked. I had to go to Kampala City Council personally and beg the health visitors to back-date the men's certificates. They obliged me, and I was able to dispatch the men and report to Amin accordingly.

These men had direct access to Amin and he relied on them to keep informed of any sabotage activities by Ugandans or others abroad. The exercise was destined to fail even before it took off. Most of the men were uneducated and became easy prey to manipulators, who in certain cases used them as instruments to maneuver good officers out of their positions.

In another phone call, Amin informed me that he was with immediate effect moving the passport section from my ministry to the Ministry of Internal Affairs, and that I was to inform all the embassies at once. It had not occurred to Amin that Ugandans who were determined to defect would do so whether they had passports or not. I did as I was bid, but Ugandans continued to defect, and there was quite a racket in illicit passports.

Of no less seriousness was Amin's move to divorce his four wives.

These were Kay from West Nile, Mama Malyamu from Busoga in the east of Uganda, Nora from the Langi tribe, and Medina from the Buganda tribe. One Saturday morning, according to my usual routine, I was in my office studying the political reports from our ambassadors. When Amin rang, I was absorbed in the ambassador to Peking's report. Apparently the president had been expecting me at a meeting that morning with an envoy from the president of another African state, and was surprised at my absence. He had just asked the chief of protocol if I had been informed of the meeting, and been told that I had. "Why didn't you come to the meeting? I can have you replaced, you know," Amin said. "That's a matter for Your Excellency to decide," I replied. "However, as you know, the OAU does not come under my jurisdiction."

"I have divorced all my wives," Amin said, suddenly. There was a long silence.

"I am telling you as my foreign minister," Amin added.

"But why, what have they done?" I asked. "Such a move will be terribly damaging for your image, both here and abroad."

"It's too late now, I've already divorced them," he told me. "If I don't want them, no one can force them on me, and no one can force me to live with them."

"Whereas the country might understand your divorcing Mama Malyamu because of your quarrel with Kibedi, or Kay because of your problems with the Lugbaras, or Nora because she is related to Obote, you can pin nothing on Medina. Why don't you keep her?" I implored Amin.

The president listened, but he hung up without giving me any indication of what he was going to do. It was clear that his fears for himself were growing; he no longer felt safe, even with his own wives. In the end, he decided to keep Medina; the others were not so lucky.

One Monday afternoon I had driven to Nakassero Presidential Lodge, where I had an appointment to see Amin. After a long wait along with other Cabinet colleagues, it came to my turn. I was about to go in when Henry Kyemba, now the minister of health, entered, looking very grim. He asked me if I'd mind letting him go in before me, as he had something extremely urgent to discuss with the president. He was still with Amin when I was called in to be briefed on my forthcoming mission. I left, leaving Henry with the president, but without the slightest idea what had occurred.

The following day was Tuesday, Cabinet day. By 10:00 A.M. we were all in our seats, with Shekanabo, the minister of public affairs, in the chair—which was always the case except on rare occasions when the president took the chair. My place was between that of Information and Finance. It was Cabinet ministers' practice to refer to each other by the names of their ministries. I was always referred to as "Foreign," and the minister of animal resources and husbandry was referred to as "Animal"—we were forever being teased because of the connotations attached to these two words.

As usual, the ministers were chatting to each other before the meeting was called to order—it was often through these chitchats that we shared important information and alerted one another to possible dangers, which we couldn't normally do over our tapped phones or at friendly gatherings, however small, without inviting suspicion. I remember, after one Cabinet meeting, suggesting to a colleague I'd just been talking to that we continue our discussion a little longer. "Not over my dead body!" he shuddered. "Amin always rings through after cabinet meetings to check which ministers have stayed behind to talk amongst themselves. If we hang around here talking, you can be sure someone will tell him you and I have been plotting something or other."

"Information," a Nubian called Juma Oris, and "Finance," Simyeyo Kiyingi, had become great friends of mine. Juma Oris suddenly leaned toward me and whispered, "Kay has been killed."

"Kay who?" I asked.

"Kay Amin," he answered.

I ran out of the Cabinet room to Joy Mawalo, the president's secretary, and asked her if I could speak to Amin. She connected me, and I asked him if it was true that Mrs. Kay Amin had been murdered. He replied in the affirmative.

"Could I come in and see you?" I said.

"Why do you want to see me?" he demanded.

"In connection with Mrs. Amin," I told him.

"You can come and see me," he said.

I went into his office and sat down.

"I don't believe that Kay has been murdered," I said. She had been my favorite among Amin's wives. She was gentle and charming, the first Lugbara to be educated at Gayaza High School and the first Lugbara to go to university.

"I've already told you, why do you ask me again?" Amin snapped. "Kay is dead."

"The country is going to hold you responsible," I said quietly. "If your hands are clean, go on television and radio tonight and explain how she came to die."

Amin picked up his phone and told his secretary to summon the minister of information. Oris came in, looking grave.

"The minister says the country will blame me for Kay's death unless I go on TV and radio immediately to explain her death," Amin said. "What do *you* think?"

Juma Oris, still standing, looked on the verge of tears. In a voice loaded with emotion, he said, "The minister is right."

We were interrupted by a knock at the door, and a Nubian called Ismali Sebi, the president's principal private secretary, walked in with three of Kay and Amin's young children.

"Go back to the Cabinet room. I'll come and address you all this afternoon," Amin said to Oris and myself.

We did as we were told, and the meeting proceeded. The afternoon session, however, was destined to be the most memorable Cabinet session I ever attended. Amin turned up accompanied by Odria, the commissioner of police, himself a Lugbara like Kay, and the head of the CID, who happened to be my brother-in-law, Mukasa. The chairman hurriedly vacated his seat for Amin, and two extra seats were brought for Odria and Mukasa.

"I know everyone will blame me," Amin told the electrified Cabinet, "but I don't mind."

With a gesture, he bade Odria and Mukasa to address us on the results of their investigations into Kay's murder. Among the exhibits the police produced as having been found at the scene of the murder was Kay's dress, which I had seen her wearing on several occasions. We were told that, according to Kay's father, who had been staying with her, Kay had been complaining of headaches and generally not feeling well on the day she died. On Sunday afternoon, Dr. Mbalwa Mukasa had come to collect her in his car and they had driven off somewhere.

That had been the last Kay's father had seen of his daughter. On the following day, her body was found in the trunk of Dr. Mukasa's car outside his clinic, her legs and arms mutilated. On the same day, Mukasa tried to take the lives of his wife and six children by administering fatal overdoses of drugs, before committing suicide himself. The wife and children were discovered by a neighbor and rushed to the nearest hospital, where they were revived. We were told that they were still in a critical condition, and had not therefore been interviewed by the police.

Throughout the police briefing, I kept glancing at Amin, looking for clues. He was wearing a bright red short-sleeved shirt which highlighted his blackness, and, for the first time, I noticed how large his arms and hands were. Were these the arms and hands of a murderer? I asked myself, frightened. Could he murder the mother of his children? The thought was beyond my comprehension. But I remembered something the Italian ambassador's wife had told me, about how Kay had called her and asked to see her, and how the ambassador's wife had invited her to tea, and how depressed Kay had seemed to be. Her hostess thought it was because Kay was still in love with Amin, even though he had divorced her. But I, and others, am inclined to think she was carrying Amin's child and was depressed at the thought of having an abortion. Dr. Mukasa was notorious for the many abortions he had performed in Kampala. The questions still remained: Had Dr. Mukasa and Kay been followed that Sunday afternoon after he'd picked her up? If he *had* attempted to perform an abortion on her, had he been caught in the act? Or had Mukasa been her lover? Did the doctor really commit suicide, or had he been forced to take his own life by someone else? Many people believe that only Amin could have arranged such a murder.

One report in connection with Kay's death was particularly disturbing. While we were in the Cabinet meeting that Tuesday, Amin had taken his and Kay's children to the mortuary in Mulago Hospital, where he had pointed to Kay's corpse and said, "Your mother was a bad woman." There is not a shred of evidence to suggest that Kay had ever been unfaithful to Amin; if she had, she would have been dead a long time ago. Was he therefore referring to an abortion, or something else? One thing was clear: Kay's death was an ominous sign for the women of Uganda. Up to this time, Amin's murderous system had claimed few women as victims; I personally know of only one girl, called Pink Kabahenda, whom he accused of having been a spy of Obote. The combination of the soldier and the Muslim made Amin not quite despise women, but made him feel they presented little or no threat—which made Kay's murder even more mysterious. I felt we were entering the murky waters of psychopathy. Was the president a sadist? Whatever he was, this latest incident boded no good for the rest of us.

12

The Last Pillar
of Conquest

One night, shortly after midnight, several police cars arrived in the compound and we heard loud banging on every door around the house. I gave orders that no one should admit anyone and, as the house was an official residence and was very secure, the banging went on for ages with no one managing to break in.

After a while, Ougambo, the cook, and the gardener, Jimmy Rwabuhesi, a grandson of the former head gardener at the palace, came to me in a state of panic, saying that the police had threatened to start shooting and begging me to open up.

I was about to be arrested! I was shocked. Although there had been many signs of impending trouble, one of the wonders of Amin's Uganda was that while the ship kept sinking deeper and deeper, there was never a shortage of rescue operations to stop us from being drowned.

Nation after nation, friend and foe, kept coming to Amin's aid. It was my responsibility as foreign minister to arouse confidence abroad, to soothe hostilities, and to encourage state visits. As roving ambassador, I had cultivated good relations with the Arab League, which was based in Cairo. On August 12, 1974, my contacts bore fruit in the visit of Mr. Mahmouhd Riyadah, the Arab League's secretary general, an important figure who had held Cabinet posts in the Nasser and Sadat governments in Egypt.

At a state dinner I gave in his honor, I made a long speech in which I said that Uganda had been a prime mover in the Pro-Arabism that had swept through the OAU in the early seventies, engulfing nearly every OAU state, including Ethiopia and Kenya. The result was close cooperation between the Arab and the African worlds. However, Pro-Arabism had bred only disillusionment in Africa, and I appealed to the Arab world to make Uganda the test case for Arab intentions toward our continent.

Riyadah was evidently moved by my speech, and told me so. In him, Uganda came to have a supporter within the Arab League, and negotiations opened up for getting the Afro-Arab Bank established in Uganda. Later that year when the League allocated loans and grants to various African states, Uganda was treated with priority, and our share was a fair one. Unfortunately the security situation worked against the Afro-Arab Bank being set up in Uganda.

The one head of state who was a stabilizing influence on Amin was President Said Barre of Somalia. Said Barre had all the qualities that Amin most admired: he was a soldier, a Muslim, a revolutionary, and was respected by Arabs and Africans alike. I myself was particularly close to the Somali minister of foreign affairs, Omar Ateh. While attending the meeting of the Liberation Committee of the OAU in Yaonde, Cameroon, I discussed Uganda-Somalia relations with Ateh and as a result Said Barre paid a state visit to our country. (Ateh and I agreed on a joint stand on many serious issues which were due to come up at the impending OAU meeting of heads of state in Mogadishu, Somalia, and I said that I would support his candidature for the secretary generalship of the OAU.) Said Barres' visit went off well; Amin gave a state luncheon in his honor at State House. The two presidents sat in the middle of the enormous mahogany table, while Ateh and I were seated directly opposite them. At one point, Ateh whispered in my ear, "Not only do you look like a Somali, but you even smell like a Somali girl!" I saw Amin interrupt his conversation with President Said Barre to stare at us. . . .

The most important state visit to Uganda, however, was that of Colonel Gaddafi. I had discussed the president of Libya's visit with his ambassador, Mahomoud, when I invited him to a dinner at my residence. "But he looks like us," my mother had remarked after meeting him. She had expected to see a white ambassador and was surprised to find that he was black—which showed how clever Gaddafi had been in his choice of envoy. The message that the peoples of Libya and Uganda were brothers had been put across most effectively, but Mahomoud himself was a modest and obliging man and, at the end of our dinner, I felt confident that the visit of his president would have significant results for Uganda.

However, Gaddafi seemed to take offense at the fact that Uganda's foreign minister was a woman, and he complained to Amin, who ordered me to keep as wide a distance as possible from the visting president. At first, I felt baffled and resentful but when, at the state banquet, Gaddafi demanded and Amin accepted that men should dine separately from women, I realized that Gaddafi's objection to me was on puritanical grounds, and that he did not mean it as a personal affront.

Gaddafi had brought his finance minister with him, an indication of the seriousness he attached to his visit. Certainly, if the negotiations had gone the way Libya wanted, financial and defense agreements would have been signed on the spot. But the Ugandan Cabinet advised Amin that Libya's proposals effectively amounted to a half share in the entire country, and Amin turned down Gaddafi's offer of massive financial investment in Uganda and was barely on speaking terms with his guest by the time of departure. Amin may have been almost illiterate, and eventually could not cope with the magnitude of the presidency, but he was not a traitor to his country, even though he desperately needed Libya's money and would have benefited personally from it.

The next few months were especially trying for me. There was a resurgence of aggression in Amin, which was demonstrated above all in the insults he dished out to foreign leaders and his ministers. Suddenly, he seemed to have a preoccupation with sending long, impertinent cables to people he felt like abusing, which he would ask me, or another minister, to draft for him. If a cable did not meet with his standards of contempt, he would say brusquely, "It hasn't got enough *piri piri* [red pepper] in it. Redraft it!"

On one occasion, he dictated a cable for me to Golda Meir of Israel, telling me to add at the end, "Pick up your knickers and go back to America where you came from." "I'm sorry, sir, but you're a head of state, and as such you cannot use such language," I told him. When, at his further insistence, I still refused to include it, he hung up.

Amin also ridiculed his ministers. Since ours was a military government, he said, we should all be drafted into the Army and made to wear uniforms and learn how to shoot. He also insisted that we had to play football and go swimming with him. When I failed to turn up at the swimming sessions, he sent a message via the justice minister, Honorable Godfrey Lule, to ask why I hadn't been going along. "Tell the president I would be making an improper exhibition of myself if I were to turn up in a swimming costume along with eighteen men and be the only woman there," I relayed back. I refused to learn to shoot for the same reason.

The president continued to be haunted by defections by top-level members of his government, and rumors persisted that I was contemplating escape. When the time came for me to go to Caracas, Venezuela, to attend the next Law of the Sea conference, Amin waited until the day before I was to travel and then canceled my trip.

I got into trouble, too, when I invited a team of British negotiators to Uganda, to discuss the issue of the British Asians and compensation for the nationalizing of British interests in 1972. Amin had agreed weeks before that these talks should go ahead, but when the team arrived, he was in his worst anti-British mood. Jonathan Ekochu, the president's principal private secretary, warned me to keep away from the team, as Amin was holding me personally responsible for their coming and had accused me in front of Army officers. This was indeed a matter for concern, as any accusation by Amin before Army officers or troops was nearly always a prelude to a personal strike against those whom he thought had transgressed. When Mr. Hennessy, the British acting high commissioner, contacted me about the team's arrival, therefore, I made some sort of excuse for not receiving the team, even for a courtesy call, and asked him to inform Ekochu, who would let Amin know that the team had arrived. On the president's orders, the team was humiliated and the discussions, of course, came to naught.

Amin was in another of his dark moods when the time came for me to go to Mogadishu in Somalia for the meeting of the OAU ministers of foreign affairs. In front of other Cabinet ministers, the president said to me, "You will go to Mogadishu later; we'll fly there together." I thought such a suggestion was totally scandalous. What, I thought, would people think if I were to turn up with Amin while the other foreign ministers had already assembled in Mogadishu? In what capacity was he expecting me to turn up with him?

Several times, the Somali ambassador asked me on behalf of his government whether I would be going to Mogadishu or not—Somalia had been preparing to greet me with enthusiasm, and I was to have been the only foreign minister to stay in a presidential lodge. I went to Amin and told him that I regarded it as being bad for my image that I should not be present at the foreign ministers' meeting and then be turning up with him. I pointed out that since I would have made no practical contribution to the meeting, my presence there would be meaningless, and I asked him for permission not to go. He granted his permission sullenly, but I went with my colleagues to see him off to Mogadishu from the airport. Before he took off, Amin addressed some Ugandan troops at the airport, and among other things he told them that some of his ministers were pro-British. This was a clear attack on me. "Did you hear what he said?" Ekochu asked, coming up to me. "I did," I replied.

However, I was allowed no time to brood, as another crisis awaited me back at my office. Emmanuel Gasana, my personal assistant, had a Reuter report to show me on a film about Amin which had just started showing in Paris. The report indicated that Amin was shown up in a very bad light in the film, which meant I would be in for it when the president came back from Somalia. I knew that accusations against me were bound to follow for failing to act effectively against my imperialist "masters" (as I was supposed to be pro-Western). It was difficult to say with any certainty what the results of the accusations would be: if I were lucky, I would just be dismissed; if not, I could disappear without trace. I therefore moved with the utmost speed to defuse the crisis.

Mugoya, the acting head of our Paris mission, came to my aid. He went and saw the film himself several times and dispatched a detailed report to me about the reaction of the audiences, and all the circumstances surrounding the film. He also called a meeting of all the African ambassadors in Paris, who viewed the film not as a personal insult to Amin but as being a scurrilous attack on Africa, and they put in a protest about it to the French government as an OAU group. But Mugoya also lodged an official complaint on Uganda's behalf with the French Ministry of Foreign Affairs.

Juma Oris was the acting president in Amin's absence, and I managed to convince him that the crisis was of unpredictable dimensions. However, I realized that the French government would try to wash its hands of the affair by arguing that it had no control over a free media, which meant that unless we could get the government to acknowledge a measure of responsibility, we could take no effective action against the film company.

Fortunately, I had personal knowledge of the French government's involvement in the film. I remembered that, in 1973 when I was still roving ambassador, the French ambassador in Kampala had invited me to a lunch at his residence, where I had been introduced to a film unit that was in the capital to make a film about Amin. The purpose of the lunch had been to persuade me to agree to be featured in the film. When I asked them whether there were going to be any other members of the Ugandan government in it, they said no, and I declined the invitation. But the fact that the French ambassador had taken advantage of Amin's benevolent attitude toward France as a nation made him and his government in my eyes accountable. My case was strengthened by the fact that the film was made by French television, which is government owned.

I summoned the French ambassador and made my protest, informing him that we regarded its implications for Ugandan-French relations as extremely serious. I demanded that the film be withdrawn immediately and that he obtain a reel for me so that the president could view it on his return from Mogadishu.

The French ambassador's reaction astounded me. I knew there had been a long history of Anglo-French enmity and rivalry in the nineteenth century, but I was taken aback to experience it in the twentieth. When I showed the Reuter report to the ambassador, he only said irritably: "That news agency is English."

"Your Excellency," I said, "I have always respected French logic. Am I to be given to understand that because the film has been reported by a top British news agency, we must hold England responsible for the film's existence and its contents?

"It's an insult to our intelligence for you to believe that we could be hoodwinked by such a smoke screen," I snapped, and on that note I dismissed the French ambassador.

When Amin returned, Juma Oris went in to see him and explain the entire fiasco. He let the president know how hard I had worked to defuse the situation, which he pointed out was regarded by the OAU ambassadors in Paris as an affront to the whole of Africa, and Amin was generally pleased with the way in which we had handled the affair.

We managed finally to get hold of a copy of the film, which was screened at Nakassero Lodge in the presence of the French ambassador, a few ministers, and Amin himself. The president's reaction was a real eye-opener for me. The film had undoubtedly held Amin up as a figure of contempt, but he saw himself as a star! In fact, the last sentence uttered by a European in the film—"Isn't this a deformed image of ourselves?" didn't faze him; and the French ambassador was clearly amused by Amin's favorable interpretation of his own depiction.

When we explained the implications to the president, however, he did threaten to sever relations with France, and an aircraft was prepared to take me to see the French foreign minister. At the last minute, though, the French government agreed to censor, and certain scenes were ultimately deleted from the film.

In late 1974 I led a delegation to the twenty-ninth session of the United Nations General Assembly in New York.

Odria, the commissioner of police; the head of the State Research, Lt. Col. Francis Itabuka; a county chief from Karamoja; and several policemen and women from Special Branch and the CID were included at Amin's behest in my delegation. Of the sixteen members of the team, there were hardly ten professional people to do the UN job. Nevertheless, this delegation was surrounded by a certain aura of glamour, and I was very excited. I had commissioned for our delegation dresses in the traditional Uganda style by an unknown but brilliant and upcoming young designer, Henrietta Lwaga, and I took Mrs. Uba, a Nigerian hair-plaiter, to attend on myself and the female members of the delegation. Our send-off from Uganda was impressive, and I traveled in the presidential plane (a gift to Amin from Israel), an unprecedented honor. I arrived in New York wearing a Zandra Rhodes robe which had been a present from Marietta Tree, and I was soon settled in the Ugandan ambassador's residence.

As was customary, the U.S. secretary of state, who was at that time Henry Kissinger, gave a luncheon for all African foreign ministers who were to attend the UN session. As the elected chairman of the OAU group I was requested to express a vote of thanks to our host. Kissinger agreed to speak off the cuff, if I would too. I did.

I began by acknowledging Dr. Kissinger's personal efforts in endeavoring to realize peaceful settlements where the Middle East and Indo-China were concerned, and went on to say that we were all committed to the success of the UN in eliminating international tensions and promoting cooperation and understanding among all nations. I agreed that nations were interdependent, but I emphasized that "there will never be peace in Africa and the world until a new economic order, which would necessitate decolonization and an equitable redistribution of world wealth, is established." I pointed out that there were many areas in Africa that were still subject to foreign domination and racial oppression. Apartheid was a policy that was completely contrary to any civilized and humanitarian principles, and continued to make a mockery of African dignity and independence. So long as colonialism and imperialism continued, the world would continue to have human rights problems. I concluded my speech by asking Kissinger to support the African liberation movements, and to visit Africa instead of depending on distorted reports about the African people and their society. As a superstar in the eyes of the West and other parts of the world, Henry Kissinger represented a concept that was nonexistent in Africa. In order for such a phenomenon to become a reality on our continent, he should come and see for himself what Africa and African hospitality was like—and let himself be seen.

After the publicity accorded me in the press, every seat was full when I came to speak at the UN General Assembly. I wore a long, narrow dress of gold Chinese brocade, a gift of the Chinese government, and my hair was plaited in a crown. With Uganda's image in the West at its lowest ebb, barely a year after the controversial expulsion of the Asians, and Amin at loggerheads with nearly every Western country, people were also curious to see how I, a Cambridge-educated lawyer, a princess who was supposedly a friend of the West, and someone who had made history by becoming Africa's first female foreign minister in a republic, would conduct myself.

I was aware that the way I delivered the speech, so as to present Uganda's—and Africa's—dilemma in a fashion that would make the world sit up and take notice, was more important than its contents. For days, Amin had been telephoning at all hours, apparently oblivious of time differences, to add passages and phrases to what was to be a major encomium of Ugandan foreign policy.

Finally, it was time for me to speak, against the impressive background of the huge UN forum, its height emphasized by parallel vertical lines of polished wood which soar a hundred feet from floor to ceiling behind the speaker's rostrum. The speech was critical of the West in every way. I said that we viewed with guarded delight the new developments in Portugal (where there had recently been a coup), and welcomed the admission of the liberated state of Guinea-Bissau to the Assembly. I underlined that we were strongly opposed to any program that stipulated any delay in granting immediate independence to the Cape Verde Islands, Mozambique, and Angola. The stern lesson that Portugal had learned over the previous thirteen years should sound a clear warning to the racist minority regimes of South Africa and Rhodesia—which were supported by the very powers that accused Uganda of racism when it nationalized its assets in the interest of the development of its own citizens. The flagrant breach of the UN charter by the Pretoria regime should mean the expulsion of South Africa from the UN.

Uganda believed in the right of every country to exercise permanent sovereignty over its national resources and all economic activities. Our objective in declaring our own economic war was to transfer Uganda's economy to its rightful owners, the Ugandans, and to assert our self-reliance. However, economic self-reliance did not imply complete isolation. Thus foreign enterprise, financial assistance, and personnel were always welcome to supplement Uganda's own resources for the development of key sectors of the economy. Also, the expansion of Uganda's trade with foreign countries remained a cardinal element in the government's development strategy.

Uganda was therefore startled when Britain and Israel started a smear campaign against the country, to the extent of persuading their imperialist allies to cease commercial transactions with Uganda. We were contributors to such international financial institutions as the World Bank and the IMF, and were entitled to receive credit from them. But we had become victims of the belief, translated into practice, of certain countries that aid was an extension of foreign policy and had to be utilized to wield undue influence. I said that we rejected this 'Big Brother blackmail policy" in aiding developing countries and urged an immediate reform of the aforementioned institutions to rectify such an invidious situation.

I concluded by stating that Uganda and other peace-loving nations of the world would work toward making the UN a truly international community, where the experiences, cultures, and contributions of the various communities represented were mixed and balanced. We in Africa felt that for our contributions to make an impact, we had to be ourselves—that is, truly African. Our mission, and the challenge we had to face, was not to opt out of our responsibility to battle with the affairs of our countries as our enemies would have us do, just because of the immensity and complexity of our problems, but to contribute whatever we were capable of contributing. After all, problems would continue to exist and even multiply so long as this world was not Utopia. And I said that I could do no better than end with a quotation from Shakespeare:

> *There is a tide in the affairs of men,*
> *Which, taken at the flood, leads on to fortune;*
> *Omitted, all the voyage of their life*
> *Is bound in shallows and in miseries.*

ELIZABETH OF TORO

On such a full sea are we now afloat;
And we must take the current when it serves,
Or lose our ventures.

(Julius Caesar, *IV.iii*)

This quotation was my only contribution to the speech, and it was intended to sum up the dilemma as I saw it: that in the life of every politician there comes a time when one's ideals clash head-on with events, but one will be judged by how one measures up to such occasions. We, the Ugandans, were finding ourselves engulfed in a situation beyond our control, and we must either plunge in and swim—or else drown.

The U.S. newspapers were unanimous in praising my speech—a personal victory for me, and a real breakthrough for Uganda. The *New York Times* had not covered speeches from members of the Third World countries since the Second World War, but even this paper gave my speech prominence, and the black population and women's organizations in the United States hailed the speech as both a boost for the black people and for the dignity and equality of women.

Although I did not realize it at the time, it was my success at the United Nations which gave President Amin one of his madder ideas, namely that it would be a good political move to marry me. I was to be the last pillar of conquest. While I was in New York, I could feel that his attitude toward me was changing.

As Obote before him, Amin regarded everything under his control, including Uganda, as his personal property, and he was incapable of seeing that my triumph on the rostrum of the UN was due to my qualifications. He seemed to have felt that he personally was responsible for my achievement, and that marrying me would now be a way of increasing his own stature.

He never said anything to me directly, but immediately after my speech I began to notice signs that he was taking a personal interest in me. The Uganda Information Service had made a film of my performance at the UN, which would normally have been handled by the Foreign Ministry and the Information Ministry, but my permanent secretary told me in a phone call from Kampala that the president had issued specific orders that no one was to look at the film before he did. I also noticed that he was checking up on me in a personal rather than official way. In the week after the speech, I became very tired, but there was a ceaseless round of work to be completed. I had to go to Washington to deal with problems connected with our embassy, and while I was there, I was almost overcome by exhaustion. I came back to New York determined to get some sleep; I saw a doctor, took some prescribed medicine, and went to bed.

At about two in the morning the president called. The Ugandan ambassador explained that I was ill and suggested that he get me to call Amin back the next morning, but the president would not hear of it. He demanded to speak to me at once, and I got the distinct impression that he was making sure I was in the residence. Luckily, I was available; that was one of the reasons I had chosen to stay with the ambassador. When you were planning any course of action, you always had to say to yourself: How will this look to Amin? There were a great many friends from my modeling days whom I would have loved to have seen, and possibly stayed with, but I knew that if the president had found out, he would have said, "Oh, she's running around with her imperialist friends."

I took the call, told Amin how ill I was, and he let me go back to bed, but I sensed it mattered to him a great deal to know that I had been asleep in the residence at the time.

These signs of the president's personal interest did not worry me unduly. I felt strong enough in my own position to be able to fend him off, and I didn't believe that, once I had shown enough resistance, he would try to force me. I had always been extremely careful in the way I behaved toward him; and I think that, up till then, I had been saved from any more intimate approaches by two things: my strictly formal bearing toward him, and the fact that I maintained rigorous standards toward everyone in public life.

My formality was indeed a matter of record; the TV cameras in Kampala had documented almost daily my meetings with the president, and the whole nation had seen that I behaved always in a dignified and correct way. From the moment I entered politics, I knew that I had to succeed by my own ability. I knew instinctively that I would never survive in politics if I was not taken seriously. I never played around with anyone—least of all with other politicians or anyone I worked with. I had the advantage, because of my status as a princess, that I was one of the few women in Uganda who could say no to approaches of a sexual nature by prominent public figures, and I made the most of it. For the majority of women, saying no was much more awkward. Right from independence, politicians had tended to adopt the attitude that they were the most important people around, and they used their newly acquired power and money to take what they wanted—and that included women.

I was an exception. I was not available, and they knew it. I possessed the education to understand the implications of my actions, and I knew that the surest way to ruin my career was to be free and easy with other politicians, or to do anything which would cause gossip. Amin knew this. He had never had a single report of me living it up in a Kampala nightclub or going about with anyone, and this helped me to keep him at bay, as he could never feel that I was rejecting him while accepting the attentions of others.

Knowing that my reputation was secure, I was unconcerned by the president's scrutiny. He was delighted with my performance at the UN and had announced that he was decorating me with a medal for my services—one normally reserved for visiting heads of state. He had gone all over the country praising me as a woman able to defend Uganda's position to the world, and upstage the great Henry Kissinger as well, and he made a point of going to Toro and telling my people, "You have given birth to a very clever girl." As a friend wryly pointed out, such lavish praise was not always a good sign. It had happened before to other politicians and soon afterwards they had been sacked or killed, but when I left New York to continue the tour to Canada, West Germany, France, and Britain, there were no indications of any strain in my relations with the president.

The Canadian visit was very successful and eventful. My stay in West Germany was fruitful and the visit was capped by the early release of funds for a major aid program, but it was there that the first small cloud appeared on the horizon.

It was really a very trivial matter. One of the officials in my delegation began to feel aggrieved because he felt he wasn't getting enough attention on the tour. I didn't take it particularly seriously, and he started to sulk. In normal circumstances, the problem would have gone away of its own accord, but on our next stop, in Paris, the problem intensified when he found a supporter.

Such intrigues are an enduring feature of Ugandan political life, and they had plagued me right from the start of my appointment as foreign minister. Before I was named for the post, there was considerable rivalry for the job, which is very sought after in any government, guaranteeing much travel, lavish allowances, publicity, prestige, and, above all, the constant ear of the president.

But I was not in any mood to be bothered with petty infighting. I was still euphoric after my success at the UN. So, although I was aware of the contrivance going on, I got on with my work and did my best to ignore the phone calls which were flying between Paris and Kampala.

In fact there was a systematic campaign throughout my stay in Paris to create the impression that I was neglecting my work and my delegation and just concentrating on having a good time. With Amin in the state he was in—thinking of marriage and believing that I owed it to him as a price for my international acclaim—that kind of poison poured into his ear had a devastating effect. Looking back, I can imagine him saying to himself, "Look at this woman whom I have helped achieve so much success and prestige, and here she is, enjoying herself and showing me no gratitude whatsoever."

Too preoccupied to counterattack, I dismissed a small protest headed by the official who had been sulking since West Germany, with the words, "Oh goodness, I hadn't realized you were so unhappy." Another ominous sign was a warning from the French security officials who had been assigned to me during my stay They advised me that there had been close inquiries about my movements, and that they had refused the information, but felt I should know.

But the first real indication that the situation was turning sour came in the form of a phone call from Justice Byagagaire, the minister of public affairs, in Kampala. He called me unexpectedly and said, "Elizabeth, the president wants you to cut short your tour and return to Uganda immediately." When the president was displeased, he would pick a messenger arbitrarily to act as intermediary.

I had no idea why Amin wanted me to cancel the rest of the tour, and neither did Byagagaire. Fortunately, the minister was an old friend, and I felt safe enough with him to put my arguments in favor of continuing with my mission. I told him I felt it was imperative to go on, so as to exploit to the maximum the favorable publicity Uganda had gained in New York, and I pointed out too that I had not yet carried out one of my main tasks in Paris, which was to organize a meeting of the OAU ambassadors of the coffee-growing states to press my country's bid to become regional headquarters of the Coffee Organization.

Byagagaire agreed to present my arguments to the president and apparently he succeeded because the following morning I had a second message to say that the tour should continue. I felt relieved, until I found to my horror that the ambassadors' meeting had also fallen foul of the intrigues.

On the day the meeting was scheduled, I was informed—just as I was on the point of leaving to attend the meeting—that the other ambassadors had not been contacted and that the gathering could not therefore take place. This was another plot. I knew that if the meeting didn't take place, I would be in real trouble. I had only one more day in Paris, and if I were to leave without having discussed the coffee issue, the president would see it as irrefutable proof that I had been neglecting my duties. Fortunately I had some good friends in Paris, one of the most trusted of them being Leslie Harriman, the Nigerian ambassador to France. When I called him and explained my predicament, he was able to round up every single ambassador at once, and the meeting went ahead as planned. It took place in Harriman's own office.

My troubles did not stop there. That night (well after midnight), Amin called me on the phone. He wanted to talk about the case of Helen Ogwang, a woman who had defected from the Paris embassy, and asked me if I had compiled a report. Unwisely, I responded sharply, as I was annoyed because I felt the president wasn't appreciating how much work was being done on behalf of Uganda during the mission. I said that perhaps he should take up the matter directly with the ambassador, as I really hadn't had time to look into it. Amin slammed down the phone without another word.

The following day, I was to receive further bad news. The Tanzanian ambassador happened to overhear a telephone conversation between Amin and a Ugandan. The ambassador was stunned by the character assassination he was hearing, so much so that he left and contacted Leslie Harriman immediately, telling him that he ought to warn me not to go back to Uganda. Leslie moved quickly to impart this advice, but by that time I had had a cable from the president ordering me to cut short my mission. I was to go to London as planned, but I was to cancel all the negotiations scheduled to take place with the British government over the expulsion of the Asians; I was to address one meeting of Ugandan students in London, then fly straight back to Kampala.

I took the cable and went to discuss it with Leslie at his embassy. He was deeply concerned. "Of course, the final decision is up to you," he said, "but you must ask yourself whether it is safe."

However, I was determined to go home. I knew I was in danger, but I felt an almost martyrlike resignation about the whole affair; it would at least be an honorable ending. I wasn't about to let down our people and throw away everything I had accomplished at the UN by running away and letting Amin and my enemies exploit my defection. I had not been raised to run from danger. I remembered a song from my ancestors: a warlike people, who were referred to as Abanyakitara, Believers in Shield and Spear:

Better move along with one's shield	*(Leader)*
Eee	*(Crowd)*
Than a relative who is a coward	*(Leader)*
Lo and behold,	*(Crowd)*
They have dropped their shields,	
Yea, peasants will stand	
Any form of war problems	
Eh! In the open extensive battlefield	*(Leader)*
Eee	*(Crowd)*
There leave me should I prove a coward	*(Leader)*
Eee	*(Crowd)*

I ordered that preparations should go ahead for our departure as scheduled, and at the airport I let the officials who were masterminding the intrigues feel my displeasure. I left them in no doubt that I was extremely vexed about the coffee conference, which could have been a disaster for Uganda if I hadn't been able to count on the support of friends.

In London, the web became more intricate. I was staying with my sister Mabel in her flat close to Buckingham Palace, and almost before I had settled in, I found myself being bombarded with advice, much of it telling me not to return to Uganda. Among the warning messages was a phone call from a group of Ugandans in New York, including my brother Stephen who had stayed behind at the end of the UN session. They were themselves divided over whether it was safe for me to go home, but the majority view was that I should return, as so much was at stake if I did not. One member of the group, Perezi Kamunanwire, who now teaches at Columbia University, told me, "What you achieved here will never be repeated by any other Ugandan; you must not defect."

The group in New York told me that Amin had already been convinced that I wasn't going to go back, and he had sent cables to all our embassies preparing them for my defection. I gave the group my assurance that I would go back, and Jack Ibale lent me moral support when he told me about being with the president on his tour of the country and hearing him praise my achievements at the UN. "Elizabeth, it was incredible," he said. "I'm sure the president can't turn against you after that."

I had already arranged to cancel the rest of my scheduled engagements through Dingle Foot, the labour solicitor-general, who was an old friend of my family. I told him that Amin had forbidden me to have the talks with the British government about the Asians which had been suggested by the foreign secretary, James Callaghan, whom I had met in New York.

The High Commission went ahead with the arrangements for the student meeting, but just before I was due to leave for our embassy in Trafalgar Square, I was told to expect a phone call from Amin. I waited and waited, but the call was delayed and the time was close for me to address the students. I sent word that the officials were to explain the reason for my tardiness to the gathering awaiting me. Then

I got a call from a security official, who warned me that the officials were carrying on as though I had failed to turn up. Infuriated, I left the phone, jumped into my car, and raced over to the meeting.

When I arrived in the hall, the official who was speaking fell silent. He was obviously embarrassed as I swept on to the platform and made my apologies, telling the students that I had been waiting for a phone call from the president. The meeting was still going on when the call did finally come through.

Amin spoke in the first instance to a security official, asking him if I had addressed the meeting and whether I had talked about the economic war. His economic war was directed primarily against the British, and he was convinced that I wouldn't have the courage to talk about it in Britain. When he was told that I had talked about it at the meeting, he asked to speak to me, but our conversation was brief and cold. His main concern seemed to be to find out if I was there, and after a few seconds he asked to speak to other people in my delegation, choosing to bypass me as its leader.

Still resolute, I took the plane the next day to Uganda. We landed at Kampala about seven o'clock in the morning and, compared with the pomp and ceremony which had marked our departure to New York, we practically crept back into the country. There were no press or TV cameras, just a group of officials from the Foreign Ministry, led by the permanent secretary. Everyone expected to find themselves meeting a delegation without its leader, so when I stepped off the plane, the reaction was one of disbelief. This feeling was echoed throughout Kampala as soon as word got round that I was back. Several people told me later that they thought they were dreaming when they saw me in the streets. Everybody was sure I would have fled—including the president himself.

Amin had scheduled a meeting of senior Army officers for that day at the conference center to announce the news of my defection, but as soon as I appeared from the plane and the word was flashed to him, he canceled the meeting. I learned later from a Mutoro waiter who had served at a luncheon Amin had attended with senior Army officers at the Nile Hotel that the president had stormed into the hotel "like a wounded animal"—but that he had also been stupefied by my return. "I must say I'm surprised and impressed she's come back," he told the Army officers at the table. "Now all she has to do is to explain about the money."

As was customary, I led my delegation that afternoon to a formal debriefing with the president at his office at the Parliament building. I entered first, leading my delegates in a line, and shook hands with Amin. During the greeting, I was aware of the hugeness of his hands, which the like the rest of his body are massive. He looked me sharply in the eye, as if he were thinking to himself, "How will she behave? Will she be ashamed of herself?" I turned to begin presenting the delegation, but he waved me aside—a clear sign of displeasure—and started talking to the delegates directly.

Afterwards, I gave my brief on the mission, speaking at length about its achievements. The president listened coldly, contradicting me at one point over a reference I made to the international press. "Just call it the imperialist press," he said curtly. Another indication of his anger came when the chief from Karamoja rose to talk about the tour; he was an agreeable old man who was grateful to me for helping him out with his financial problems in New York, and he began to speak warmly about my UN triumph—but Amin cut him off roughly, obviously unwilling to listen to any praise of me.

I, too, was cut off abruptly when I announced that I was able to confirm that President Tito of Yugoslavia would be visiting Uganda. The confirmation had come in New York, and I was particularly pleased about it because I had done a lot of work to cultivate good relations with Yugoslavia. But Amin made it clear that he did not wish me to have any credit for such an important visit.

His own briefing to the press on the mission could not have been more low-key, in complete contrast to his usual extravagant style when addressing the media about the good work his delegates had done on foreign missions. He also failed to turn up at a reception in our honor. The diplomatic community was lavish in its praise, and the photographs taken that night show me dancing as cheerfully as though nothing had happened to cloud my relations with Amin. I knew how serious the situation might become, but I didn't care; my mission had succeeded and nothing could take that away from me.

The following days were tense, but there were no dramatic developments. It was a whim of Amin's to force his ministers to take a month's leave at short notice, in order to break their links with their own ministries and, he hoped, to humiliate them. The rest of the Cabinet had gone on leave while I was away, and at the debriefing the president had told me that I should also take a month's leave.

I returned to my official residence and took the phone off the hook. Not even the president could call me, and eventually he had to send an emissary, the minister of internal affairs, Obado, who came with an odd message: "The president says that if you would like to see him, do ring and make an appointment." I told Obado that I didn't particularly want to see Amin, but that I would submit my written report on the mission shortly.

I spent many hours writing the report and, during that time, my personal assistant Emmanuel Gasana came to see me. He had arranged leave and wanted to clear it with me. When I gave my approval, he asked if he could leave an attaché case with me containing the financial records of the trip. He was going to Burundi to see some relatives and he felt the case would be safer with me than left at his own flat. I took it and put it in my bedroom, not realizing then that its contents would help to save me from disaster.

I finished my report and passed it on to Amin's principal private secretary. Then I more or less collapsed, feeling exhausted from my trip, and I checked into the Rubaga missionary hospital in Kampala. I was given medication and advised to take several-days' rest.

Before I left for Toro, I had a phone call from Roy Innis, who headed the Congress of Racial Equality in the United States. I was only slightly acquainted with him—we had met at a few functions in Kampala—but I knew a lot about him, in particular that he was a close friend and confidant of Amin.

I was surprised that he had called and puzzled when he asked if he could come around for a chat. I received him in my sitting room and we talked mostly about politics. Innis compared the Ghanaian leader, Kwame Nkrumah, with Amin, saying that Nkrumah was an outstanding leader but lacked Amin's larger-than-life character which pushed him to extremes of behavior and set him so far apart from the herd. He termed Amin a psychopath, but he intended it as an expression of praise, indicating that the president was driven to great acts. Then he said suddenly: "If Amin asks you, will you marry him?"

"It's out of the question," I said. "The president is a married man." Amin had two wives at that time, Sarah and Medina—he had divorced the others.

Innis replied, "If he asks you, I shouldn't refuse if I were you. It will be very dangerous."

Again I said there was no question of my marrying Amin. I understood now why Innis had come; he had been sent by the president to take soundings, and I thought it was best to make my position as clear as possible. Innis left, but I could see he was alarmed.

Even after that, I had no inkling of the full extent of the turmoil going on in Amin's mind or of the conflict that had been set up between his admiration for what I had done in New York and the malicious rumors and lies that my enemies had fed him from Paris and London.

I went off to Toro, where I rested and spent most of the time with my family and close friends. I enjoyed the pleasure that the success of my mission had given to the Batoro. I remember in particular talking to an old valet, Masa Owabandi, who had worked for my grandfather, father, and brother. He spoke no English, but he said immediately how proud he had been of my speech. "How did you know about it?" I asked. "You have no radio."

"No. But my son has one, and he explained everything to me," he replied. Many of the ordinary people had no idea what had happened at the UN; they simply understood that their princess had done something big and important.

But the congratulations were mixed with expressions of grave concern. The word on everyone's lips was "flee." The warning was put most forcibly by my uncle Kawaya. He came to my home in Toro and said, "Look, you have served Toro and Uganda well in the positions you have held for Amin, but now you must get out of the country." I told him that I wasn't afraid and that I intended to carry on with my leave and see what happened when I returned to Kampala.

Meanwhile, Amin was continuing his investigation into the reports he had been receiving.

I stayed aloof from it all and, at the end of the month, I went back to the capital. The first day back was a Tuesday—Cabinet day. I went to the office in the normal way, and found the atmosphere in general very agreeable. There were congratulations from every side, and a lot of joking about my success in New York. They were aware of the trouble looming over me, but trouble had loomed over many people, including some of them, under Amin's capricious rule, and they knew that often it simply faded away. They were prepared to wait and see.

The next day I went to my office as usual and almost immediately had a phone call from Amin's secretary: Could I come at once to the Cabinet room? I went upstairs and was confronted with a most unusual gathering; the Cabinet members were all seated round the table, but with them were several outsiders, including the chief of police and the head of intelligence who had been with me on the delegation.

I sat down and started chatting with some of the ministers. Then a message came to say that the president wanted to see me.

His office was divided from the Cabinet room only by a secretary's office. I walked through and found Amin alone, seated at his desk. I closed the door behind me, walked over to a sofa, and sat down. He stared down at his desk for a moment or two, then he said without preamble and in a quiet tone, "Is there anything you would like to say to me?"

Equally quietly, I said, "No. But if you have lost confidence in me, it's right that I should no longer remain your minister."

"All right," he said. "Go and hand over."

That was it. There were no explanations. I walked out and went back to the Cabinet room, where I collected my papers, smiled and waved to the other members of the Cabinet, and went back downstairs to my own office. The police were waiting for me and they watched as I formally handed over to my permanent secretary. During the hand-over, I snatched the opportunity to tell my secretary to phone the news to my brother Patrick in Nairobi. Before anyone had time to intervene, she managed to make the phone call.

When the hand-over was complete, the police led me downstairs. This time I was not saluted. I was put into the back of one of the two police cars waiting outside the Parliament building. With a policeman sitting on either side of me, we drove off. Not a word had been said about where we were going. However, I soon realized that I was being taken to my official residence.

At the house, I broke the news to my stunned family. My mother's comment was: "The people in your world are mad." There is no exact translation (she spoke in Rutoro), but what she meant was, what kind of a world was it when I could be praised to the heavens one minute and brought down so low the next.

More police arrived to search the house. While they worked, one policewoman, who was from Toro, whispered to me, "For goodness' sake, don't say anything. Just co-operate." They didn't find anything, but they missed one document which could have been very damaging. Amin had told me some time in 1971 that he might be sending me on a mission to Israel, and I had mentioned this to Marietta Tree, the once U.S. delegate to the United Nations. She had written to me later, enclosing a letter of introduction to the mayor of Jerusalem. Given the current state of relations between Uganda and Israel, the letter could easily have been twisted in a court to portray me as a Zionist spy.

As the search was going on, police cars were taking up positions around the house; my cook overheard the police sealing off all the roads out of Kampala, and he urged me not to try to flee.

In the meantime, the president had gone straight from his office to the Cabinet room, where he announced his decision to depose me and launched into the monstrous and astonishing lie that was to go right around the world in the media and cause me far more embarrassment abroad than it ever did at home.

Amin said that he had sacked me because of my unsatisfactory behavior during my recent mission, and that what had displeased him most about my conduct was that I had had sexual relations with a white man in a toilet at Orly Airport.

The first I heard of the story was when I watched the president making the statement on the five o'clock news on Uganda television. I was shocked, but not outraged because it was too ridiculous and farcical for me to react in that way. I didn't anticipate that the international press would be stupid enough to repeat the story in a fashion that would seem to give it credence, and I knew that inside Uganda no one would believe it, especially coming from the lips of Amin. Israel Mayengo told me later how he had met the secretary to the Cabinet, Peter Uchanda, in the street, and how Peter had said to him, "I've just attended the most sickening Cabinet meeting ever." That just about summed up everyone's reaction. Israel said that when the report was broadcast, he hadn't seen a reaction like it since the announcement of the assassination of President Kennedy. He saw people staring at the television with tears of horror and disbelief streaming down their faces.

The story was fed to Amin from Paris just when he was feeling particularly sensitive about me—as he was preparing to broach the issue of marriage. It says a great deal about the president that he believed it. It was so grotesque that, with anyone else, it might have been better to concoct a more subtle story which the majority of the people might have been prepared to believe. But one of the vital features of Amin's makeup was that he lacked the basic common sense which protects most people from extremes of behavior, and he could not bear to be seen to be ridiculed. The story wounded him because it seemed to him that not only was I rejecting him—as I'd made clear to Roy Innes—but that I was preferring a white man to him.

That same night, I was arrested. After banging on all my doors, the CID officer in charge learned from two servants which room was my bedroom. He came to the shuttered windows and identified himself as my own brother-in-law! He was the head of the CID in Kampala and I found out later that when the president had given him the order to go and arrest me, he'd said no on the grounds that I was a relative. But his wife, Joy, my sister, had told him, "Don't be a fool. If Elizabeth has to be arrested, it's far better that you do it rather than someone else."

When I realized who it was, I allowed my uncle to open the door, and my brother-in-law, accompanied by several policemen, came to my bedroom and said, "We've been asked to take you to the police station." The order, he said, had come direct from the president. I was still in my dressing gown, so I told them to wait outside and I changed.

The police wanted to take me alone, but my aunt, Princess Ruth, insisted on coming with us and eventually the police gave up trying to prevent her. With the rest of the family watching from the veranda, we were put into a car and taken to the central police station, a small wooden colonial-style building in the middle of Kampala.

I was taken briefly into an office, then put in a tiny cell on the lower level, bare except for a bed and a narrow mattress. It wasn't very clean, but I knew that I could have been incarcerated in far worse places. I was not maltreated; and I was left alone to sleep for the rest of the night.

I spent all the next day in the cell, unaware that my arrest had triggered a worldwide wave of protest which was being translated into vigorous pressure on Amin to release me. As soon as he heard the news, my brother Patrick went to see President Jomo Kenyatta of Kenya. Kenyatta phoned Amin at once, and warned him not to mistreat someone whom he regarded as his daughter. He also reminded the president that one of my most successful missions as roving ambassador had been my mission to Kenya, and that Amin would do well not to forget the service I had rendered to my country. At the United Nations, the OAU ambassadors met under the chairmanship of Nigeria and agreed on a joint message to Amin, threatening to break off diplomatic relations with Uganda if I was harmed.

Inside Uganda, the word of my arrest spread like a bushfire, and before long there were hundreds of people sitting in silent vigil around the police station.

Amin was taken completely by surprise by the reaction, and although he was still determined to see me humiliated, he bowed to the intensity of the international outcry, and to pleading from Ayume, the solicitor general, Ayisu, the head of the Special Branch, and Godfrey Lule, minister of justice, and ordered my release from the cell by five o'clock that same day.

I was driven back to my residence, where an emotional scene ensued, with my mother breaking down and sobbing, and the rest of the family joining in. I cried as well, and the tears brought some release. I was formally told that I was to remain under house arrest, although my mother and my aunt would be allowed to stay with me. When everyone had quieted down, a senior CID officer informed me that I must write a formal statement, setting out in detail my movements during the mission abroad and a detailed account of the funds which had been spent on the trip. He did not tell me immediately what was behind the request, but I gathered during the conversation that I was being asked to defend myself against allegations that I had wasted my time while abroad, especially in Paris, and that I had squandered public money.

I said I would make a full statement about my movements and activities, but that I couldn't do the accounts because they had been the responsibility of my personal assistant and I did not have any records or receipts. The attaché case that Gasana had left with me had been confiscated during the police search on the day of my arrest, and I did not expect to see it again. However, it turned up with Gasana—miraculously, it had not been broken into before his return from Burundi—when he took the courageous decision to come back from Burundi to try to help me, as soon as he learned from the radio that I was in trouble. When his family tried to dissuade him from returning, he said to them, "If I don't go back and Elizabeth's head is bashed in Naguru [one of Amin's torture chambers], I'll never forgive myself, and will be haunted for the rest of my life."

I did not know that Gasana was back, but when I told the CID officer that I would need his help, he was brought to the house, and we worked on the accounts together for nearly three days. When the work was completed, I realized that Gasana had been able to account for every single penny of the funds and, in the final outcome, it was that which saved me.

I spent a week under house arrest, and during that time I had only a sketchy knowledge of what was happening outside.

The worldwide campaign of protest was growing daily. There were appeals and warnings from every quarter—from women's groups worldwide, from heads of state, and from all kinds of organizations and individuals. There was also an unprecedented statement from the French government to say that the alleged incident at Orly Airport had not taken place. The French authorities gave a formal assurance that I had been strictly guarded by the security services throughout the entire departure, and that there had been no incident whatever on which the lie could have even been based.

I gathered later from friends that Amin was being driven into a frenzy of frustration at this time because he was unable to achieve his goal of publicly humiliating me. He had wanted me to be detained in a cell and he hadn't been able to maintain that because of the international outcry. Then he had wanted to put me on trial, but his advisers told him there were simply no grounds for one. A dossier had been compiled of all the evidence from delegates and handed to the attorney general, the solicitor general, the CID, and the Special Branch, and the upshot of it was that there were no charges to be preferred.

Amin was furious, and an eyewitness told me later that he had stormed up and down the room at one of the meetings, shouting, "You've got to find a charge!" It was a deadlocked situation. As Gasana had kept such careful accounts, there was no question of charges of embezzlement or misappropriation of funds. Finally, responding to his pressure, the attorney general and the solicitor general advised Amin that at the very worst I might be accused—although in fact quite wrongly—of allowing officials to spend too much money. But this was hardly a criminal matter, and the president was advised that he could take only administrative action. He could sack me, which he had already done, and, he was told, he could fine me, which seemed to be the only solution left if Amin were to save any face at all.

At this time, we were getting only garbled fragments of information, interspersed with radio announcements and rumors from various sources, including the policewomen who were sleeping on the floor of my bedroom. Toward the end of the week, rumors became persistent that I was likely to be facing a fine, but the figure being proposed fluctuated wildly from hundreds up to millions of shillings. My aunt Princess Ruth spent a great deal of time and energy trying to raise money to meet these fluctuating fines. She was our main contact with the outside world, thanks indirectly to her strong Christian devotion; on the first Sunday of our captivity, she had told the police aggressively, "You can do what you like, but you're not stopping me from going to church." When she was allowed out, she decided to extend her license and went out every day, not to church but all over the city in her attempts to ferret out information and raise funds.

When the order for my release finally came through, it was as sudden as the arrest. Amin appeared on television one afternoon, receiving a delegation from the Palestine Liberation Organization, and announced that I was soon to be released. My mother was watching the program, but she speaks very little English and did not fully understand. She came rushing to me with a garbled version, and I got the full story from a policewoman who had also been watching.

The release, like everything else under Amin's regime, was carefully stage-managed for the press and the television cameras. When the day arrived, a car turned up at my residence and I was escorted by Uganda's most famous policeman, the international athlete Akibua, to the president at Makindye Lodge. Makindye Lodge is a beautiful residence—it was the home of the governor in colonial times—and stands on a hilltop surrounded by magnificent lawns overlooking rolling countryside.

The president was sitting in an open-sided grass-thatched hut in the center of the lawns, flanked by various ministers and officials and with TV and pressmen, as always, in attendance. When I got out of the car, it was quite a long walk to where Amin was sitting, and the cameras followed me every step of the way.

I was told to sit down facing the semicircle, a setup which resembled a miniature trial. Very formally, the attorney general, Godfrey Lule, read out a statement saying that I was to be released but with a fine of 15,000 shillings, the equivalent of about £750. Then Amin spoke. He began by asking me to take off my head scarf. I obeyed without understanding why, and he said for the benefit of the TV camera, "There, you see, the imperialist press said I had shaved her head. But they lied. I did not." I was still mystified, but I was told later that there had been rumors circulating that my long hair—which was famous throughout Uganda to the point of being virtually my trademark—had been cut off, which had aroused specially bitter resentment.

The president then went on to inform me: "I have been very, very kind. I could have sent you to Luzira, or Naguru, or Makindye," naming his three most notorious prisons. "But I sent you to a police cell instead."

"A lot of people appealed to me on your behalf," he continued, "even the PLO, and now I'm releasing you—but I warn you, if you undermine my government, I shall have you arrested again."

Before coming to the lodge, I'd received a message from Lule to say that, whatever happened, I should not argue with the president, but I was so angry over the whole situation that I'm afraid I forgot the warning and assumed a defiant attitude.

"What is the fine for?" I demanded. "For what do I have to pay 15,000 shillings?"

Amin was livid. "Look, this is not a court of law."

As he was speaking, I caught Lule's eye, and saw his terror. But I was not about to become a whipping post for Amin, and this little scene of his was a travesty.

Looking back to that day, I am reminded of a story that illustrates the cloth from which I am cut, a cloth I would not stain by cowering before Amin. It is the story of one of my aunts, who is over eighty years old. Often, at my insistence, she recounted the story for me, as I had begged her many times before.

She was a young girl in Kibira, in the county of Mwenge, herding calves with some of the other village children. It was an ordinary day, hot and bright, as she and about twenty other children walked in a field, behind the grazing herd. Some of the children amused themselves by playing with the rich earth, shaping it into ships or milk pots. My aunt stood on an anthill, watching the other children play. Suddenly, she felt a wind as the calves came running in the direction of the children. My aunt saw three lions approaching. One, a female, stopped in front of my aunt, holding a calf in its front paws, raising it toward the heavens. The children watched from afar, and then ran off to the village for help. The two other lions, a male and a female, stood behind the aggressor. My aunt had been walking with a stick, which she raised to the sky. "I'm going to beat you," she warned the lion, noticing its enormous pointed fangs and huge, widening eyes.

My aunt tells the story slowly, easing her body off the couch onto the carpeted floor, her legs and arms becoming limbs of a lion. Slowly her face seems to change, to resemble the lion. My aunt begins to growl, explaining that this is what the lion had done. The growl of my aunt seems to move from the front of her mouth to the back of her throat, a low deep rumble, a distant thunder.

"I am going to beat you" became my aunt's refrain as she stood in that field alone. After a while, the lion hurled the calf to the ground, turning and thrashing furiously around, digging up the grass and spraying her with it. Then the lion coiled its tail and urinated, splashing her. She just stood there, the children long gone, having run off to town, frightened, certain that she would be dead by the time they returned with help.

Her older brother soon arrived, relieved to find his sister still alive. With one swoop he speared the lion, hitting her in the shoulder. Injured, she retreated, her companions following.

My aunt became limp and fell to the ground. She was lifted and carried back to the village, where she was confined to bedrest and silence. Her arm, which had been upraised during the entire episode, was strained severely, and rendered nonfunctional for a month. At night, in her sleep, the little girl could be heard yelling out, "I'm going to beat you, I'm going to beat you."

My aunt eases herself back up on the couch, her metamorphosis reversed, and she laughs self-consciously at her performance. But she grows serious, and says this would not happen these days. The importance of protecting the herd is not felt as strongly. "The children now, they go bare-handed." She shakes her head.

I could not go bare-handed that day, and so I stood proudly before Amin, who had become my lion. The air was heavy with concern. Many who had angered Amin less than I, had disappeared without a trace.

Standing before Amin, the air was heavy with fear. I noticed my friend, Juma Oris, the information minister, had begun to weep. I could see in his eyes and others present that they had already begun to mourn for me. But that was unnecessary. While I had forced Amin to witness the strength of my people, I believed I could still get out with my life. I turned and began to walk slowly toward the car, my head raised, my steps unhurried and measured. The television cameras followed my silent procession. That was the last time I saw Amin.

I asked to be taken to my brother Stephen's house, where I found my mother and my aunt. I was still bent on remaining in the country—I could not face the thought of another exile—as an ordinary citizen. I therefore decided that the best course of action was to try to pursue a normal life as though nothing untoward had been happening. I even went shopping, just as any ordinary citizen would do.

Meanwhile, I had scores of visitors, all well-wishers. Among them was the ambassador of Ghana, who said to me, "Amin hasn't shamed you, he has shamed Africa, so there's no need to torment yourself." Mr. Mukamba, Zaire's ambassador, also came, with an encouraging message from his president, Mobutu. It was that, as I had served Africa so well, Zaire would be prepared to help me in any way it could, starting by settling the fine that Amin had inflicted on me.

Then a man called Ekodeo, who was married to a cousin of mine and was a permanent secretary in the Ministry of Information, turned up. He told me that he had been informed by certain officers in the Army and police force—and by a fellow Teso, Ayisu, who was head of the Special Branch—that my life was still endangered, and that the only way I could hope to escape death was by getting out of the country.

Ekodeo's visit was soon followed by that of a Toro man who was a top official in the Post Office. When he asked to have a word with me in private, I was dubious as I had never seen him before, but my mother and aunt knew him and could vouch for him. That very same day, he said, when we were alone, some men from the State Research had come to the Post Office and arranged to have my telephone bugged—in other words, any conversations that were carried on over my brother's telephone could be listened into.

My older brother Stephen had been serving under me in the Foreign Ministry and I had always tried to be good to him, allowing him easy access to my office and so forth. In fact, it was partly on his account that I had begun to fall into Amin's bad books. Stephen had very much wanted to be included in the delegation to the UN session in New York, and I had fixed it for him—which was when the president stepped in to make his own selection. Stephen owed it to me not to exert pressure on me to leave his house, but obviously he was concerned for his own family's safety.

My routine at that time was simple. I'd get up in the mornings, wash and eat, and then go to sit under a tree in the compound, where I would spend the days reading, writing, and pondering my predicament. (I had actually been warned not to make a habit of sitting outside, as the road passed right by the compound.) At that time, I was under twenty-four-hours' surveillance. One morning I was sitting under the tree as usual, when my former housekeeper Ongambo and gardener Jimmy came running up. They said that there were some Europeans at the gate, who wanted to speak with me. I had no idea who these people might be, but I suspected it might be dangerous for me to be seen talking to them, so I went indoors and hid in my bedroom. By a strange coincidence, two Batoro girls also arrived, both of whom I knew to be employed by the State Research. (One of them was known to be living with Minawa, the head of the SR). They informed me that the Europeans were from a German magazine and wanted to interview me. I replied that I had no interest in being interviewed, and eventually the Europeans went away.

One evening, a car rolled up outside, flying a pennant. I was puzzled, as I could not think which minister would be daring to pay me a visit; then it transpired that it was no minister but the archbishop of Uganda, Janan Luwum, who was the head of the Protestant Church in Uganda (three years later he was murdered by Amin). He told me that the Church was praying for me, and asked if there was anything it could do to help me. I said yes—that I would appreciate a house to rent and some sort of employment if possible. The archbishop promised to make inquiries, and I was allocated a small house within the Church compound on Namirembe Hill. And as I was qualified as a lawyer, I was asked to lend my expertise in compiling a constitution that the Church was in the process of drawing up.

I was very happy to be going to Namirembe, as being within the Church organization, right away from the pressure centers, inside the friendly compound offered me the peace I needed. I moved into my little house with my mother and aunt Ruth, and got down to work. I continued to receive visitors, although my house was difficult to find (the archbishop had generously told me that he would make himself answerable to Amin if the president demanded to know who had given me the house).

One morning, about seven Aunt Walusimbi and my brother Emmanuel drove up. When I asked why they were looking so grave, they looked surprised. "You mean you haven't heard?" Apparently, a photograph of a nude woman had been shown on television and appeared in the press, and Amin was claiming it was of me. However, my aunt and her husband, Walusimbi, had been so concerned that they thought I should be warned and moved straight away. Accordingly, my aunt had rung my brother Emmanuel at 6:00 A.M., and they'd come as soon as possible to try to persuade me to leave Uganda.

I realized, of course, what Amin was up to. One of the greatest weapons that one can wield against a dictator is ridicule—and Amin in the eyes of the world *had* been ridiculed when he'd failed miserably to have me branded as a bad woman, or anything else. He was working hard at that time to become the next OAU chairman, and so it was important for him to be able to convince Africans, above all, that I was indeed what he said I was—especially as our ambassador to the OAU headquarters in Addis Ababa, Matiya Lubega, had reported to him that all the OAU ambassadors were expressing explicit indignation over his vendetta against me.

Now this nude photograph, which had first appeared in the German magazine *Das Bild* on January 11, 1975, struck him as providing the proof he needed to turn the tables on everyone who was laughing at him for his gullibility or disapproving of his relentless persecution of me. I knew it was imperative that I go underground immediately.

Leaving my mother and aunt behind to cover for me, my aunt Walusimbi drove me to the suburb of Tank Hill in Kampala, where Mr. and Mrs. Israel Mayengo (my friends from New York) lived. Regina Mayengo was so frightened that the Army or police would burst in and kill or arrest her family that I stayed with them only one day and then moved to the Walusimbis' house in Rubaga suburb. Here, a number of escape plans were proposed and discussed.

There was no shortage of offers of help. Mrs. Scherer, a German UN employee who was a specialist in landscape gardening and had designed my garden at the foreign minister's residence, planned with my former chief gardener, Osinyi, to drive me in a car bearing a diplomatic plate to Uganda's eastern border with Kenya. My uncle Rwakatale, together with Jonasani Kironde, a close friend of my father's, planned to ferry me out via Lakes George and Edward in western Uganda to Zaire. In Nairobi, a Ugandan lawyer, Christopher Mboijana, planned with others to smuggle me out in a petrol tanker, with a special compartment built into it, which traveled between Kampala and Mombasa.

President Museveni, then the leader of a guerrilla organization called FRONASA, which has now been assimilated into the national resistance movement in Uganda and was already engaged in guerrilla activities against Amin, sent a Ugandan called Charles Katungi to see Patrick, offering to smuggle me out, and in Los Angeles, Edward Mosk, who had been one of the producers of the film I had starred in in Nigeria, succeeded in persuading Amnesty International to adopt my case as a prisoner of conscience. In England David Harlech, in cooperation with my sister Mabel, contacted Henry Kissinger, who agreed to try to enlist Arab leaders in support for me.

There were a couple of other desperate schemes, one projected by some Toro sisters who wanted to get me out via Jinja and across the eastern border, and the other by a close friend of mine, Marina Roper—whose husband was the cultural attaché at the French Embassy, in conjunction with the ambassador of Zaire.

One afternoon, while I was still ruminating on the various avenues of escape, my mother turned up—on foot. She told me that two plainclothes policemen had come looking for me at Namirembe. They had been very polite, and said that the president wanted to see me. My mother explained that I had gone out with friends, but that she would get me to ring them when I returned. They left a telephone number and went. Careless and in a panic, my mother rushed out into the compound, where she met a sympathetic European missionary and got a lift to Rubaga, where the church worker dropped her off a short distance from the Walusimbis' house and promised to wait for her.

I had to make a rapid decision—whether to appear briefly before Amin and then to continue with my escape arrangements or to make a bolt for it at once. The Walusimbis advised me to get out. We arranged that my mother should tell the police that I had gone for the weekend to Toro, and that I would be back on the Monday. Meanwhile, we got into the Walusimbis' old Morris Minor and drove off before my aunt's house could be surrounded and our exits sealed off.

We had to find a safe house where I could go underground until the escape plan was finalized, so we drove, avoiding the main roads, to the village of Salama, where a loyal friend of the Walusimbis called Lwasa lived with his wife and children. Lwasa had been for about fifty years the organist at Namirembe Cathedral, the seat of the Protestant Church, and when we arrived at his house, he was absent at the cathedral. His wife let us in and nervously we awaited Lwasa's return. Lwasa had been at school with my father and shared a bedroom at the palace of King Daudi Chwa, whom his sister had married. He told us he could not but help the daughter of his friend. Nevertheless, he decided it could only be for three days.

I was hidden in a tiny dark room which I had to share with a girl and her baby (the girl's father had been murdered by Obote's army when it ransacked the Kabaka's palace). The Lwasas were very kind, even bringing out their best cutlery and china to entertain me, although I had to stay in my cramped quarters all the time so that their relatives, children, and servants wouldn't see me. My ears were assailed by the strains of Beethoven and Mozart, which was incongruous music to hear in an African village.

In the meantime, the pressure was growing on my family to reveal what they knew of my whereabouts. We heard that the minister of finance, Emmanuel Wakweya, had defected, and pressed by journalists at press conferences, he admitted that I had disappeared. Because of the ensuing uproar, Amin was anxious to produce me on television so that everyone would *see* I hadn't been quietly done away with, and the police insisted that that was the only reason he wanted me back.

On the third day, my aunt, Emmanuel, and another relative, a former policeman called Samuel Mugamba, came to see me and reported that the pressure being exerted on my family was such that some of my relatives were muttering that I should give myself up, while others said absolutely not. Mugamba advised me to flee at once.

Meanwhille, Israel Mayengo, together with two relatives, Semeji and Abdu, had organized an escape route which involved paying a group of smugglers about 30,000 shillings to disclose a smugglers' route out across the Ugandan-Kenyan border. The money was raised and, late on the afternoon of February 8, Sam Mugamba came to collect me in his car. By this time, the Army and the police had been issued with my photographs, and a reward was being offered for information as to my whereabouts. There were also announcements being given out about me on the radio and television.

Mrs. Lwasa gave me a book of Psalms, and said, "You will go through peacefully." Avoiding the main roads, Sam and I drove to Wankulukuku Stadium, where Sam decided we should wait until it was dark. Then we left for Jinja in eastern Uganda, with me lying on the backseat of the car. Someone in Jinja directed us to the house of a Mutoro girl who was married to a Muganda, a couple called Simbwa. To my surprise, she turned out to be my first cousin, Komuntale. I stayed with them for one night while Sam returned to Kampala to find out whether the next stage of the plan was ready. The following afternoon, disguised as a simple village girl (the art of making up which I had learned as a model came in handy here), I was picked up by Sam, Semeji, and Abdu, who had borrowed my aunt Ruth's Peugeot car—without her knowledge. I sat in the front with Sam and Semeji, while Abdu sat at the back, and we set off for the border along the main road into Kenya.

Semeji deposited Sam, and myself outside a house that was being constructed by the roadside, a few miles from the official Uganda-Kenya border, while he and Abdu went off to see the smugglers and hand over the money. The smugglers had no idea it was a person who was being smuggled out—they were told it was elephant tusks. The workmen guarding the building arrived and demanded that we leave, but when Sam told them that I was his wife, expecting a baby, and that we were waiting for a car to pick us up, they felt sorry for us and allowed us to stay until Semeji and Abdu returned with the car.

We drove back along the main road until we came to a dirt road, where we turned off and found a local shopkeeper to whom we entrusted the car. Because it had a Ugandan registration number, he agreed to look after the vehicle—for a fee—until we could return for it after a few hours. Then we set off to walk four miles through the bush, crossing a river on the way, and eventually came to the border. I could hardly believe that I had actually made it to Kenya.

About eight o'clock at night, we encountered some Kenyan villagers, from whom we bought a torch and asked how far it was to the nearest place where we might be able to hitch a lift from a car. We were told that it was about fourteen miles. Realizing that we had Ugandan accents, they arrested us, and demanded to see proof of our identities (that particular area of Kenya, known as the Valley of Death, is renowned for having the highest crime rate). Fortunately, Sam managed to save the situation, as he spoke good Swahili and told them that we were on our way to Uganda. Sam had told me, "Never say where you are really going, but say you are going where you are coming from." They released us, and we walked on, arming ourselves with sticks. We had just paused for a rest when two cyclists turned up, claiming to be some sort of officials in the area. They told us that they were going to arrest us. At first, we refused to be arrested, but eventually Semeji and Abdu agreed to go with them to the police station and sort things out, while Sam and I remained where we were by the roadside.

Three quarters of an hour later, Semeji and Abdu returned. The cyclists had not been officials after all, and Semeji and Abdu had practically had to fight their way out of the place they had been taken to, where everybody had apparently been sitting around smoking *Bangi*, or pot. We walked on along a road, hoping that a passing car would stop and give us a lift—but of course drivers were by law forbidden to give lifts in this dangerous area.

About eleven o'clock, we were accosted by a couple of drunkards who accused us of being criminals, and they began blowing on a horn they had with them to summon the village. As we were pleading with them, a car approached. Sam and Semeji stood in the middle of the road so it had to stop. Inside were two Brazilian padres. This time I decided to speak. "You men of God—save us!" They said that by law no one is allowed to pick people up in that part of the world, and the drunkards added their voices, saying the padres would get themselves into trouble if they did.

At that point, another car arrived and was forced to pull over. There were two Kenyans inside, who interrogated the drunkards, pronounced them bogus, and agreed to give Sam and Abdu a lift, while Semeji and I traveled in the padres' car. We were driven four miles back along the road we had come, to a Catholic mission. There, we were given a small house in the compound for the night, and the padres told us that in the morning they would drive us to Kakamega, where we could pick up a taxi to take us to Nairobi.

We lay awake all night worrying about the car we had left behind with the shopkeeper, for if it were found, we knew that the police would inform Amin, and then my family would start to be harassed, and Sam, Abdu, and Semeji would be unable to return to Uganda. At

5:00 A.M., therefore, Sam and Abdu got up and went off to make their way back to Uganda and retrieve the car.

Semeji and I breakfasted with the padres, and we had a fairly innocuous conversation, about Brazil and New York among other things. I think it was beginning to dawn on the padres who I was, and they drove us 160 miles to Eldoret—further than they had said they would—and even offered us the money for a taxi to Nairobi. On the way, one of them said casually, "By the way, what has happened to that princess in Uganda?" Semeji replied nonchalantly that he didn't really know, he presumed she was still around somewhere, but he didn't really know much about her.

We managed to get a taxi to take us to Nairobi, and went straight to my brother Patrick's office. He, meanwhile, had received a mysterious phone call from Sam's niece, Jolly, asking him not to leave his office at all that day. He was enlightened as soon as we turned up, and he took us back to his flat.

We were fearful of interrogation of family and friends—the gestapo tactics—as the real search for me was apparently only just beginning in Uganda. My aunt Walusimbi's house was searched, and she herself was interrogated. She did not deny that I'd been staying with her, but she was adamant that she didn't know where I was now. My aunt Ruth's car was also confiscated for a few days by the police, although I don't know how much, if anything, they suspected. I had to stay in hiding in Patrick's flat, as I didn't want the press getting wind of my arrival and perhaps exposing my family and friends to more danger.

President Kenyatta, who was sympathetic to my plight and looked upon me as a daughter, offered me asylum, and I moved into his daughter Margaret's house.

"Phone Amin and offer your condolences for the death of his father. That will preempt a move to persecute your family," advised Kenyatta.

I dialled Amin's number, asking the disbelieving operator to put me through to the president (I could hear the tapes recording our conversation as I spoke).

"Your Excellency," I said to him, "I am speaking from Nairobi. I came here by train from Kasese [in Toro]." I went on to offer my condolences to him on the death of his alleged father, and assured him that I wished him well and bore no grudge against either him or his government.

"But wouldn't you like to come back?" Amin asked. "You can have back your position, and your house . . ."

I told him that I'd rather stay with my brother in Nairobi, but that I would be grateful to him if he would be kind to my family. The president assured me that he wouldn't molest any members of my family and would even receive my mother and aunt Ruth. On this amicable note we parted, and the news of my call was broadcast on the radio and on the television news, and the fact that I had been offered back my position.

Because of the proximity of Kenya to Uganda, I could not stay where I was indefinitely, so I started to make inquiries about getting asylum abroad. At that time, there was a crisis between the United Kingdom and Uganda over the Dennis Hill affair (Amin threatened to hang Hill, a lecturer at Makerere University, for calling him a "village tyrant"), so I felt it wouldn't be diplomatic to approach the British authorities immediately. Austria, however, was quite prepared to accept me. I moved for a short time into the home of the Austrian ambassador, Dr. George Reisch, and his wife, Monica, and then left for Vienna under the assumed name of Marina Crosse. My old friend Marina Roper and a friend of hers called François Crosse, a French journalist, had liaised with Luiz Carlos Wiel at the World Council of Churches in Geneva, who arranged to supply my ticket.

In Vienna, I was given a warm welcome and was assigned security officers and a room in a pension. Later, I moved to a hotel. Unfortunately, someone recognized me and tipped off the press, and in no time at all the foyer of the hotel was full of reporters and TV cameras. I managed to slip out through the back unnoticed with the help of the hotel manager, and was taken to stay with Mrs. Odette Yankowitsch, the wife of an Austrian member of Parliament.

Mrs. Yankowitsch took me to see Bruno Kreisky, the chancellor of Austria. He had himself been an exile, in Sweden during the Nazi period, and understood what it meant to be on the run. He told me that his daughter had just moved out, and offered me her apartment. He also suggested that since Vienna was the headquarters of certain

United Nations agencies, such as Atomic Energy, he would help me find employment.

However, I felt I could not settle down properly until the damage done to my reputation by the international press for reporting Amin's allegations against me had been repaired. I decided to go to London, where I had friends who would be able to advise me. I left first for Geneva, and contacted David Harlech in London who saw that I got permission from the Foreign Office to come to the United Kingdom.

My arrival in London caused a furor among the Fleet Street newspapers, and there was cutthroat competition, especially between *Daily Mail* and *Daily Express* reporters, to "scoop" my story. I was already well known to the press, and I was to be constantly harassed and hounded by newspaper and television reporters, until I was forced to go "underground." I could have made a great deal of money from selling my story, but knowing that my family in Uganda was still in jeopardy from Amin and that I had the libel suits pending, I evaded the attentions of the press.

First I went to stay in Harley Street with Joan O'Connell, my old Cambridge friend, but when we were subjected to a virtual siege by reporters and cameramen, I made my escape, with the help of Charles Douglas-Home (later editor of *The Times*), and Peter Cross of Curtis Brown, to a place in Kilburn. From Kilburn, forced out by floods, I went to the Guides Club in Belgrave Square, and it was from there that I was to conduct my libel actions.

At a lunch with Charles Douglas-Home and Robin MacEwan at Douglas-Home's Club, I explained the situation. MacEwan disappeared to make a phone call. On his return, he told me that he'd just been speaking to Peter Carter-Ruck, then senior partner of Oswald Hickson, Collier & Co., who had agreed to see me. I went immediately to his offices in Essex Street, where after an initial chat he told me, "It's rare that I say to a client in a libel case that this is an open-and-shut case. I can tell you that, in your case, it is."

The libel actions were to take several years to follow through. A Nigerian, Chief Eke, very kindly donated the £1000 that was necessary to brief counsel and set the libel actions in motion. The British newspapers which I sued were the *Sunday Telegraph, News of the World, Daily Express, Daily Mail, Daily Mirror, Evening*

News, and *Sun*. The *Sunday Telegraph* had alleged that I was expecting a baby, and the other newspapers had all repeated Amin's allegations, more than once.

The trouble is that, once an allegation is repeated often enough, it takes on a ring of truth, at least in the mind of the public. The newspapers claimed in their defense that they had only been reporting what a head of state had said, and that it was in the public interest to do so, but he proved successfully that the press had a responsibility *not* to repeat unnecessarily such wild allegations.

In the case of the Orly Airport accusation by Amin, officials at the airport had disclosed as early as 1974 that such an accusation was completely false. I had made only two stops at Orly, each about fifteen minutes' duration, and on both occasions I was surrounded by delegates, security men, and other officials, who pronounced that I "could not have, even if she wanted to, taken part in the slightest extravagance." As Sir Peter Rawlinson pointed out while conducting the case against the German magazine *Der Spiegel* and its UK distributors, Seymour Press Ltd., the allegations, and the nude photographs purporting to be of me, were particularly damaging to me as a royal princess and a symbol of morality in my own country, and as a member of the bar.

All the allegations were found to be entirely without foundation, and apologies were printed in all the newspapers, as well as statements to the effect being made in open court. Every single libel action I undertook was settled out of court, including those against *Das Bild*, *Der Spiegel*, and *Stern* in West Germany. The actions against the French magazines *Paris Match* and *France-Soir* and the Italian *L'Espresso* and *Corriere della Sera* were successfully conducted in England. They also conducted the action in Italy against Italian *Playboy*. I was to receive a large overall settlement, amounting in the United Kingdom alone to over £50,000. I was also indemnified against all my legal costs. The German publications paid over 23,000 deutsch marks. Large amounts were paid by the French and Italian ones.

I had kept quiet about Amin's regime, and my place in it, for my family's and others' sakes, to the extent that even Amin was impressed. It seems that all my life I have been walking a sort of tightrope—ignoring the advice of colleagues personally to benefit from the high positions I have held, by accepting commissions or bribes. I had always striven to maintain an impeccable reputation, and eventually my policy paid off. The money—honorably won—and the vindication I attained from the libel actions were proof that, in the long run, there is little to be gained from narrow self-interest.

THE ULTIMATE
MYSTERY OF BEING

13

Wilbur

I found myself on a cargo plane bound for Uganda, stashed precariously between crates of chemicals, agricultural equipment, drugs for humans and animals, school and office supplies, rural water supplies, clothing and bedding—all requirements for emergency relief and rehabilitation for Uganda. It was April of 1979 and Idi Amin had just been deposed by a combination of Tanzanian forces and Ugandan exile groups.

I hadn't been home since I made my escape in 1975, and the excitement of returning eclipsed everything else. As the plane came down out of the clouds, I could see the familiar grass-thatched roofs of the African fishing villages below. Soon I spotted Entebbe, which rested on a shore of Lake Victoria, calm and shimmering bright blue.

An official van came to pick up the supplies. The driver offered to give me a lift home, as long as I didn't mind stopping at the State House, the official residence of the Ugandan president, to unload the cargo. I accepted his offer. Entebbe Airport, closed to commercial flights, had been damaged by the fighting, so another ride might not have materialized soon.

A reception was in full swing when we arrived at the State House. A few people came out to greet me, beckoning me to come join the party. But exhausted and dressed in jeans, I decided it would be inappropriate. As I stood by the van chatting, a young man whom I didn't recognize slowly walked toward me. He held an African ceremonial stick in his left hand.

"Hello, Elizabeth. I am Yoweri Museveni," he said as we shook hands.

I had never met Museveni, even though he had offered in 1974 on behalf of FRONASA and through a third party to smuggle me out of the country when I had had to make my escape from Amin, provided I joined and worked for FRONASA, a guerrilla movement fighting Amin, later to become the NRA, the military arm of the National Resistance Movement. Museveni was its leader. Soon after I was very impressed and inspired by a speech he had delivered at Makerere University analyzing Uganda's problems, which was reported in our press. It was clear that we had a lot to talk about and that we shared the same vision for Uganda. We agreed to meet again, and later met frequently at his home for intensive political discussions about Uganda's future.

The Uganda I came back to was not the one I had left. It was now occupied by Tanzanian forces, and with the occupation came a heightened sense of uncertainty and anxiety. There was an ominous finality about our situation. Petty squabbles among the Ugandan leadership enraged Tanzania's president Julius Nyerere. However, his mistaken decision to reinstate Obote shocked us. The majority of Ugandans knew that to have Obote return would lead to disaster.

While Amin had been a truculent and unpredictable ruler, there had never been the slightest doubt that he would eventually fall—the only variable had been when. Amin had been responsible for the killings of many thousands of Ugandans, but with Obote's reappearance, death squads were murdering people at an even higher rate.

One morning about five months after I had returned home, I found myself at a Kampala café in the company of old friends, relatives, and my brother Patrick, who had also returned from London. Instead of falling prey to despondency, we kept our spirits up by going out electioneering and socializing. With all the campaigning, we were caught up in the election fever, although we knew in our hearts the elections were predetermined. This particular morning we had lingered over coffee for quite awhile before we finally decided to disperse. Just as we were descending the stairs, a young man bounded up.

The others started shouting, "Wilbur, Wilbur!" and pulled him outside. He smiled but looked a bit uncomfortable, obviously embarrassed by all the loud attention.

Who is this breathtakingly handsome stranger, I wondered. I thought I had noticed all the beautiful people in the world, but here was someone who outshone them all.

"Who is this one?" I inquired.

"He is Mama Buli's child," someone answered.

"You are the one who married recently," Patrick called to him.

"No, no, that was my brother Fred," Wilbur replied, embarrassed and eager to correct the mistake. I found myself secretly sighing with relief that he was not married.

I was drawn to him instantly; it seemed that every detail of him, his face, his hands, his nails, his body, his smile, was perfectly formed. Very tall and dressed in blue jeans, a light beige corduroy vest over a long-sleeved white shirt tucked in by a belt, and boots, he looked like a movie star.

Wilbur's extraordinary beauty and civility was a product of carefully selective breeding spanning several generations of the Abacaki clan on his father's side and the Abasongora clan on his mother's side, clans famed for their beauty and etiquette, culture and patriotic nationalism. His father, Leo Sharp Ochaki, who died in a car accident when Wilbur was a baby, was reputedly the most handsome and best-dressed man in Uganda—so much so that my sisters and I used to play his wives and had childishly resolved that when we grew up we would marry him and live with him happily thereafter in one very big house. Two of his paternal grandfathers and a maternal grandparent had distinguished service as chiefs and were adorned with coronets qualifying them as members of the Sacred Guild—the highest honor in the Kitara Empire.

The greatest influence exercised on Wilbur came from "Mama

Buli" and "Amoti of Kigaya," his paternal and maternal grandmothers respectively, who were acknowledged authorities on history, rituals, and traditions of the Kitara Empire. Their great wisdom explained Wilbur's acute sense of propriety in his manner of speech, conduct, and attire, his sensitivity and closeness toward nature, and his maturity and caution in life with his fellowman.

It was Mama Buli in her wisdom and sense of history who entrusted baby Wilbur to me in my capacity as the Batebe of Toro and as her trusted relative. (She was my mother's first cousin.) She made me Wilbur's godmother, and although I was too young to remember it, I attended his christening at the village church of Bukuku built by Wilbur's paternal grandfather. Mama Buli constantly reminded me, "Elizabeth, remember your child."

This is how destiny had bound us together. So many times throughout our six-year marriage, Wilbur had played John Lennon's song "Woman," to affirm our belief that it was written in the stars that our destiny would be linked together.

On this memorable day—outside the café that I, alone, always now return to every time I have a chance—after the rest departed, I lingered behind to chat with him. He told me he was an engineer and that he had a temporary job at the International Conference Center. We agreed to meet one another there later the same day—well aware that any romantic involvement between us would be taboo, in our culture, even if we were second cousins once removed.

Due to the fractured state of public transportation, I was unable to get a ride to meet Wilbur. My efforts to track him down by telephone were fruitless. I had only met him once, but he was all I could think about. I was miserable.

I decided to ask the advice of my cousin Nightingale Rukuba, whom we called Nightie. She was studying law at Makerere University, and since my return to Uganda, I had visited her often at the university. I confessed to Nightie that I was completely taken with this gorgeous cousin of ours, and heartbroken over our failed rendezvous.

Nightie laughed. "That's Wilbur," she told me. She undertook to arrange a meeting and to explain to him what had occurred, but Wilbur being his cautious self refused to believe her, fearing it a hoax.

Meanwhile, I returned to Toro for the upcoming elections. Patrick was running as a candidate in Toro for the Uganda Patriotic Movement (UPM), the forerunner of the National Resistance Movement, the first time a Ugandan king had stood for elections. As feared, the election was a mockery. Obote usurped power and embarked on a campaign of persecution against all of us who had opposed him. After he singled out my brother Patrick and myself for an attack at a public meeting, I decided to fly to Nairobi and monitor Uganda events from there.

One afternoon shortly afterwards, Wilbur called me from Uganda, asking if Nightie's message was true. Overjoyed, I assured him it was. Encouraged by his initiative to call me, I told him I would love it if he came to Nairobi. Happily, Wilbur was working as an engineer for a Swedish company called Asseyah, which had its East African headquarters in Nairobi, so he was able to find a plausible reason for a week's sojourn to Kenya.

I made elaborate preparations for Wilbur's arrival in Nairobi, and the excitement was simply too much for me to sleep the night before his arrival. By dawn, I was ready, dressed up in white and waiting for the Range Rover I had borrowed from a Ugandan friend to take me to Embakasi Airport in Nairobi. The driver was late, so by the time I got to the airport, the plane had already landed. I looked everywhere, but Wilbur was nowhere to be found. I was stunned, all my orientation gone, when a young stewardess approached me and casually said, "Wilbur was looking for you. You've just missed him." He had arranged for a company car to pick him up in case I didn't show up.

Revived, I rushed off to the car and we headed for the Pan Africa Hotel. And there, sitting on the veranda of a packed coffeehouse was Wilbur. His beautiful big eyes met mine. I rushed to him and gave him our apartment number within the same hotel. Then I left him to finish his coffee while I waited for him at the apartment—fearful that if I sat with him someone might recognize us.

He soon joined me. We talked for many hours about relatives, friends, politics, and home. The conversation centered around his future.

"I would give anything to be able to fly" Wilbur told me forcefully. I told him about my friend Lord Harlech, who, I assured him, could very easily get him into a flying school in England.

When the evening fell, Wilbur slipped into one of the two beds with a novel and started reading, some of the time conversing with me across the room where I sat at the table. Then he said quietly, "Come and lie next to me." Timidly I joined him. He held me closely in his arms. My heart opened up. I fell in love for the first time in my life, and resolved to be the best woman Wilbur could ever want on this earth.

We were totally carefree. After breakfast every day, we went our separate ways and had fun with different friends during the day, and whoever returned first, collected the key and waited for the other at the hotel. We moved from the Pan Africa to the Kilimani Hotel, which was nicer and more private. Our first night out was at Nairobi's Florida nightclub. I was astounded when, five years later, during a conversation we were having in our London home, he remarked, "You were wearing gold boots!" I still vividly see Wilbur rising from our table and taking me to the dance floor at Lionel Ritchie's "Something Told Me You Are the One" played. I tried to dance, pretending we were not lovers. But he pulled me toward him and held me tightly. I let myself go, held him closely, and danced with unmistakable passion.

We had been in Nairobi for one month when one morning Wilbur got up before me and went down to have breakfast in the garden of the hotel. I later rose, got dressed, and sat on the balcony, enjoying the morning sun and the view of the rolling hills and valleys, while the chambermaid cleaned our room. I was considering going down to join Wilbur for some breakfast when he stormed into the room, marched onto the balcony, closing the sliding doors behind him, and positioned himself close to me.

"When are we getting married?" he asked.

"We will," I answered when I recovered from the surprise of his request, "but we should do it secretly, in London."

"Either I marry you openly or not at all," he responded firmly.

We reached a compromise that we should leave for London where Wilbur could start flying while we prepared for our wedding. Fortunately our visa applications were approved quickly. We prepared to leave Africa for London for what would be Wilbur's first trip to England. One morning while we listened to music in our room, Wilbur suddenly turned the radio up. I listened carefully. It was Barry White singing, "I Am Like a Blind Man." I marveled. Blindly, but through the means of love, Wilbur and I were taking the first steps into the ultimate mystery of being. Our journey into the unknown had begun. It was the journey not the destination that counted. The journey was the destination. The invisible hand of love would nurture and protect us. Music was our food.

We bade farewell to no one and arrived at London's Heathrow Airport in the middle of the bitter winter of 1981. The icy February wind hit Wilbur so hard that he recoiled. I gave him a smile. Fortunately a taxi pulled up for us. We jumped into the back of it and huddled together all the way to our new home—an apartment looking on the Regents Park on one side and Primrose Hill on the other.

As we settled down to our new life, I discovered that Wilbur was Utopian in his makeup and outlook. This gave him the inexhaustible patience and capability to build a wall of immunity around himself to distance himself from all things contemptuous, insensitive, vulgar, profane. His deep emotions of love, pain, happiness, were expressed through music, and the first shopping we did soon after our arrival was for a stereo, records, and tapes. The flying gained him independence and freedom whenever he wanted to detach himself from social contact or discord. Flying so much impinged itself on our lives that when he flirted with me he sometimes used flying language! Above all, it was *love* that ran deepest in Wilbur's psyche. Music, flying, freedom, money, and his country were all but means to secure him the love he created his Utopia with. After we had been married for five years, he once told me, "The one most invaluable thing you did for me, Akiiki, and which I always thank you for, is that you showed me that *money is not important*," and in a long telephone conversation he had with his brother one evening, he told him irritably, "What is money, Fred? Money is not important."

To Wilbur, who had never known a free Uganda, had only dreamed of it, this was a transformation and a revelation. He belonged to an imperiled generation in which the mania for money had become all important, cheapening life itself. Betrayal and not loyalty was the

207

order of the day. He was vulnerable without love. That's why his life pursuit was harmony and happiness through love. For Wilbur, only true love proclaimed, affirmed, to him his conception of himself—*that of a noble man.*

At the height of our love, he had a dream. In the middle of the night. He was startled. I grabbed him and whispered, "What is it Akiiki sweetie?"

He awoke and said, "I dreamed that you were gone. Promise me that we will never part."

I promised him that we would never part. I was always convinced that I would be the first one to die. So once I asked him, "What will you do when I die and people mistreat you?"

"I will disappear and people will forget I ever existed," he said almost angrily.

Knowing him as I did, I am certain he would have carried out that "threat." Wilbur admitted very few people into his world, as few as three. By my fortune I was one of those to be let in; the other two were Fred Karugonjo, his Uganda friend, and Ahamed Gobir, his pilot friend from Nigeria.

As I became totally submerged into Wilbur's world, I often sang Lionel Ritchie's, "Baby, You Are Going to Change My Life Around." I was reborn. He liked neither my hairstyle nor my old wardrobe. So I acquired new hair styles and a new wardrobe which showed off my figure (now half the size it had been when I first met him) and features at their best. I looked radiant. I adjusted to sleeping or doing serious reading with music playing twenty-four hours. Beauty meant so much to Wilbur that I made it a habit to buy flowers for our home every Friday. The first arrangement I ever made was of chrysanthemum, my favorite English flowers. When Wilbur entered the flat and saw them, he exclaimed, "What beautiful flowers!" He moved them where he could keep glancing at them as he listened to music and watched TV simultaneously. He even influenced me to look kindly upon nature. If a harmless insect happened to stray into our home, we spared it because he had taught me, "Why do you want to hack it to death? Pick it up in a tissue and throw it outside."

Endless surprises opened up for me. He was science oriented and I was not taught any sciences apart from elementary biology. Through a serious study and discussion of the articles from *Science*—a weekly that he brought home every Thursday—and watching science fiction films and TV shows like "Star Trek," I began to acquire an interest in and elementary knowledge and understanding of science issues. But I did get into trouble with my cooking! I thought I could get by on "take-out" food. So initially I used to walk across Primrose Hill and bring home either fried fish or chicken, or ribs with chips. I did it twice; the third time Wilbur was livid, "We can't live on junk food." We bought some Cookery books and he taught me to cook. We became food connoisseurs. Dining reflected dignity and propriety just as it had always been in the homes of his paternal and maternal grandparents where he was brought up. In return I gave him true love and looked after him. I brushed his hair daily, washed his feet with warm water, and massaged his body. One day, watching me run up and down the stairs of our maisonette to fetch and change water for washing his feet, he looked at me and told me, "You know how to look after your man."

We were wrapped up in each other for months. We ate together, went everywhere together, and did everything together. We shared the very air we breathed. But then out of the blue, Wilbur, in a very stern tone, said to me, "We have been living as if the rest of the world does not exist. It's time we talk about what we are planning to do." After we had a discussion, we agreed that he should pursue his flying career and that I should push on with the writing of my autobiography. We went to see David Harlech at Harlech Television on Baker Street to ask him if he had any ideas as to how Wilbur could go about entering a flying school. I had never known David to fail to come up with a solution to a problem. David liked Wilbur very much. He talked to him about his goals. The next thing we knew, he had contacted Sir John and Lady Astor, whose parents had founded a private flying club called Marshall's of Cambridge. Wilbur was admitted. We decided to get married before he left for Cambridge.

The night before our wedding, Wilbur went out with his Somali friend Mohammed Abshir. When he returned, we sat on the floor of our sitting room and played music until we retired to bed. Early next morning, Mohammed took us in his car to have our hair done at "Splinters," a black salon. His wife, Faiza, arrived at 9:30 A.M. and they drove us through Regent Street, Trafalgar Square, White Hall, to St. Margaret's Church at Westminster.

We were married secretly on April 25, 1981, at St. Margaret's Church (the church of the British aristocracy) by the Reverend Canon John Baker, who had once said to me, "I hope one day I shall be the one to marry you." Collingwood of Conduit Street, the jewelers of British royalty, designed our wedding rings.

For the wedding Wilbur wore a cream jacket, black trousers, black leather boots, and a cream silk shirt and bow tie. They were selected by Wilbur and his friend Lawrence Kirshell from Cecil Gee, where Lawrence worked. I wore a short white-and-gold dress designed by Regamus of Beauchamp Place. The only people we told about the wedding were our witnesses, Mohammed and Faiza. At 10:00 A.M. St. Margaret's doors were closed to the tourists that flock to London from all over the world every year to visit this fifteenth-century church, and we took our positions before the altar.

Everything went smoothly until it was Wilbur's turn to say, "With all my worldly possessions I thee endow." I noticed his hands had begun to shake, perhaps because all he had to give in the way of worldly possessions was his 911SC Porsche. But I didn't care, he was giving me perfect love. After the ceremony, Mohammed and Faiza took us for breakfast at the Cavendish Hotel on Jermyn Street and treated us to a champagne celebration at a nightclub, "String Fellows," in the evening.

We kept our marriage secret against our friend Henry Elwell's advice to announce it in the London *Times* by a small paragraph. But one day in Trafalgar Square Wilbur and I hopped on one of those red double-decker London buses and there was my brother Patrick, who was also living in London after the mock elections in Uganda had resulted in Obote's presidency. "My God, there is Patrick," I gasped, and hurried to the top of the bus.

When we got up the stairs, Wilbur was calm. "Why are you running? Let's go and greet him. How long can we continue to run?" Wilbur said. Wilbur insisted that I meet with Patrick and tell him of our marriage. I did.

"I'll support you," he said simply.

Then I went to tell my mother, who was living in London with

Patrick. "My goodness! What have you done?" She looked horrified. "Well, I suppose there are such people on earth who do such things and go on living in this world."

When the time came for Wilbur to leave me for Cambridge, he was unhappy. He wondered whether he should not stay and do something else. "That's something you have always wanted to do. It's time for us to make the sacrifice," I told him. So on that Friday in May 1981, we took a train to Cambridge from King's Cross Station. When we arrived at Cambridge Station, I pointed out to Wilbur the sight of so many bicycles crowded together, wanting to explain that that's the mode of transport of everyone—whether they be undergraduates, graduates, or professors. But Wilbur was totally disinterested. He was moody and talked very little. After we checked into a hotel near the station, I tried to take him on a sight-seeing tour of Cambridge, but Wilbur would not have it. So I went out for a walk by myself but got soaked and rushed back to him. We spent the rest of the weekend quietly at the hotel—talking very little, but each one of us obviously wondering what living apart was going to mean for us both. On Sunday we checked out of the hotel and took a taxi to Marshall's of Cambridge to meet with Wilbur's instructors. That completed, he said, "I will take you to the station." At the station, our passion turned into agonizing pain as we tried to say good-bye. Wilbur gasped with such agony that it was audible. He was fearful that our love might not survive the test of separation. It might mean betrayal. I did not worry, though, knowing I would never be unfaithful to him. I told myself Cambridge and London were close and every Friday one of us would go to the other.

I went back to London and spent a miserable week. He had no phone where I could call him, so he called me that first evening, as he was to do every single day of the following week. During the same week an aunt, who had been visiting my mother, asked if I could do some shopping for her and take her to Gatwick Airport on Friday. Wilbur was agreeable, so I had her over to our home to stay a few days during which I was able to assign her the special mission of calling on Mama Buli with greetings from us and to tell her about our marriage. With two of my cousins, David and Xeda Kassami, I took her to Gatwick Airport by train, but because her plane was late I did not get back to our flat until around eleven that evening. When I opened the door, sitting on the chaise longue and directly facing me was Wilbur! He was waiting to see if I would enter with some man. He smiled. Without warning, he had come down for the weekend. As a matter of fact, he had been in for some hours, because I saw that he had had a bath and was beautifully dressed to go out for the evening. Happily I welcomed him home and sat down to greet him. Instead he inquired, "What are those cigarettes doing there?" referring to the cigarettes on the table. I explained that they were David Kassami's, who with his sister Xeda had accompanied me to Katwick to see our aunt off. In a happy mood, he phoned his new Cambridge friends and arranged to meet them for a drink at a pub. He left and returned home late.

Nothing had changed. We had a blissful weekend. We were both reassured. Throughout his entire time at Cambridge he drove down in his Porsche every Friday and returned Sunday. From Monday to Friday I stayed in working on my autobiography and I saw nobody, surviving on his telephone calls. Come every Friday, my life started. I rose early, got on bus 74 to Camden town market where I bought fresh vegetables, fruit, and flowers, moved on to the butcher for fresh meat, and ended at the bakery owned by Cypriots for freshly baked bread, all bought inexpensively. When I got home, I made our bed with clean sheets, bathed, and dressed up. When the flat looked beautiful and I was perfectly sure I looked my very best, I sat by the window, listening for the sound of the Porsche's engine, which I had learned to distinguish from all the other cars. With Wilbur's arrival my life started, and it ended with his departure on Sundays!

There were many exciting moments, among them when we attended Diana Ross's concert at Wembley Stadium. She was informed we were in the audience and surprised us by coming to us and greeting us warmly. Wilbur quickly photographed her. I myself looked radiant with love, so much so that Miriam Kavuma, the wife of my close friend, Godfrey Kavuma, exclaimed, "You look so young, Elizabeth. I thought it was some young sister of yours." Unforgettable also was Stevie Wonder's and Teddy Pendergrass's concert at Victoria Astoria. I escaped being stampeded by the crowd. Even more exciting for Wilbur but "troublesome" for me was the arrival in London of Wilbur's best friend, Fred Karugonjo.

Up to this moment Wilbur had not had an intimate friend of his own in London. With Fred he was to build his own circle of friends in which I was not always included. When they wanted a change from our home or to talk men talk or to get drunk, I wasn't welcome. Often I was left home to wait for long hours. It did not help that Wilbur was always exquisitely dressed and would go out looking simply too gorgeous—in his Porsche. Every girl in London wanted him. I panicked. I just could not bear to think of him holding someone else. I started becoming too possessive. We quarreled and he asked me, "What has happened to the woman I knew in Nairobi?" reminding me how carefree I used to be with him.

But Fred had the ability to turn "tragic" situations into hilariously funny ones. So whenever they returned, however late, I was happy to see them and reassured. He said to me, "Wilbur is a very proud man. He needs his freedom. Give him time to adjust to being married." I accepted Wilbur's going out with his friends while I stayed home. I fully trusted him. I began to enjoy being alone at home—having more time to make myself and our home beautiful for him to come back to. Fred brought so much warmth and happiness to our home. When he returned to Uganda, leaving his belongings in our care, and Wilbur took him to the airport, it was as if someone very close to us had died in our home. It was as if we were in mourning for a long time.

The commuting between Cambridge and London continued. Whatever doubts I entertained during Wilbur's absences were wiped out during one weekend. No sooner had he arrived from Cambridge for his usual weekend than he muttered to himself, "I must go out and buy Randy Crawford's record." These songs were dynamite. They telegraphed his passion and love for me. Listening to them now makes me helpless and desperate for Wilbur. They are a priceless memento of his Cambridge days.

I also learned more about flying than I ever imagined I could. Often, as we sat together in bed drinking our morning tea, he would sketch planes for me, teaching me about the function of the tail, the throttle, the nose, the cockpit. One day his pilot friend John Kassami phoned us. During the conversation he asked, "Liz, since when did you become so knowledgeable about flying?"

"I live with it," I answered.

After six months, Wilbur completed his training at Cambridge and obtained his private pilot's license. His instructor told me, "I've never known any student who loves flying so much. It has been such a joy to train Wilbur." Wilbur gave a farewell party for his instructors and bought them gifts. But flying had its tough moments for Wilbur. I recall him coming home one weekend and throwing himself on the sofa in the sitting room. He was speechless. I tried to chitchat. "You don't know what I have just gone through. The spin almost made me give up flying!"

In October 1981 he joined Oxford Air Training School in Kidlington—the leading flying school in the British Commonwealth. He continued to commute between Oxford and London every weekend. He was very happy at Oxford and it was here that he met Ahamed Gobir, a fellow pilot and one of the two life friends he had, the other being Fred Karugonjo. But Oxford was so expensive we had to sell his Porsche and also move to a cheaper flat. Even then, we would not have managed to pay Oxford fees without loans from friends and the bank. Finally, in 1982, Wilbur became a full-fledged commercial pilot with instrument rating.

We searched everywhere for a flying job. Every airline informed us that it gave priority to its nationals. Private airlines gave priority to experienced pilots; they could not risk beginners. Without experience he was unemployable, without a job he could not get job experience—a catch-22 situation. This more than anything else convinced him Uganda had to be free for him to have a future. Our love acquired a political dimension, and our lives, one single purpose.

14

The Struggle

The sports stadium was packed and buzzing with people. Ojok and Okello, Obote's strong men, sat prominently in the front row to instill more fear in the tense crowd assembled for Toro's national rally. Then Museveni, whom Obote had just ousted as minister of state for defense, entered the stadium. The crowd fell silent. It was a daring stunt on Museveni's part to show up in this manner. He raised his fist to the sky. I rose from my seat to my feet as a sign of support, and tentatively others followed. I was not about to turn my back on the brightest hope for Uganda.

I believed in my heart that the best way to help my people was to promote collective leadership as opposed to personal rule, and the one man who could pull Uganda out of murderous tyranny was Yoweri Museveni. We had held frequent meetings in 1979 upon my return to Uganda after Amin's demise. During those meetings I had become convinced that Museveni had the rare and necessary combination of intellectual ability (having been educated at Ntare School in west

Uganda as well as at Dar-Es-Salaam University in Tanzania) and military muscle, as leader and founder of the guerrilla organization FRONASA.

After Amin had been deposed, the country was nominally ruled for a short time by NLF (National Liberation Front) under president Yusuf Lule, a coalition of opposing factions until the Consultative Council, which was overseen and supported by Tanzanian Forces, replaced him with Godfrey Binaisa, a former attorney general during Obote's first regime between 1962 and 1971, and my personal friend and in-law. The country was under pressure from Western powers to go to elections in order to gain international respectability, although it was common knowledge that they would be rigged and lead to Obote's regaining control of the country. Binaisa was powerless himself in the face of the power of the Tanzanian Forces.

One day, when I called on him at State House, he said, "Elizabeth, I don't have to hide it from you. The intelligence reports say you are an avid supporter of Museveni." It made no difference. When Museveni formed the Uganda Patriotic Movement, I joined it, supported it financially, and accompanied him on his campaigns. When it was clear Obote was being supported in his *coup d'état* by Tanzania, I decided to leave for Nairobi where I could be near enough to follow the election and when terror and murder started against the Uganda Patriotic Movement I could raise the alarm abroad.

The mock elections came and, of course, as expected, Obote grabbed power. A campaign of murder and terror ensued. Museveni had promised the country that if Obote usurped power he would go to the bush to lead the resistance against Obote.

From inside the bush, Museveni with twenty-seven men founded the National Resistance Movement (NRM) with the National Resistance Army forming its military arm, and its civilian arm outside Uganda was led by the External Committee to rally diplomatic, financial, moral, and material support. The war was conducted differently from past guerrilla wars which, traditionally, are staged from neighboring countries. But in this instance, no African country wanted to risk the repercussions of aiding a popular effort to topple a fellow African government. Wilbur and I worked with the External Committee, rallying material and diplomatic support outside.

Toward the end of 1981 Museveni came out from the bush and flew to London to coordinate the External Committee with inside operations. The situation was becoming difficult, as they were running out of weapons and supplies. Museveni met with Wilbur and myself in our Ormande Terrace apartment on several occasions and during that time we were given our assignments. We were to cover Nigeria, Austria, Germany, France, Africa, and Europe, making use of my former diplomatic connections.

We decided that London would remain our base as we traveled in Africa and Europe, with the dual purpose of gathering support for the movement and looking for a flying job for Wilbur.

Our campaign started with a very wealthy Nigerian businessman named Isiaku Ibrahim. We briefed him on Uganda and the movement at his very large, beautiful home in London overlooking Hyde Park. Mr. Ibrahim gave a luncheon for us in his home to which he invited about a dozen people including bankers and businessmen from West Africa whom he thought might be interested in our efforts. After lunch we presented a well-documented case: photos of people being tortured while in police custody, complete with names and dates smuggled out of prison and the numbers of those killed, plus statements explaining that Obote was no improvement over Amin and was in fact committing even more serious atrocities. Mr. Terence Terry, a well-connected attorney from Sierra Leone, visibly moved by our presentation, offered to go to Sierra Leone and meet his law partner, Abdulai Conteh, the then foreign minister of Sierra Leone, who would arrange for Wilbur and me to meet President Siaka Stevens, an important offer because of Siaka Stevens's influence in the region. Mr. Terry, a director of Air Afrique and other airlines, also undertook to aid Wilbur in his search for a flying position.

Before we set off for Sierra Leone, Wilbur's older brother Fred and his wife, Olive, arrived in London for a very important visit. Wilbur wanted to go to the airport alone to greet them, wanting to tell them that we had been married since we left Africa. They accepted the news happily and we had a pleasant reunion. They brought their little baby Steven, Wilbur's godson, with them, and after visiting for a few days, we left them our apartment. Unfortunately they became prisoners in it due to a horrible blizzard. Wilbur enjoyed calling home to hear Fred complain about the snow—he laughed so much—especially since Fred was an older brother.

In Paris we went Christmas shopping in Saint-Honoré where Wilbur bought some lovely leather black boots and had a suit made. Like his father, Wilbur expressed his sense of individuality in his clothes. Looking at his newest impressive wardrobe, he turned to me and said, "What would you do with my clothes if I died?" I was not worried by the question—always confident that I would die first.

From Paris we caught an Air Afrique flight to Freetown, Sierra Leone's capital. It seemed less developed than Kampala. The first part we drove through was a depressing little pocket of slums and I was sure we hadn't arrived in Freetown.

Wilbur said softly to me, "This is it! We have arrived."

Finally, the scenery began to change and we found ourselves in a very wealthy section, where Mr. Terry lived. We pulled up in front of his spacious and elegant home and were escorted inside where we found our host waiting for us at the bar, having a cocktail.

In Freetown Christmas is party season and we went out partying, but with business in mind. Mr. Terry introduced us to his legal partner, Abdulai Conteh, and the following day he arranged for us to meet with President Stevens.

The State House (in Freetown), a beautiful former residence of the colonial governors, reminded me of an old castle. We entered his office, and the president stood up behind his desk to welcome us. He was an imposing very black man, well over six feet tall, in his mid-seventies. His features were strikingly prominent, well-defined, resembling a fine weathered statue.

When he saw Wilbur, he remarked on Wilbur's appearance and regal presence. "He looks royal, is he?"

I answered, "We're cousins, but he's not from the royal family."

We sat down and began to present the documented situation in Uganda, appealing for his support. He said he knew Obote. His speech was very deliberate and his manner stern. "I have had full reports about his abuse of power and I foresaw the trouble he would be in and warned him in Addis Ababa." We were impressed.

We requested that he share the information with his fellow heads of state at the next meeting of the OAU and at regional meetings. He took the photographs and information we had brought for him, and called in Abdulai Conteh, asking him to follow up. We then asked for his support for a flying job in his country's airline. He assigned the same to Conteh for a follow-up. His manner was fatherly and warm to us; he seemed genuinely concerned about our efforts on behalf of the movement, as well as our personal set of circumstances. We were particularly impressed by his concern during a time when there was a lot of tension in his own life and country. To have a head of state receive you is always an honor, but this was even more appreciated because we knew there was a lot of criticism circulating then against his regime and himself. We had even heard rumors of a coup d'état. But here he was calm and focused on our situation, committed to raise Uganda with his colleagues regionally and at OAU. We had won our first ally for the movement.

We returned to London where we stayed until Christmas of 1982 when we embarked on our next diplomatic mission: Vienna, Austria, the country that had given me asylum when I fled Amin and had gone into my second exile. With little money, we resisted hotels. We phoned Peter Jumba, activist student cell leader. "Don't move," he replied and immediately came and took us home, where we spent one of our happiest times. "Sharing" in the true sense of the word sums up our relationship with Jumba and Regina, his wife. We shared their small apartment, grocery expenses, tram tickets, everything. They cooked for us, and even when we moved to the hotel, we only slept there.

As usual, it was impossible for the girls not to take notice of Wilbur, especially Viennese. They are sensitive and warm. Once at a Christmas party it got to be too much. I pretended to have a headache and we went home. I went to a separate room, but in the middle of the night he came and carried me back to our bedroom.

In Jumba's apartment, we rehearsed what we would say when we went before the scheduled meetings of Austrian officials. The day arrived and Jumba, Immanuel (another Ugandan student), Wilbur, and I set off for the palace. We were escorted on a historical tour around the palace, which was filled with portraits, antiques, and tapestries. Then we entered Bruno Kreisky's offices and greeted the chancellor. He was very warm, remembering my past stay and inquiring how I had been in the interim. I started off by introducing Wilbur and my

Ugandan colleagues and thanking him for the protection he had provided me in 1975. I gave him an update of what I had been doing. We then explained that while we had got through the problems with Amin, the current situation with Obote was even worse, and we backed up our findings with the documentary evidence of people being tortured while in police custody and all the rest of the horror and murders.

We explained that the violation of human rights in Uganda had for more than a decade attracted international concern. Organizations such as Amnesty International had exposed Amin for the extermination of hundreds of thousands of innocent Ugandan lives.

When Amin and his band of murderers were routed out of Uganda, our hope and prayer was that the principles of the struggle against dictatorship and fascism were eventually, sooner rather than later, going to lead to a properly elected and therefore democratic government, committed to the service of all in Uganda.

Unfortunately, before long, the people of Uganda were already smelling doom because of what they saw during the electioneering period: political opponents being murdered; government powers being usurped to serve the interests of one of the four political parties; illegal army recruitment exclusively of the northerners on the pretext of militia service; mass murders in West Nile and Madi districts on the pretext of repulsing Amin's invading forces; security forces being deployed in strategic places throughout the country and increasing widespread killings of innocent civilians by government soldiers.

The Commonwealth election team came, *but came too late*, only to witness the final phase of what other political parties in Uganda have termed, among other things, fraudulent elections, whose results they have refused to accept—challenging them to the extent of waging an armed struggle in order to topple what they call a fascist regime.

For the purpose of our presentation, we separated political problems from the human-rights violations, leaving the former to political organizations opposed to the Obote regime to handle. It is an unpleasant task to undertake to compare evil against evil in fascism and dictatorship, but qualitative differences had become irrelevant. Innocent Ugandans forced to draw a comparison between Amin's and Obote's regimes found adequate evidence that *Obote's regime had turned out to be worse than Amin's regime in the extent to which it committed acts in violation of human rights.*

The mass murders openly committed by the current Obote regime added a new dimension to the killings carried out by the Amin regime and made the Obote regime more dangerous to the people of Uganda.

Eyewitness accounts from West Nile district and Bulemezi in Luwero district provided clear evidence of the Obote regime's decision and determination to carry out atrocities and total extermination of the tribes which did not support his political party.

Eyewitness accounts of personal experiences of torture provided equally shocking revelations. The following testimony was among the many documents that we presented to Chancellor Kreisky that day. It was written by Bakulu Mpagi Wamala, who was born in the Mengo District of the then Buganda Kingdom. He was educated at St. Henry's College, Kitovu, and Kings College, Budo, before joining Makerere University, where he took a degree in French and philosophy. He then went to the University of Kent at Canterbury, England, and took a master's degree in philosophy, returning to lecture at Makerere University.

On Thursday, March 26, 1981, he was abducted from his home by Obote's troops and was badly wounded in the process. In absence of news of his whereabouts, several newspapers and major radio networks around the world carried the news of his death. Among them: the BBC, the Voice of Germany, the Voice of America, Radio RSA, *The Times* (London), *The Nation* (Nairobi), and third-world countries.

The following is his account of what actually happened:

> Thursday, March 26, 1981. It is about 5:30 P.M. and I have just returned to my flat at plot 176 Port Bell Road in the Kampala suburb of Mbuya. Shortly afterward commotion begins outside in the compound below. Suddenly a stern voice barks out an order for everybody to come out of their flats.
>
> From a window of my top-floor flat I peer out to see what is happening. Between 35 and 40 soldiers of Obote's army have taken up positions all around our apartment block. They are in full combat uniform and battle camouflage, their guns at the ready. From the same window I can see somebody below pointing up at my flat. An-

other, harsher, order is barked out for everybody to get out.

I know they have come for me. Only weeks ago, Obote's troops burst into the residence of several of my colleagues on the party executive of the Uganda Patriotic Movement (UPM) and abducted them. Among them was Jabel Bidandi Sali, UPM Secretary General, Rev. Father Christopher Okoth, UPM Vice-President and Mrs. Rhoda Kalema, UPM Secretary for Women's Affairs. Each of them has been a government minister before. Leaders of other political parties, like the Democratic Party, among them several members of Parliament, have also been abducted from their homes in the last few weeks. Hundreds of other officials from both parties at the branch level have been either rounded up or killed.

As national secretary for publicity and information of the party, I have naturally been one of the most outspoken members of our party executive. For that outspokenness I was once threatened with virtual physical extermination by military commission government leader Paulo Muwanga, currently Obote's vice-president. Now, with Obote's soldiers waiting for me outside, I fear for my life. I advise my wife, Florence, and other members of the household to go down immediately.

I snatch a few minutes to compose myself and then get out of the flat. Suddenly a burst of gunfire, and bullets begin flying past me. Instinctively I take cover by falling flat on the concrete landing of the flat. Miraculously, none of the bullets hits me.

Somebody, presumably the commanding officer, gives an order to his men not to shoot. He orders me to go into the compound. Half dead with fright, I proceed down, my hands up.

By now a large crowd has assembled from the adjacent Silver Springs Hotel. There are almost two hundred people. As soon as I get to the compound a soldier gives me another order in Swahili to lie down on the tarmac access road. I do so immediately, and the soldiers begin to stab me with their bayonets, rifle butts, and military boots. Somebody among the residents, probably my wife, screams. Children and women begin screaming and crying. I am bleeding profusely, but have not begun to feel

222

any pain. The stabbing, butting, and boot kicks continue for what seems to me eternity.

At last the bayonet stabs, rifle butts, and boot kicks stop. I am barely conscious, but I can hear the order that I should be driven to Nile Mansions, the luxury apartment hotel that serves as a home for almost all Obote's ministers. Also at the hotel, room 105 and two other rooms serve as torture chambers for Obote's nascent Secret Service.

Four men grab me by the limbs and throw me, as you would a sack of dry beans, onto a white Datsun 1200 pickup van. One soldier stands with his heavy boots on my swollen head, another stands on my stomach while a third stands over my thighs. Bleeding intensifies. I can feel it. The van sets off. The soldiers sing and dance, jumping up and down on top of me. I should report that somewhere along the road I am thoroughly searched and stripped of any valuables I have: my watch, a pocket pipe, pipe tobacco, Shs. 7000/- cash (equivalent to U.S. $1,000 at official rates), a trouser belt, shoes, socks, and a pipe lighter. My identification papers are also taken from me. A fist fight ensues over who should take my watch.

Later we reach Nile Mansions. Again like a sack of beans, I am thrown off the van onto the hard tarmac, and I begin bleeding from the nose. Every inch of my beige safari suit is covered with blood from bayonet wounds and other injuries. I am subjected to another round of bayonet stabbing, boot kicks and rifle-butt blows. Then I am frog-marched to the entrance of Nile Mansions.

Without the aid of my spectacles I cannot see very far. All the same I can see there are many people about the place. As we pass I recognize two of Obote's ministers who knew me. The soldiers are given orders to take me to "Operations Control Room." I am not sure whether this is the same as room 105, the notorious torture chamber. We are moving up the steps of Nile Mansions. An army officer is coming down the same steps. He is told something by one of the soldiers guarding me. He looks at me and replies in Swahili, "I am tired, take him to Makindye (barracks)."

I am pushed down the staircase, and land on my head in the lounge of Nile Mansions. I am picked up by the soldiers and taken back to the waiting Datsun 1200 pickup van. Once more I am thrown onto the back, face down this time. The soldiers resume their positions standing on me. We drive off, I am not sure where to. I have a suspicion that I am going to be killed and that my body will probably turn up in one of the forests around Kampala, like so many others have done in recent weeks.

From a corner of my eye I catch a glimpse of one of the soldiers. He tears up my identity papers, and says "He won't need them anymore." I am now convinced that I am going to my death. I become unconscious at this stage. A total blackout engulfs me.

When I open my eyes again we are already in the notorious Makindye military barracks. It is barely daylight. I am thrown off the van. I am beaten and kicked once again, but no bayonet stabbing this time. Everybody seems convinced that I am "finished" (euphemism for death).

One of the soldiers who has brought me tells those we find on duty in Makindye that another "maiti" (dead body) has been brought. I am careful to note that no statement has been made by those who have brought me in. No record at all is made that I have been brought into the barracks. Anybody can do anything to me now—kill me, smuggle me out, or whatever, and it could not be traced to Makindye barracks.

My hands and legs are tied with a rope. I am pushed into a room—nay, a dungeon, right next to the main gate to Makindye barracks. No ventilation of any kind. Heavy metal door. Urine all over the floor and other human excrement in a corner. Fresh blood was splattered about the walls. Maybe somebody has just been killed here. There is a nauseating smell of death and filth inside the cell. When I am pushed into the room, I fall down and become part of this filth. I guess it is about 7:00 P.M. local time.

Shortly I become aware of pains, sharp pains, all over my body. Both sides of my chest are painful and I cannot lie down sideways. I have to lie on my back, though this too, is considerably painful.

The heavy metal door opens. Somebody is brought in; another prisoner or someone to spy on me? My hands are tied to his, but his legs are free. I cannot possibly shift my body now without his cooperation.

Other prisoners are pushed in; I suppose about ten in this tiny, ten-by-ten-foot dungeon. It is unbearably hot. I feel I am about to faint, but I must not allow myself to do so. I have a bad temperature. I want to undo the buttons of my safari suit, but with my hands bound up and tied to another person this is nearly impossible. However, with a lot of pain and effort I maneuver my hands into a position to unbutton the jacket. With even more difficulty I manage to shift my jacket so that my back remains bare. My hands have been cut by the sisal rope.

I feel cooler, now that my bare back is lying in the cold urine on the floor. Since my watch has been appropriated by the bandit soldiers, I cannot tell what time it is exactly. But I think it is around 8:00 P.M. There is complete darkness inside and outside. The soldiers on guard outside our dungeon are smoking marijuana. Another voice, presumably an officer, joins them. The door of the dungeon is thrown ajar and one of them begins thrashing about the dungeon with a stick. A yell of pain from one of the prisoners. Most of the prisoners have been standing, since there is no room for them to lie down or sit. Only I, rope-mate, and one of two others are lying on the floor. When the thrashing begins there is a stampede in the room, each prisoner trying to dodge the mad swing of the sticks. Several times I am trodden underfoot, but I am too ill to protest. Yells of pain from prisoners who are caught by the stick. Sadistic peals of laughter from the marijuana-loaded soldiers outside.

At last the mad stick stops. The door is bolted from outside. One of the drunken voices outside vows in Swahili, "*Lazima hapa watakufa maiti mbili leo*" (I swear there will be two dead bodies here tonight). He orders his men to fit his pistol with a silencer. Now I know for sure that I am going to be killed. I seem to be the most "dangerous" prisoner in the room. I am the only one bound hand and foot, and certainly the most roughly abused so far. The voice which has promised itself to kill two of us tonight says now he is going for supper and will return later.

A heavy cloud of death is hanging over us. My thoughts

inevitably gravitate toward my children. My youngest child, a son, is only about 8 months old. My eldest child, a daughter, is under 9 years old. In between there are three other daughters. What will happen to them after my death? What will happen to my old mother, whose husband (my father) was killed by the Amin regime? And what will happen to this poor country?

My thoughts are interrupted. A prisoner in this cell is pleading with the guards outside to allow him to go and relieve himself. He is harshly told to shut up. Other prisoners mumble among themselves. I suppose everybody wants to relieve himself. An order is given by the guards that all those wishing to relieve themselves have to do it on the floor. For the next five minutes all other sounds are drowned by the sound of urination. I am still lying on my back, and can feel the urine level rising on the concrete floor. My clothes, every inch already covered with blood, are receiving an extra drenching of filthy urine! But I am too preoccupied with other thoughts to worry about the cleanliness of a body I know will shortly be lifeless. I go back to my thoughts. Where will my dead body be thrown? Will it be recovered and be laid to rest in my ancestral burial ground beside my father and my grandfather? How will this be possible when my identity papers have all been destroyed? I wish I could find a pen and paper to write my names down somewhere!

Another interruption—this time from outside. A drunken soldier has been coming into the barracks through the gate, with his equally drunken girlfriend. A quarrel ensues between him and the soldiers on guard. It seems that this particular girlfriend was in the barracks earlier in the day with another soldier. The arriving soldier and his girlfriend are making a lot of noisy protests. They, too, are pushed into our dungeon. Their noise grows even louder. The guards outside open the door again and remove the wailing woman, whom they take turns raping on the veranda. There are now about five different excited voices outside. A number of women passing by on the adjacent road are stopped by the soldiers. They too, are brought into the barracks and raped on the veranda. Finally all the women are pushed into our dungeon. I reckon there are now about 15 people in this little room. The urine level on the floor is ever rising, as is the nauseating stench of putrefaction.

I think it now about 11:00 P.M., but it may be later. I am only guessing. I go back to thoughts of my impending death. What will become of X? What will become of Y? All the people with whom I have shared my life? A million other thoughts and questions.

I emerge from these thoughts and realize that our drunken "executioner" is probably asleep and most likely not coming back tonight. It is about 1:00 A.M. I may last the night if I do not bleed to death. My thoughts now turn toward my body for the first time since my arrest. I feel an awful lot of pain everywhere, and my mind is full of questions. How badly injured am I? If I do not die tonight, will I get emergency medical treatment tomorrow?

Will I survive the notorious crude torture of Makindye barracks, to which I shall certainly be subjected? Is anybody outside this barracks taking interest in what is happening to us here? What is happening right now to my family, who remained at the mercy of Obote's soldiers when I was abducted? In incredible physical and psychological pain, I spend the remaining hours of the night till dawn. For the first time in my life I have spent a night without sleeping even one second, without even dozing.

It is about 7:00 A.M. on Friday March 27, 1981, and I am still lying on my back in the urine, bound hand and foot. The soldiers outside seem to be changing guard. Shortly afterward the door of our small dungeon is thrown open. Some fresh air—sweet, fresh air comes in to dilute the stench of sweat, urine, and other human excreta. Outside there is a heavy downpour of torrential tropical rain.

A soldier peers into our cell and recoils—probably from the stench. He orders the women to run out and go back to their homes. The rest of us he orders to lick, with our tongues, the urine off the floor. He says he will be back in five minutes and must find the room clean. The inmates take off their shirts and start drying the floor. I cannot join in since I am still bound. Moreover, my clothes are thoroughly drenched in urine and can absorb no more. The urine is too much for men's shirts to absorb. They cannot wring them dry because the urine will pour back on the floor. They put back the shirts on their backs and remove their trousers which they use to dry the floor, and hastily wear again.

The guard returns and orders all of us to run out of the room. Everyone runs out except me and my rope-mate. After giving me a nasty kick in the ribs, he unties the rope. I try to stand but collapse on the floor. The guard gets hold of me by my hair and drags me out into the rain where the rest of the inmates are.

Lying on the grass in the rain, I begin to feel a bit of life return to me. Also I feel somewhat cleansed of last night's filth. I can now sit, and even stand! Though with pain. For almost four hours the torrential downpour continues unabated. It is supposed to be a punishment to us, but I am relishing it. I begin to examine myself but only one eye can see. The other is too swollen. I have several wounds which are still bleeding, but in the rain the blood is beginning to coagulate and prevent further bleeding. I know I have bad wounds in the back, but I cannot see them.

After about 4 hours, we are ordered to get out of the still pouring rain and are herded into a clerical office at the quarter-guard.

Each is informally asked by a corporal why he has been brought to the barracks. Obviously the soliders on duty do not know anything about any of us. Each one explains. A schoolboy, about 15, had been returning home in the evening from a school when soldiers grabbed him at Mulago trading center, took his watch and shoes, and brought him to Makindye barracks when he protested. Another boy, about 16, had gone to buy sugar from the trading center at Mulago when both the sugar and the boy were hijacked to Makindye by soldiers. And so on and so forth. When the corporal comes to me I mumble something. No records taken. I don't know any of the prisoners.

It is now about midday. We are taken out of the clerical office to the adjacent quarter-guard cells. One cell, which acts as a "transit" room for inmates, has a number of prisoners brought during the previous two days. There are about 15 in all. To this our own number is added. In an adjacent cell, separated from the "transit" room by a metal grille, one catches a glimpse of other prisoners—

mainly army and air-force men detained for one reason or another. But there are other civilian prisoners as well.

In the "transit" room I manage to sit up, with my back pressed against the wall. My clothes get stickier at the back. I look at the wall to check and find a blotch of fresh blood on the wall where my back has been pressed. A wound in my back is still bleeding!

One of the prisoners in the "transit" room has recognized me. An exclamation of shock. Two or three more inmates recognize me. We talk briefly. An examination of my wounds. I have eight bayonet wounds in all, one of them between two ribs in my back. Later examination reveals that this particular bayonet stab barely missed my heart by a fraction of an inch. Other bayonet wounds are on the limbs and at the back of the neck. I fear that savage boot kicks in the chest may have dislocated a rib—because I can feel a lot of pain. It turns out on later examination that my spleen has been damaged. My face and head are swollen from rifle butt hits and boot kicks. Only one eye can see.

After about one hour in the "transit" room all of us, including those we found there, are taken out for interrogation in the administrative quarter of the barracks, about two hundred yards farther down the hill inside the barracks. We are made to sit in the rain on the concrete pavement in front of an office which, I later learned, belongs to Intelligence Officer 1 Mukhwana.

There are about 25 prisoners in all. There are also about 10 soldiers towering over the prisoners with various torture gadgets—most of them very crude and rudimentary: a bundle of barbed-wire lengths, a pair of tongs, a club, etc. It is now about 1:30 in the afternoon.

The office of Intelligence Officer 1 Mukhwana is still locked. Meanwhile the captives are subjected to torture by the soldiers, who seem to be amusing themselves. Barbed wire is used on the bare backs of the captives, and when the teeth have sunk into flesh, the barbed wire is pulled, violently tearing the flesh of the victim. All prisoners are subjected to this form of torture except myself. I look more dead than alive. Then another form of torture starts: a soldier with a pair of tongs slits the lower lip of a prisoner, the upper lip of another one, the nose of a third, and the right ear of yet another!

229

The more you scream with pain, the more torture you invite because the soldiers find you more fun. A soldier breaks a bottle into several pieces and is determined to "shave" off my long beard with one of the pieces! He is stopped by an elderly Acholi soldier who says that more respect should be given to the dead than to the living. He too was billing me as good as dead.

The office of Intelligence Officer 1 Mukhwana is now opened, and Mukhwana himself appears shortly. A vicious-looking character appears with him. I later learn that his name is Roger, and that he has taken the lives of many prisoners. On this occasion eight of the prisoners, apparently the healthiest, are selected. An order is given by Roger that they should be taken to the "Go-Down" and given the "V.I.P. Treatment." Sticks, clubs, and boot kicks begin to rain on the eight as they are dragged to the Go-Down.

The Go-Down occupies one side, the lower side, of the administrative quarter which is a sort of square complex with a square green in the middle. The Go-Down is at right angles to the offices occupied by intelligence officers. It is only five yards away from where I am sitting now. But to get into it one has to go outside the square, to the back of the block where the only entrance to the Go-Down is.

About three to four minutes later, the eight inmates begin yelling and crying in pain. There is a sound of whips, clubs, sticks, and metal bars coming down. Louder cries of agony. After about 5 minutes the cries gradually weaken until they cease altogether, but the swishing and landing of the sticks continues with intensified ferocity for another five minutes. When this, too, stops, eight limp bodies are dragged out to near where we are sitting. Five of them, identified as dead, are thrown in a heap in one corner of the square. The other three, barely still breathing, are laid out in the rain. Two of them die the following day, but one of them miraculously survives.

As soon as the "V.I.P. treatment" is thus concluded, Mukhwana addresses the remaining inmates, threatening to subject the rest of us to similar treatment unless we cooperate with him. It is not very clear to me what "cooperation" in this case means, but I suppose it means we must give the answers desired by him—not necessarily the truth—at interrogation sessions.

Three prisoners, one after the other, are taken into Mukhwana's room to make a statement and undergo interrogation. No torture. Before any more prisoners can take their turn, the interrogation session is stopped when Mukhwana is called away to go into town. The prisoners are now divided into two groups. Some are taken back to the quarter-guard cells while the rest of us—about six are taken to what is called "Death Cell" at the bottom end of Makindye barracks.

From the administrative quarters, Death Cell is about 20 yards behind the Go-Down. The two are separated by two rows of barbed wire. The prisoners are driven with sticks down the path to Death Cell, a dull gray concrete building with corrugated iron roofing.

One of the soldiers opens the metal grille entrance to the cell, lets us in, and locks up again. This one is about 90 feet by 30, and is subdivided into 7 cubicles, each of which is separated from the main corridor by a metal grille. It has internal flush toilets but no water; so that the first thing that hits you, yards away from the building, is the stench of urine and human excrement. When you actually enter, your eyes are stung by airborne acid from the urine!

In this pot of filth we find about 180 inmates, most of them reduced to mere skeletons, and all of them so dirty that one can peel off layer after layer of dirt. Their eyes are filled with horror, and it is difficult to imagine a more terrified group of emaciated men. Among these men we take our positions. Even in this group of trapped scared rabbits a certain social hierarchy is apparent. And, as new prisoners do in every prison, we take our position at the bottom of the social ladder.

On arrival in this cell I am thoroughly dehydrated; I collapse on the floor and start sweating profusely. Other inmates give the only first aid they can, they unbutton my safari jacket and my shirt, and fan me with them. Later, when I have recovered a little, I ask for some water. I am told there is no water anywhere in the cell. I am still lying on my back, and it is about 3:00 P.M.

231

As soon as I taste the food I feel like throwing up. It is virtually uncooked, has got maggots in it; and there is no salt. However, as I have promised myself not to let myself die of starvation I have to eat it. I shut my eyes and eat without looking.

After eating, the "patrone" gives me a drop of water, and we begin talking. For about an hour I am educating myself with the help of these inmates who, for some reason or other, seem to have a lot of respect for me. Later I learn that a former student in one of my philosophy classes at Makerere University is among the inmates and has told them about me. For weeks while I am here hardly anybody knows my name in Death Cell—they all call me "professor."

At sunset, about 6:30 P.M., I note an ominous silence in Death Cell. I cannot understand it. Nobody wants to speak or be spoken to. Suddenly I hear the clanking of keys on a chain. Each prisoner is visibly nervous now. A soldier approaching the metal grille to Death Cell announces his arrival in Swahili *"Nimekuja mimi Muwuaje."* ("I, the killer, have arrived".) At first I miss the significance of this statement.

The soldier calls out six names. Someone in the main corridor is sobbing. But all six people proceed to the door where a soldier opens for them. Meek and subdued, like sacrificial lambs, they walk out and the metal grille closes behind them. I shall never forget the faces of those men!

A few minutes later the ritual of torture, whipping, clubbing and cries of agony begin in the Go-Down. Finally the cries subside, but the beatings rise to a crescendo and finally stop. We know that the inmates are dead. It is a sunset ritual that one witnesses many a time at Makindye.

Miraculously, Bakulu Mpagi Wamala's family soon smuggled him out of prison and found safe passage for him to Canada through London where he stopped overnight with Wilbur and myself. At first, embarrassed to even mention the grisly details, Wamala hesitated to speak about the torture that he had endured. But as Wilbur and I encouraged him to tell us the whole story, he told us more and more about Makindye. (I could not help recalling that this was the prison to which Idi Amin might have sent me.) We convinced Wamala that the world had to be informed of the truth, and all night he sat on a mattress on our floor, writing.

In 1986, the year I was appointed Uganda's Ambassador to the United States, Wamala was appointed our Ambassador to the United Nations, but he died from an illness related to his prison wounds. His death robbed Uganda of an irreplaceable voice. As a Roman Catholic from an aristocratic family of the Baganda tribe, he had been a coup for the movement, and he remains one of its heroic figures.

Listening to his story and reviewing the rest of the documents, Chancellor Kreisky was visibly moved.

Right then he called in his assistants and began dictating a letter to Obote demanding an explanation and warning him that he would raise the issue with Olof Palme of Sweden, Willy Brandt of West Germany and Spain's Felipe Gonzalez of the Socialist International.

We had had great hope for Kreisky, as he had a history of supporting those under oppression. We left Austria with a sense of accomplishment, trusting we had gained another ally for the movement. His party gave our movement financial support.

Our next mission was to Nigeria in 1983. It was three-pronged. First, we went to launch the Nigerian version of my autobiography, *African Princess*. Second, we wanted to follow up Wilbur's application with Nigerian Airways that Ahamed had been pursuing, and third, we hoped to mobilize Nigeria and West Africa for the NRM.

African Princess had both a national and state launching. It was sold out in Nigeria immediately, and the intense publicity served as a terrific vehicle for publicizing the NRM and to mobilize allies for NRM in Nigeria. Chief Akinkgube drove us in a big convoy of cars to Ota Farm to meet with a Nigerian former head of state, General O. Obasanjo, who upon hearing our documentated case on Uganda agreed to become a spokesman for the movement to rally diplomatic and material support for NRM. He introduced us to Chief M. K. Abiola, who owned Radio Communication Nigeria (RCN), which had an aviation division, and pursued Wilbur's application with Nigerian Airways. It was miraculous news for us when Abiola not only offered Wilbur a flying job but also rallied diplomatic support for NRM.

Ota Farm became our base every time we returned to Nigeria. Obasanjo and Abiola made appointments for us to meet influential

Nigerians. In the absence of our mother country—Uganda—Nigeria became our African home.

African Princess continued to gain recognition with serialization in *The Sunday Times*, the leading paper in the quality press in United Kingdom. Wilbur and I were not the only beneficiaries of this success; the NRM gained a platform from which we broadcast its message and its victories. President Museveni told me later that he listened to all the broadcasts from deep in the bush. Needless to say, this support boosted the morale of our fighters and common people inside the bush.

15

I Lose My Baby

The intense publicity surrounding my book did not escape the gaze of Columbia Pictures, which was searching for the right person to play the "Shaman," a leading role in the film *Sheena*. They invited me to audition.

I asked Wilbur to read the script and see what he made of it before I phoned Columbia. He picked it up from the casting director at Columbia's headquarters in Soho Square and settled down in our living room to read it.

"There is a part for a pilot!" he shouted from the living room. I came running to glance over it and was excited at the prospect.

"I'll phone and ask if I could audition for it," Wilbur said. The casting director agreed to give him a chance, and gave both of us the same date to audition.

When the day arrived, I put on my favorite outfit at the time—a turquoise-and-black-striped cotton workman's overall, a matching turquoise blouse and belt, and silver cowboy boots—and parted my hair in the middle with each side tacked away in an African plait. I wore no jewelry or makeup.

John Guillermin, the director, summoned me in first. Before him and the casting director, I read my lines and discussed the role. He could not contain his excitement. He stood up and paced a few steps.

"How did you find her? She is perfect for the role," he exclaimed.

"Our P.R. person spotted her through the press. She phoned me and said, 'She is the one you want!' " answered the casting director.

"The only problem is that she looks too young for the Shaman. But we can get round that with the aging makeup if she will agree to it," John Guillermin added.

Naively, and astonishing Guillermin, I proceeded to interview him. I inquired, "What films have you directed?"

Guillermin just laughed. When the casting director returned to the room, he amusingly told her, "Elizabeth asked me what films I have directed!" She roared with laughter.

I now realize that to ask a John Guillermin what films he has directed is like asking a king, "Are you really a king?" How is he supposed to prove it? He cannot put on the crown just to prove he is one, for to do so would be to ridicule the institution. I apologized to Guillermin for my ignorance, explaining that I had spent a very short time in the acting world and had not seen many films. Of course he had not seriously minded my questions but had just been amused. He offered me the part and I gladly accepted, even agreeing to the aging makeup!

I exited and Wilbur entered. He auditioned for his part and they discussed the role. Both men came out and Guillermin took us out to lunch at an Italian restaurant around the corner—Soho abounds with them.

"I like Wilbur very much," Guillermin said. "He is very sensitive. But I had someone else in mind for this part. I will see what I can do."

For the next few days we waited anxiously. Shortly after, the casting director called us with the good news that Wilbur had got the part.

We both thought very little of the story and the film script itself. It was badly written. But for me, *Sheena* expressed a certain truth, a certain reality, namely, that an indigenous culture, a way of life of a people, had suffered an assault at the hands of an alien one. The role of the Shaman, the defender of the indigenous culture in *Sheena*, had parallels with my own life and what had come to pass for Africa and our people. To Wilbur, the cockpit and the reunion with Africa were worth everything.

Fate has its own way of imposing itself. While our minds and plans were totally preoccupied with the forthcoming shooting of *Sheena*, my aunt Ruth phoned me from Heathrow Airport, announcing her arrival in London! A few weeks before, my sister Mabel had consulted me whether she should go on struggling with her plan to bring Aunt Ruth to London for treatment of her rheumatism. "It is time you match your words with actions," I said impatiently. "You can go on delaying it until it's too late." Weary of waiting, I had given up on her coming. The more surprising it was, therefore, that in spite of enormous organizational and financial problems, Mabel had managed to pull it off.

The reunion with my aunt was an important moment in my life for two reasons. First, I had been living with a secret fear that if she were to die without sharing with me her last moments and words on earth it would have meant a curse upon me and a bad omen for me as the heir to the position of the Batebe, and would have plagued me for the rest of my life. Second, the time for Wilbur and I to receive her pronouncement on our marriage had arrived. If it was condemnation, we were prepared to ask her forgiveness.

Without Wilbur, I spent the day with her at Mabel's flat in Victoria. I did not discuss Wilbur but agreed on a date for her to come and spend a day with us at our home.

That day we made our home look its best and prepared the best dinner that we were capable of. When she was seated on the golden velvet-covered chaise longue, Wilbur knelt and greeted her. She touched him on the shoulder and greeted him by Akiiki, his *Empako*, the Kitoro endearing name. From that moment on there was absolutely no awkwardness between them. Too much bound them together. Sensitivity, love, warmth, and laughter characterized their relationship. The feeling was like that between a mother and a precious son.

I waited on my knees and addressed my aunt, "Akiiki, we wronged. We ask your forgiveness."

She stared at me seriously. "What wrong did you do?" she asked me. I stared back in disbelief. "I, myself, did precisely that. Our clan does not regard that as taboo." She had adjudicated. No one could overrule her. Only Patrick had the right and power to overrule her, but in these matters he always listened to her as an elder. This woman, I thought to myself, is truly larger than life. We heard for the first time about the meeting, initiated by Mama Buli, that the two held alone.

"Mama Buli came to see me to discuss your marriage. I told her that you had not wronged. She answered me that her only concern was whether you, Wilbur, are old enough to carry the heavy burden of marriage. Otherwise she approves your marriage," she told us.

Wilbur went to the liquor cart, poured himself a beer, and sat down. He had been tense, but now he relaxed. For him it was Mama Buli's verdict that mattered more than anyone else's. To seal her approval, Mama Buli had written to us for the first time, enclosing a red-beaded Toro necklace for me, the traditional gift to a Mutoro bride. My aunt now handed these to us.

My aunt was essentially a political animal. It was thus in character that the conversation turned to the politics of Uganda. Her descriptions of NRM and Museveni, the victories and battles against Obote, by then legendary, were simply hilarious, just as the activities of Obote's cronies were. By the time she left us that evening, Wilbur and I were pulsing with new life.

Our small flat could not accommodate her and her daughter Angeline, who arrived from New York to be with her mother. So I arranged for them to stay at a lovely house in a London suburb, belonging to my cousin, Dr. Tom Mutazindwa. This would also give the many Batoro living in London free access to her. Dr. Henderson, my own doctor, arranged X rays and tests for her and treated her for rheumatism. Otherwise, she pronounced her to be in good health for her age of eighty-four. Aunt Ruth then remained under Dr. Tom Mutazindwa's observation.

Tom's house was always full of Batoro visiting her. In fact, Tom gave a party in her honor. She had two wishes, though, that I had to take care of before her return to Uganda. First, she asked me to arrange Angeline's ticket to New York, which I did. Second, she made it quite clear that it would be extremely painful for her if she were to leave England without visiting Dr. Jo and Mrs. Church, the English missionaries who belonged to the same religious movement as she did and who had worked in Toro and Uganda for many, many years. I hired a car and we spent a day at their home at Shelford, Cambridge. She asked Dr. Church, "My brother in God, what can I do about this pain?" pointing to parts of her body inflicted with pain as I translated from Rutoro into English.

"Nobody can cure rheumatism completely. The medicine will only relieve you. You must pray about it," Dr. Church told her. I could see that she was disappointed. She had had more expectations from Dr. Church than from Dr. Henderson. All the same, the visit was very important to her and a source of satisfaction to me.

When we returned, she asked Patrick to arrange her ticket back to Uganda at the same time our departure for Nairobi was approaching. So I went to be with her for a few days. We shared the same bed and talked round the clock. She could not bend easily in the bath, so I helped bathe her.

"Tell me, Akiiki, when you die, shall I come for the burial?" I asked her.

"No. What good will it do to bury two people?" She meant that my going to Uganda during Obote's time would have been suicidal.

"Akiiki, I want to know about everything from you. I don't want to be misled and confused when you are no longer here," I said. She told me everything about my father and my mother, and explained controversies in our history.

When it was time for me to leave her, she said, "Call your brother Jimmy. I will move to his house and that will be my last stop before returning to Uganda." No amount of argument would convince her to pass through Germany for further treatment under German doctors. Jimmy took her to his home where she spent a lot of time with Patrick and my mother. Patrick delivered to her her ticket to Uganda via Nairobi about the same time as Columbia Pictures delivered to us our tickets to Nairobi via Rome, in order that we might see Stella Mbabazi, Wilbur's older sister, and do some shopping for ourselves.

Not by design, we departed for Rome on the same day my aunt left for Uganda via Nairobi. I phoned her before leaving. "Bye-bye,

Akiiki. We will see you in Nairobi. I will phone you the minute we land."

Wilbur and I had left Nairobi four years before as secret lovers. Now we returned in broad daylight as a married couple, accorded star treatment by Columbia Pictures. Prominent Africans associated with *Sheena* received us warmly at the airport, along with representatives of Columbia Pictures, who drove us to the Norfolk Hotel, the hub of the white settlers' community of Kenya and an epitome of luxury and comfort. (Tragically it was a target in 1976 of a bomb attack by people wanting to revenge the Israeli raid on Entebbe. I do not know whether the Norfolk was a target because it belongs to my friend Tubby Block, a Jew, or the target was Kenya because it was alleged that Israel's planes refueled in Kenya before proceeding to Uganda to attack Entebbe Airport.)

Right away, I phoned Aunt Ruth. I felt desperately helpless when she told me she was ill and I promised to visit her at the earliest opportunity.

It was clear that John Guillermin was under pressure to complete shooting within a tight time frame due to budgetary constraints. He announced that he would start right away with the airport scene. Wilbur and I exchanged quick glances. When we retired to our suite, I suggested to him that he should use me as a sounding board to practice his lines.

"It is a small part. I am not bothered," he said.

I disagreed. "Those small parts look deceptively easy. They are tougher because you have little maneuvering space." He, however, would not be persuaded. So we both had a good laugh when he discovered the hard way.

Guillermin summoned him and the other two Americans, extremely experienced and good actors, to a practice at Nairobi Airport. Hours later, he walked into our room and threw himself on the bed. "John Guillermin made me read those lines and act them out in front of everyone before practicing with me alone!" he told me.

"It serves you right, Wilbur. You refused to practice with me. You underestimated that part!" I said.

After this he practiced quite often. When the film was released in London, Wilbur and I went to see it, and I know he was pleased with the scene. Little did I know that it would assume priceless value for me. After completion of the airport scene, the entire *Sheena* film company, including the elephant, the lions, the leopard, and the rhino, traveling in convoys of trucks and four-wheel-drive vehicles, and by plane, left Nairobi and set up headquarters in several lodges in the Aberdare mountains—all for the shooting of the death scene of the Shaman, when the "Shaman," the spiritual leader of the Zamburis, bequeaths the Powers of Prophecy, on her deathbed, to "Sheena," the American actress Tanya Roberts.

My call sheet announcing my wake-up call at 2:00 A.M., my makeup call at 3:00 A.M., and shooting at 8:00 A.M. was duly delivered to our bedroom the evening before the day of the shooting. The aging makeup was a real killer and it took four hours to apply, in spite of the great expertise of the Italian artists. It was painful, dangerous, and I detested it. At 7:00 A.M. I was ready, dressed in the animal-skin-and-barkcloth dress, with the Zamburi headdress on my head and skin sandals on my feet, and looking the seventy-year-old Shaman. With my left hand resting on the hand of the makeup artist and a long traditional ceremonial stick in my right hand, I was led from the makeup caravan and we slowly ascended a steep hill to the Shaman's deathbed and the grave, which the animals (the elephant, the leopard, and the monkeys) had prepared in a forest in the Aberdare mountains for her. I was laid on the deathbed. Sheena knelt by my side with her hands rested in mine. The animals were brought and placed in their positions around me. John Guillermin, accompanied by Columbia's executives, the two producers, arrived.

"Good morning, Elizabeth. How do you feel this morning?" Fearing to crack the makeup around my lips and thus inviting more makeup to be added, I did not answer but just looked up. "Won't you even say good morning to me, Elizabeth?" John asked, puzzled.

"It's the makeup, John!" I said.

Relieved, he proceeded to introduce me to the distinguished visitors as I lay on "my" deathbed! I uttered not a word but just looked at them!

Everything, including the cameras, was in position. John Guillermin took a look through the camera lens. "That's fine. I like even the mist," he said to the cameramen. "Tanya, Elizabeth, everybody, are you ready?"

"Action," John Guillermin called out.

"Your hand. It is so cold!" was Sheena's opening line.

"The flame departs," the Shaman answered.

We had gone halfway through the scene when John Guillermin stopped us. "It is a very strong scene. Tanya, it will not do."

I understood precisely what Guillermin meant. It wasn't because I was a better actress than Tanya. The difference was, she was acting and I wasn't. Good acting comes from life experience. There were parallels between the Shaman's and my own life. As the Batebe, I held the position of leadership among the Batoro just as the Shaman did among the Zamburis. Right then and there, as the death scene was being played out, the battle not only for my people's survival but for their way of life was raging between the NRM and Obote's fascist forces within Uganda. I was in the forefront of that struggle to defend my people and their culture under assault by an alien culture just as the Shaman was the defender of her people and their way of life. Her spiritual role was similar to the secular and spiritual role of our monarchy. In the character of the Shaman, I was living out my own experience and crisis.

It did not take Tanya long to summon her acting skills. She adjusted and we shot very good scenes. Guillermin was intending to shoot more repeats when, out of nowhere, hell broke loose! A thick fog/mist covered the entire area where we were and visibility became difficult. Then there was lightning, which agitated the animals, especially the leopard. The heavens opened, and there was a hailstorm and thunderstorm. The animals cried. The cast and crew ran for their four-wheel-drive vehicles. Some got through, but later on the roads became impassable. Some people were stuck in the mountains. Luckily, we got out by plane.

As I was acting the death scene in the Aberdare mountains, Aunt Ruth lay dying in the Nairobi hospital. Frantic relatives, terrified at the thought that the Batebe might die in a foreign land without either Patrick or myself present, relayed the news to Wilbur and me.

"Why have you delayed?" She told me angrily when I arrived at Nairobi Hospital.

"Delayed, Akiiki! I was buried in the forest up in the mountains. Your news just got to us," I told her.

She smiled. That had always been the way between us. No matter how tragic a situation was, I always teased her and she always responded. Her doctor informed us that he was carrying out blood and other tests to determine what was wrong. She was very weak and the hospital kindly allowed me to arrange for Aboki Mary Mugenyi, her cousin and life friend who had grown up with her, to stay in the room with her. The Norfolk made her a Christmas cake, which we shared with relatives and friends at the hospital on Christmas day.

The thought of her dying receded from my consciousness. But then on the morning of December 27 her doctor, without informing me or anyone in the family, decided to operate on her because, he told me afterward, her condition had suddenly deteriorated. As I was preparing to leave for the hospital, Aboki phoned me. "Hurry up. Akiiki has just passed away." I lost my bearings. Everything I touched fell out of my hands.

I arrived at the hospital just as they were wheeling my aunt from the operating theater. I followed her to her room where we placed her on her bed and covered her in white sheets. I could not reach Patrick or my mother on the phone. So I phoned Mabel.

"Mabel, listen to me carefully. *Akiiki atulize* [she sleeps]. Inform Patrick. Ask him to phone me about his arrival." I hung up. I told the crowd of Batoro, Ugandan, and friends who were streaming into the room and wailing, "They are going to drive us out of the hospital. It is better that we are allowed to be around her than kept away from her because of our wailing." They painfully refrained, waiting for me to find a proper place for mourning.

There were two homes of members of our family, and however humble they were, as long as they were ready to have us, I felt it would be improper to go to other homes. My brother Stephen explained that his home was too small, so I requested that Prince Selvano Katama and his wife offer their home and they agreed. I had got over my first hurdle. But no African death is ever controversy free.

243

There were worse obstacles yet to be overcome, beginning with the Nairobi mortuary. The stench of human bodies and blood is something one would not be able to bear without special reason. But I said to myself that if the Batebe could be lying there, who am I to shrink away from it. I found myself there several times a day—sorting out all sorts of problems. Since it was Christmas, the men in charge were impossible to locate. I had to go to their homes in the villages. The home of the Indian supervisor was guarded by man-eater bulldogs to protect him from the public and he was thus inaccessible.

I had paid the first lot of guards to protect the body and to give us access on demand. They went off duty and the next lot who came on shift said they knew nothing about earlier payment. I paid again with no guarantee that they would be there at the crucial time. After the Christmas holidays I managed to locate the supervisor, and I said to him, "The woman lying there is a public figure. I am personally accountable for delivering her to our country *on time*. I have paid all my dues. If you fail to deliver her to us on demand, you will be held personally accountable, and I will expose this matter to the press. Every time I come here I have to make fresh payments to different men. Is this a business, sir? I beg you to control your men." I implored him. He summoned his men to our meeting and he promised to deliver his part of the bargain and to bear upon his men.

Meanwhile, in London, Patrick held meetings of the family, the Batoro, and other Ugandans, including ex-President Godfrey Binaisa. He received information from Uganda that Obote and his government were attempting to take over supervision of the funeral arrangements in order to manipulate the Batebe's death to gain political advantage. He was furious when he called.

"I am phoning you to convey to everybody my warning that I will not tolerate anyone, including Obote's government, exploiting my aunt's death. Unless I am satisfied that there is no manipulation, I will not allow the body to go to Uganda. We will temporarily bury her abroad until such time that she can be buried peacefully and properly in Toro," he said in a stern voice.

I called a meeting of all the mourners and conveyed Patrick's message. Monumental as this problem was, still of more immediacy was the guarding of the body until Patrick could arrive and bid farewell to his aunt. That responsibility fell solely and squarely on my shoulders. That the Batebe should be whisked off to Uganda before the arrival of the heir to the throne of Toro, and by virtue of that head of the Babito clan, was to somersault our culture. To allow it was to allow myself to be entrapped in a permanent curse for the rest of my life. Complicating matters even more was my unfinished work on *Sheena.*

Since the death I had not been in touch with the producers. Apart from going to the Norfolk to wash and change clothes every morning, I had abandoned the hotel and in accordance with tradition was alongside other mourners, sleeping on a mattress in the sitting room at the mourners' house. *Sheena*'s representatives located this house situated in a crowded suburb of Nairobi and delivered my call sheet summoning me to the shooting of the opening scene of *Sheena*. In terms of the meaning of *Sheena*, it is this scene, when the Shaman first introduces Baby Sheena to her tribes' men and women, the Zamburis, and the death scene that are the most important. Torn between my responsibility to the clan and to *Sheena*, I reluctantly decided to risk leaving Nairobi for the briefest possible time.

John Guillermin had selected the East African Rift Valley as the location for the opening scene, the Shaman's house, the prison in which the Shaman is imprisoned and rescued by Sheena on a zebra and the animals, and the giant cave from which Baby Sheena emerges for her first encounter with the Shaman. A helicopter flew me to this breathtakingly picturesque location. We landed in the valley below. The steep climb to the cave had to be done on foot, but I had to be carried in order to reach the Shaman's home on top of the gorge.

Everything was in place for the shooting of the opening scene. I disappeared into the bush from which I was to emerge with the leopard following on my trail. Baby Sheena entered the cave with her "real" parents, from which she would emerge alone after the earthquake explosion that killed her parents, to be discovered by the Shaman. The Zamburis stood guard with their spears.

"Action," John Guillermin called out, his voice echoing across the valley. A terrified Baby Sheena ran from the cave just as I was walking to meet her. But then I felt the leopard too close on my heels. Instead of continuing my journey to reach Sheena, to lift her in my arms to be hailed by the Zamburis, I fled to the Zamburis for protection. The leopard was following me but was frightened by the spears and colorful costumes. The animal man called back the leopard. "If the leopard follows you here to attack us, we will spear it," a Zamburi told me. John Guillermin heard them and was furious.

"If you spear the leopard, I will spear you," he told the Zamburis. For the first time on the picture John Guillermin was annoyed with me. There was repeat after repeat of that scene until the fear of the leopard was drained out of me.

Shortly, Patrick and my brother Jimmy arrived and checked into the Norfolk. My mother had stayed behind to look after Jimmy's infant son. I briefed them. He got in the car and led us to the mourners. As soon as he appeared, there was stormy silence. The men stood and the women knelt. He shook hands warmly with all the men.

By tradition, a king never sets eyes on a dead body. Patrick decided to waive that tradition. My father did the same with Queen Victoria and his grandmother. I led him and Jimmy to the mortuary to the Batebe's body and handed it over to Patrick. He took over the operation, although I continued alongside with others to help him. He phoned Uganda from the Norfolk. He was informed that the family and the people, and not Obote's agents, were in control of the funeral arrangements. He assembled the mourners and in a quiet voice thanked them for their support and announced that the body would be flown to Uganda on a Uganda Airways flight on the same day we were to hold a memorial service in Nairobi.

What he did not announce was the bitter controversy raging in Toro about Akiiki's burial place and which was tearing the family and the clan asunder. Patrick allowed no public discussion in Nairobi. He carried out discreet soundings. He asked my view.

"As you know, I shared a bed with Akiiki in her last days on earth. I asked her bluntly, 'Where do you want to be buried, Akiiki?' 'At the church,' she told me. I labored to make her realize that her decision not to be buried at Karambi had far-reaching implications for the monarchy and our culture. As you know, the wish of the dead is sacred in African culture and tradition, and has to be respected at any cost," I told my brother.

Characteristically, he said nothing but registered a mental note.

The day of the memorial service, Nairobi Cathedral was packed. Patrick entered and took his seat. A procession of the coffin bearers including Wilbur carried the body inside. I followed behind them. The Reverend John Wilson, her life friend and member of the same religious movement as my aunt, preached a moving sermon. After the service we returned the body to the mortuary and joined the mourners until late that night when we put it aboard a Ugandan Airways flight for its last journey to Toro.

I was now not only without a father but without the one person who had been my very best friend and who had guided my steps to this moment. I held on to Wilbur, knowing that there was nothing we could not face together. We said goodbye to Patrick and flew out to the location to film the rest of my scenes, knowing that we still had important family matters to resolve.

No African woman becomes fully the wife of a man whose parents have not accepted her. She is referred to as a "prostitute"! I could never regard myself fully as Wilbur's wife until I had been accepted by his mother, Abwoli Salai Mbabi.

With his innate sense of dignity and propriety, Wilbur arranged for his mother's first encounter with his wife. His brother Fred accompanied her on the twelve-hour bus journey from Kampala to Nairobi. Alone Wilbur went to the bus station and picked them up, looking worn and covered in dust. He took them to the apartment we rented, where they stayed until his mother was well rested and refreshed. Then he brought her to our suite at the Norfolk. I had made myself beautiful, put on my favorite recent acquisition from Rome, and left to make way for their arrival.

Now, as I returned, I could see them in the sitting room of our suite. Rather than walk in a straight line, I skirted around on the veranda until I reached the door where I entered, knelt before her, and welcomed and greeted her. She was overwhelmed and quietly cried. But then she wiped the tears with her handkerchief, touched me on the shoulder, and greeted me. I remained seated on the floor as is customary for a daughter-in-law and carried on a conversation with them. Her tears were the seal of approval of our marriage.

Listening to her talk, observing her demeanor, made me understand much about Wilbur. It was from her that he had inherited the serenity, the sensitivity, the civility, the inexhaustible patience, and the goodness. She was, like Wilbur, above anything profane, crude, and contemptible. In their world, fame, money, glory, and anyone else became irelevant to me. I desired nothing more outside of them.

I spent a lot of time with her during the weeks she was with us. We stopped eating at the Norfolk, preferring her traditional cooking of African food that we bought from the markets of Nairobi and its suburbs. I was able to take her to the Swedish dentist, the best in Nairobi, and to my hairdresser at the Norfolk. Wilbur and Fred completed a plan for her retirement and we gave her our financial contribution toward building her house. She had actually attended my aunt's funeral in Toro and we did get, for the first time, an eyewitness account of the funeral. She told us that without Patrick's letter informing the Batoro, the family, and the clan of my aunt's wish to be buried at the church, which was read to the mourners, fighting would have broken out, and no one knows how that problem would have been resolved. Other than that, she told us that my aunt's funeral was almost as big as my father's funeral.

The only discomfort in her visit occurred one night as we discussed a solution to the killings and atrocities being committed by Obote and his agents. Surely, we argued, the solution lay in a military struggle.

"By all means, you can fight, but will you find us?" She asked with pain in her voice. She had expressed a classic dilemma of all times. A dictator instills fear in the population by terrorizing it so that they don't support his removal. The freedom fighters cannot, though, surrender. Loss of life is the terrible price that has to be paid. This is what we discussed before she and Fred returned to a Uganda gripped in fear, violence, and genocide. We were not sure whether we would see them again. She and I cried as we parted, she to return to our homeland, and Wilbur and I to go back to London, where I discovered that I was expecting a baby.

Wilbur and I were very happy but I felt wonder and a sense of deep reflection. So I am carrying Wilbur's baby! Would I ever love someone else as much as Wilbur? How am I going to handle motherhood? So many thoughts went through my mind. I spent a lot of time to myself and mostly lying down on our bed as if not to hurt what was inside of me.

"Why are you spending so much time in bed? You are not a sick person." Wilbur laughed as he pulled me up and led me to our living room. "We better modernize this flat or the baby will freeze." Now I laughed too. We installed central heating, hot water, and a washing machine, tiled, painted, and built new cupboards in the kitchen and bathroom, and put up new mirrors on the bathroom walls.

I was hoping to stay at home more, but we were suddenly called to Lagos to follow developments for NRM. The trip entailed traveling to Kaduma in northern Nigeria, Abeokuta, and Ibadan. While still in Nigeria, we learned of Museveni's arrival in Europe. We phoned him and promised to touch base with him once we were in London and to go wherever he would be to present a report.

When we arrived in London I felt exhausted and suffered acute pains. I asked and received Wilbur's permission to explain to Museveni why I would be unable to travel with Wilbur to Sweden to see him. I disclosed to Museveni that I was expecting. Wilbur went alone and returned. My pains continued though, and I lost the baby. I locked myself in our bedroom and cried day and night. I would not eat.

"We were happy until you became pregnant. I don't mind us not having children." Wilbur's kindness and strength knocked me out of my painful nightmare. I emerged from the bedroom and went about caring for him and our home, resolved not to think about my tragedy.

Museveni phoned. "How are you?" he inquired.

"I lost the baby," I answered. "I am very, very sorry," he repeated emphatically and several times. He had been the *only* person we had told about my pregnancy. He has kept my secret.

16

"Knowing Is the Prerogative of the Gods"

After five years in the bush, Museveni emerged, leading the guerrilla army from the Mountains of the Moon, and marched through the streets of Uganda to rescue it from the lion Obote.

The Batoro sang, "*Kankaihe, nkatwarre Museveni nuwe aliretta obusinge komungeye.*" They sang about him as a man who would bring peace.

Later on when I accompanied him on a tour through Uganda, Museveni turned to me and said, "Let's sing that Kitoro song together. I had to fight back the tears the first time I heard it."

One of the challenges ahead for Museveni's government was to repair and rebuild relations with other countries—the United States in particular, largely because Museveni and our movement had been labeled Marxist and friends of Libya: When the question of who could take on this challenge arose, someone said, "It is Elizabeth who will help to manage that place for us."

So I was appointed Uganda's ambassador extraordinary and plenipotentiary to the United States, reversing my earlier appointment as

Uganda's envoy to West Germany, the area of my operation during the armed struggle.

"You must see the country before going to the United States," Museveni said to me. So I went with him to Karamoja in northern Uganda, to eastern Uganda, and to the Luwero Triangle. I saw how Uganda's social structure had collapsed. I witnessed the breakdown of communications systems, sanitary systems, and health services. I saw the killing fields of Obote's soldiers and agents in the Luwero Triangle, Toro, and elsewhere.

Then I flew to meet Wilbur in our London home so we could spend two weeks together before I went to Washington. He was preparing to leave London to start his type-rating training in Lagos with Radio Communication Nigeria (RCN). Wilbur was happy about the switch from Bonn to Washington.

After the fractured reality of Uganda, the metropolis of Washington, D.C., made me feel as though I had landed on a movie set.

Only drunkards and madmen drive in straight lines because of the potholes in Ugandan roads. In Washington, D.C., cars seemed to shoot at supersonic speed along roads that seemed to extend to the limitless horizons. Passing wooden houses on Foxhall Street, I thought of the American television program *The Waltons*. I saw black people everywhere, images of people who resembled my uncles, aunts, brothers, or sisters. Later, I would watch television and marvel at how black people danced and at their outspokenness.

I had imagined the capital of the world's first industrial power to be a city of skyscrapers. Instead, it was one big forest. With so much greenery and so many black faces, Washington reminded me of Africa. I became very fond of it as a city. The drama of small things seemed heightened. In Africa dark clouds move in to signal the rain. You notice it. Here, I couldn't anticipate its coming. I heard the splash and that was the rain.

When I arrived at the embassy (the chancery), I found it in a state of total disrepair. Here I was, in the hub of the diplomatic universe, and the phones had been disconnected, the roof was leaking. All I inherited were bills, and every inch of the place cried out for a good scrubbing. I was welcomed by an overgrown bush garden and two abandoned Yellow cabs.

On my first workday the embassy driver took me for a ride to familiarize me with the city in a blue van with a smell that prompted a garage employee to ask, "Is this a car or a tractor?" It was the only car.

"The official car was hit while parked. No one saw who hit the car!" the driver explained.

I had hardly settled in my chair when a string of former embassy employees started knocking at my door demanding to be paid. Word had spread that the ambassador had arrived. When I had to tell them that I did not have enough money to meet their demands, some broke down and cried. My predecessor had laid off some employees to reduce expenses, but as soon as he departed, they were reinstated. Our credibility was so bad we couldn't get anyone to insure us. Neither my financial attaché nor my personal secretary had housing. They stayed in the residence with me. The other two embassy officials and their families shared one house. But I had faced bigger problems.

My staff and I set out to create an efficient and self-sufficient embassy. We did not want to be parasitic on the home government's scarce foreign exchange. We planned to generate trade for our country and that way earn our own way.

We agreed to a payment plan with the telephone company, and our communication lines were opened. By using the same domestic staff at the embassy as at the residence and dispensing with entertaining at restaurants, we managed good savings. I cut our traveling expenses and ruled out the hiring of lobbyists. Instead, I set up a task force of Ugandans who availed us their free expertise—for example, the task force on health was charged with a number of medically related issues including water safety and AIDS. We brought in Ugandan consultants to set up our computer system and advise on engineering and other matters. Through a newsletter we published, we kept our own community and the American public up-to-date and informed.

Recognizing that a bad image is an obstacle to development, I consented to interviews with *60 Minutes, The Washington Post,* and *The New York Times,* and other newspapers and television programs in the United States. By the end of my two-year tenure, the appalling image of Uganda had dramatically changed and I had neutralized opposition to the NRM government in the United States.

It was right after one of these interviews that Wilbur called to tell me that Chief Abiola of Nigeria, who had supported President Museveni during the struggle, would visit Uganda in September. Wilbur wanted me back in Uganda ahead of time to insure a successful visit. Furthermore, Chief Abiola would be flown in his own executive jet piloted by his own chief pilot and copiloted by Wilbur, marking the end of Wilbur's exile from Uganda.

It was almost overwhelming for me to realize that only two years before we had fled Uganda and eloped. We had common and individual dreams for freedom in Uganda and for Wilbur to become a pilot. The day he touched down at Entebbe Airport was a glorious moment for us.

I was with Patrick at his hotel in Fairway when Wilbur called. Patrick picked up the phone and said to me, "It is Wilbur." I snatched the phone from him.

"Where are you,' I asked.

"I am in the lobby," he said, and I dropped the phone and flew out of the room and down the stairs.

Wilbur seemed unusually quiet. When we were alone, he told me they had nearly had an accident in the plane.

"We had a turbulent flight over Zaire, and at Entebbe the central tower refused to permit us to land, saying they were not informed of our arrival. They only consented after I identified myself and spoke in our language." But his narrow escape soon vanished from our minds, blown away in the diplomatic and social swirl of Chief Abiola's visit.

When Wilbur left, I rushed back to Washington.

In the United States, an ambassador must present credentials first to the deputy secretary of state and finally to the president. The deputy secretary of state happened to be John Whitehead, an old friend from my *Vogue* magazine days, when he was an executive at Condé Nast. It was good to see a familiar and friendly face, but I was still surprised that a rule forbade me to take anyone into the meeting with me. The Americans were represented and reinforced, and recorded the proceedings. I was alone and armed only with a sense of mission and urgency fueled by the human suffering of my countrymen and women.

I said in my presentation that the NRM leadership believed in doing good for its own sake and sought after truth and ideals we believed to be universal and shared by many Americans. My government's message was that we sought friendship and cooperation and trade from the United States, not primarily aid—though we would not turn down aid, if offered. We wanted to be partners in trade on mutually beneficial terms. In response to what I said, John Whitehead congratulated the NRM for restoring human rights to the Ugandan people and pledged the support of the United States government. The one concern that he did express was regarding our friendship with Libya.

I reminded him that the United States was friendly with Libya during Amin's regime at a time when Museveni was fighting Libya. Now that the Museveni government had no problem with Libya, the United States was fighting them. We Ugandans felt that a new era of cooperation had arrived replacing conflict. We had to cooperate with any nation that meant us no harm. What happened between the United States and Libya would not be our concern.

I was asked if we intended to support U.S. government policies, and I replied that we could not give the United States blanket approval, but that we would always subject each policy to careful scrutiny.

Americans prefer frankness, so I gave them a frank exchange. We believe that the era of dominance was over, and we would not allow Libya or anyone else to compromise our independence, I continued. Uganda saluted the United States as its example to the NRM of the positive results of equality and freedom. I explained that our relationship with Libya was distorted, but that would change as I kept the lines of communication between Uganda and the United States open.

Before the presentation of my credentials to President Reagan, Wilbur came. He arrived on his birthday. He had deliberately not mentioned it to test me. But he found flowers and a card on his side of our bed in our Washington home. That night just the two of us had a champagne dinner by candlelight. Later on I unrolled a colorful woven mat given to us by Mama Buli for Wilbur's feet whenever he stepped from or sat up in our bed. When he saw it, he smiled.

My life was full again with Wilbur here. He spent the two weeks with me exercising, resting, and preparing for his final flight exams. We lunched, shopped, and simply spent the time alone. The only function we attended was a dinner that the Kenya ambassador gave at his residence for African finance ministers, the World Bank, and IMF officials.

One Sunday morning as we sat sipping tea, gazing out the window, Wilbur said, "I have made a choice. I am quitting flying in January. I have my country now, and I would like to do business between the United States and Uganda. Now is not the time to thrash this out, though. We need to talk once I move here in January."

"You are moving here in January?" I asked, excitedly.

"Yes."

"Thank God. These lonely nights have been too much."

He then organized his dressing room and selected the clothes he was leaving behind and the ones I was to take for him to wear for Patrick's wedding in Toro. He asked me to buy some material for Mama Buli and his mother for traditional costumes for my brother's wedding.

I wanted to go with him to the airport, but he told me to go and attend the conference and World Bank meeting that had been scheduled long before. Then he phoned me later from London.

On November 21 I presented my credentials to President Reagan. I telexed Wilbur, asking him to be present, but he was already on a long flight to Dwala in a Cameroon, then to Abijan, Ivory Coast, and Dakar, Senegal. He phoned me from Dakar to wish me well.

Only family members are allowed at these presentations, so I went alone in a limousine with the U.S. and Uganda flags flapping in the breeze, with priority over other nonofficial cars, sailing through traffic lights to the White House.

We pulled up to the porch of the White House and were met by Mrs. Selwa Roosevelt, the chief of Protocol, who was another friend from my early days in New York. She, along with a group of officials from Protocol and the National Security Council, led me on a tour of the Cabinet room.

Along the way Selwa asked me how matters stood at the embassy and I reported that at long last it was functioning and that I myself took a hand in the cleaning.

"Only a woman could have done that," she said.

It was time to go into the president, and Selwa announced as we entered: "Her Excellency the Princess Elizabeth Nyabongo of Toro, the ambassador of Uganda."

"Welcome, Your Royal Highness," President Reagan said, at first shaking my hand then leading me to the mantelpiece, where we stood facing each other. "I want to welcome you most warmly to the United States."

"Thank you, Mr. President," I responded.

"And I want you to feel at home here. We will do everything to see you are properly settled. Let me congratulate your president and your government for having corrected those terrible abuses of human rights. However, I must express a little concern about Libya. We do not think it is a good thing for Uganda to be close to Libya."

I smiled, and, coolly, without indulging in the ironies, gave him my response.

"I thank you, Mr. President, for your warm welcome. I wish to assure you on behalf of my president and our government that we will never allow Libya or anyone else to tamper with our current independence. We've fought heavily for it."

I noticed a shift in the president's posture. Our visit was past due to be over.

"I hope, Mr. President, this will contribute a little to your knowledge of Africa." He accepted my gift of *African Princess*.

The room vibrated with warmth. It would have been perfect if Wilbur had been there, but I had not time for regrets. Washington lives and functions in a social whirl, and if I were to prevail, I had to plunge into it. So I went to a party given by my close friend in America, Mrs. Evangeline Bruce. She and her husband, David Bruce, were instrumental in helping me launch my modeling career in New York during the sixties, when he was the American ambassador in London.

When I mentioned to another guest that this was my first Washington party, he said, "Goodness, you have just arrived in Washington and find yourself in Mrs. Bruce's drawing room? You cannot help but be a success."

My social success did not make me ignore the political reality of Third World ambassadors in Washington summed up by one African ambassador as, "suffering impotence without complaining."

As busy as I became in the following days, my main preoccupation was with preparations for my brother Patrick's wedding. I was responsible for buying the wedding dress and bridesmaids dresses, shoes, linen for the couple, fabric for other relatives, plus printing the wedding invitations.

For some reason, I feared that something might happen to imperil the wedding. I said this to Wilbur in the frequent phone conversations we had between Washington and Lagos, his current base of operation. I felt that someone might die resulting in cancellation of the wedding. Wilbur brushed off my pessimistic thoughts.

I had not been sick in years, but two days before Wilbur died I called Wilbur for comfort and told him how in the night I could not breathe. I felt I was suffocating.

I believe it was telepathy. Danger cannot fall on someone you are very close to and you feel nothing.

Finally the day came for me to get on the plane that would take me home. I packed my bags, including Wilbur's dress clothes that he had left with me for the wedding. That morning he called from Paris, on his way to Zurich and then Dakar. We said good-bye, both cheered by the fact that we would soon be together again.

I arrived in Entebee tired but happy, and phoned the State House to ask for a car to take me to Kampala. Commander Innocent came on the phone and said, "I am sorry about the accident."

"What accident?" I asked.

"Your husband's accident," he said.

"Where?" I was shocked and felt desperate as Innocent fell silent, realizing that I did not know. I insisted that he finish telling me what had happened. "Phone Patrick," he said, "at the Fairway Hotel."

I called. "Patrick, what has happened?"

"Akiiki, Wilbur had an accident." He was crying.

"Where is he?"

"He is dead. It was a plane crash."

I threw myself to the floor and started wailing, *"Ebyange bihoire"* ("I am finished"). But I knew I could not afford to collapse and managed to pull myself back from the emotional abyss. With great effort and concentration, I went to the State House to President Museveni.

"You have heard what has happened to me?"

"Yes," the president said.

"All I want is a one-way ticket to Casablanca. You'd better find another ambassador," I said.

"You cannot have a one-way ticket. Where will you go" he said.

"Can you give me a car so that I can drive to Nairobi?" I asked, thinking that I could make connections from there.

"No government car can leave Uganda without written authorization of relevant authority. Even if I give you a letter under my signature, you will be arrested. You'd better go tomorrow after we have made all the proper arrangements for you."

There was nothing I could do but wait. I met my brother Patrick at the Lake Victoria Hotel to hand over the things I bought for the wedding. When Patrick reached me, he broke down and sobbed.

I cried, too, saying, "I have nobody."

"But you have me."

"You can never be Wilbur."

"I am going to postpone the wedding," he said.

"Postpone it until when? Forever? You mean you'll never marry because I have gone? Go ahead, because I might never return." Patrick wanted to accompany me, but I insisted on going alone. At 4:00 A.M. I took leave of him and was driven to the Uganda-Kenya border to begin the journey from Nairobi to Lagos, to Casablanca. I had feared that the plane crash had not left me a body to recover, but just ashes. I would not return to my country without my husband's body to bury.

At Lagos Airport Ahamed, Wilbur's close friend, and his cousin Mohammed waited in the crowd to take me to the apartment where Wilbur had lived for the past few months while he trained on charter planes. These boys had worked and shared meals with Wilbur. In the evenings Ahamed and Mohammed used to drive Wilbur to a hotel to call me.

They drove me through the crowded streets to the flat in the quiet tree-lined neighborhood where Wilbur had lived. All night we talked about Wilbur. Ahamed told me that Wilbur had been listening to a lot of jazz. "Now I understand why he had this urge to talk to you daily. He must have felt something coming. He'd been very moody lately, too," Ahamed said. When they left, gray morning light filtered through the curtains.

On Wilbur's dressing table stood my photo and a birthday card that I had presented to him in Washington, D.C., "Welcome to Washington." Tennis and squash rackets hung on the wall in the passage. I crawled into our bed and wailed myself to sleep.

The next day Ahamed and Mohammed returned to drive me to Wilbur's barber. I asked him to cut my hair. "Cut more, cut more," I ordered, until Ahamed said, "That's enough." But I did not care to make myself as beautiful as I had for my husband, not anymore.

The men returned to the house with me to pack up Wilbur's possessions. From among his many clothes, I selected a national costume of the Hausa Tribe from northern Nigeria, the "Babanriga," a white tunic and jacket with a matching cap, for his burial. The captain of the HS 125 executive jet that belonged to Chief Abiola, Wilbur's employer, arranged to take us to Casablanca. Ahamed and I got our visas and left a day later, accompanied by two company officials and two pilots.

Officials had taken Wilbur's body with the others to a mosque. There, Ahamed helped me bathe and dress him in the clothes I had brought for him. I felt very fortunate that I hadn't been left with ashes. He seemed completely unharmed, only having been suffocated from the flight fumes.

After I had laid Wilbur's body in the coffin, the police took me to the open, dry brown field where the accident had occurred. Ahamed was with me as they explained how it happened.

The captain flew from Zurich intending to refuel at Amfak in Morocco before going to Dakar in Senegal, but when the plane arrived at Amfak, they were told, "No, you can't refuel now. It's six o'clock. Refuel at Casablanca." At Casablanca, the control tower told them they had to circle while they were clearing another aircraft. They circled and tried to land but were told to circle a second time because the aircraft had not been cleared yet.

The captain told the control tower, "Allow me to land because I'm not so sure about my fuel situation."

They said, "No, circle again." The captain circled again and began the descent. They crashed four seconds from the runway. Out of fuel, they couldn't get enough lift and smashed into a house, killing a mother and her daughter. Then the plane caught fire.

Of all those on board—the captain, the owner, their wives, the nanny of the owner's children, and Wilbur—there were no survivors.

I visited the body each day for seven days until the government approved our taking it out of the country.

We arrived in Entebbe on January 4, 1987. Four months earlier Wilbur had arrived here as a copilot of the same HS 125, ending his exile. The thought overwhelmed me. I was about to break down. Then I pulled out a photograph of Wilbur when he could not have been more alive. I held it to my heart. It made me feel strong.

"Akiiki, I am bringing you to the land of your ancestors. I am going to lay you next to your father, your grandfather, and your great-grandfather," I said to Wilbur.

The airport was crowded with mourners. I was surprised that so many people had got the news in time to meet us. Government leaders, family, Wilbur's friends, and many of our clansmen and women were there. But we were flying on to Toro, and the pilot advised us to hurry because of threatening rain on the horizon. He was right. The flight was turbulent and one of the Radio Communication Nigeria (RCN) officials was visibly frightened. But the tougher the weather got, the more pleased I became. I said to myself that the best ending for me would be to die now with Wilbur. We made it though. By the time we touched down it was late afternoon, yet we still found a crowd, which included Prince Kassami, the son of King Kabalega of Bunyoro, his daughter Xeda, and my brother's trusted aide Kassim, who would supervise the last leg of our trip to Kabarole, the capital of Toro.

Wilbur's dream was to start a farm in Toro to lift up his family and our people. It was Wilbur who had opened my eyes to the riches of Toro—the crater lakes, the mountains, the extensive plains, and the unbelievably fertile land. The dream had fallen and still Toro's potential was not developed, the people still left impoverished after years of negect by the successive governments.

We slowly drove the last eighty miles to Kabarole Cathedral. On our arrival bells began ringing to summon people to come. Crowds gathered and we entered the cathedral. I led the procession to the front, where I sat on the floor next to the coffin, and the service started. At the end of the service, we started on the last journey to Ibonde, Wilbur's homeplace. As we approached, the wailing of the women was deafening. On arrival I found the men sitting around a fire that had been lit on the news of Wilbur's death and that had been kept burning throughout the nights.

I did not wail now or cry. I concentrated on being with Wilbur. I was with Wilbur's mother and Mama Buli—Wilbur's grandmother—when Wilbur's great-uncle, Byabacwezi (of the Ancestor Gods), sent for me. He was over one hundred years old and the head of the clan, and he had been brought to Ibonde on a stretcher from the seat of the Abacaki clan at Kihwera.

As I entered his room, one of his daughters announced, "Wilbur's wife has come to greet you." I knelt beside him and took his hand. He was over eight feet tall, well-built and light-skinned, with elongated ears. Wilbur had told me much about him, and about how there were few people who looked like him in Uganda anymore. He had been a chief, a virtual library of historical knowledge—our link with our past. He also was the father of the customs official at the Uganda-Kenya border who turned out to be Wilbur's uncle. He was blind but managed to touch my shoulder.

"I don't know why I have been left alive to see my friend's death. You see, I am wearing his gift of the tunic and jacket," he said. "I want them to be the clothes I will be buried in." He was crying. On the burial day we carried him to the grave and he buried Wilbur by throwing earth on the coffin.

Wilbur's return to Ibonde was complete. Yet, in that moment of utter finality, I felt reborn both physically and spiritually. The past, the present, and the future joined in unity and continuity. His death was given meaning here, and that, in turn, gave me a direction and a reason to continue living.

Afterwards, I told President Museveni that since I had given Wilbur a proper burial in his homeland, I could return to Washington, if he so wished.

"I, of course, have done nothing to replace you," he told me.

17

From Symbol
to Individual

In the season of Wilbur's passing, I had an embassy to run and there was so much yet to be done to improve relations between my country and the United States that I immersed myself in work. My goal: to arrange for President Museveni to come to Washington and meet with President Reagan. This administration had a history of meeting only leaders they considered allies, and I worked hard to dispel the myth that had been created by our enemies that my leader was a Marxist. It is a very difficult thing for an ambassador to set up such a visit. Luckily, I had Deputy Secretary of State John White-head, Donald Gregg, Vice President Bush's political adviser, and Attorney General Meese as allies. I spoke with them and many officials trying to orchestrate the visit. The administration remained reluctant to arrange a meeting between Presidents Museveni and Reagan.

In Uganda there was a hot debate among government officials over whether President Museveni should just go to Washington and meet with Vice President Bush, without meeting with President Reagan.

My friends in Washington advised me, "If you can get an appointment with Vice President George Bush, then you'll have a foot in the door." The State Department offered for President Museveni to see the secretary of state. I said that was out of the question and kept pushing. I went to see Don Gregg, and requested a meeting between his boss and mine. The White House consulted foreign policy advisers and they were told, "Museveni has been very good on human rights" and was someone the president and vice president should see.

Museveni arrived in Washington in October of 1987 and met with President Reagan and then Vice President Bush on October 19. Vice President Bush told him, "We are so relieved that the killings have stopped in Uganda."

"I don't have to be congratulated for not killing my own people," Museveni told the vice president. President Reagan congratulated President Museveni on restoration of Human Rights but repeated his concern to Museveni about Uganda's relationship with Libya, although he expressed himself a bit more strongly than he had when we discussed the issue during my first visit to the White House. Looking back, I suppose he tempered his remarks to me because I am a woman. The visit was a resounding success and the most important achievement of my political career.

In late January 1988, Wilbur's heir, Henry, his 15-year-old nephew, came to live with me in Washington, His parents and I had decided that the experience of living in America and being educated here would be invaluable. Henry is a smart, quiet boy, who reminds me of Wilbur with his shyness and kind heart. In the late winter I was able to arrange to take him along with me to the White House for a farewell reception to the diplomatic corps. We had our pictures taken with the Reagans, which was a great treat for Henry. While the photo was being taken, the Reagans told me they had seen my interview with Harry Reasoner on *60 Minutes* and that they had enjoyed it very much. That one segment brought me more attention than I had ever imagined.

I was bombarded with invitations to speak to the press, television, universities, and churches. In all these forums I attempted to correct

Uganda's international image by underscoring that the press had consistently and insistently misled the international community by insinuating that Uganda is the land of AIDS and Amin.

My task force on health led by a noted Ugandan scientist, Professor Ibulaimu Kakoma, had briefed me well on AIDS to enable me to educate Americans by stressing that AIDS was a politically complex and sensitive issue, especially as it relates to Africa in general and Uganda in particular. In line with my government's policy, I confirmed that the problem of AIDS was not merely African or Ugandan but a recognized pandemic. Uganda health authorities led by President Museveni had mounted an admirable strategy of mass education about AIDS, making Uganda one of the few countries to resist politicizing AIDS and face the reality of this deadly disease. Furthermore, Uganda took the lead internationally by establishing a National AIDS Task Force Committee even before the U.S. government had taken such a step. I explained how impossible it was to accurately determine the number of AIDS cases in Africa until diagnostic technologies were standardized for field use and the general public was well informed. The fact that the world Health Organization had commended Uganda for its stand and policies strengthened my crusade.

As my two-year stint as U.S. ambassador came to a close, I was appointed ambassador to France. I carefully considered the offer, but delayed my decision until after attending the Democratic convention in Atlanta, which was the last duty of my tenure as Ambassador. It was intriguing to see the American political process in action, especially in comparison to my own country's.

Presidential candidate Michael Dukakis took me by surprise when he approached and said, "Please, tell me who you are."

"I am the princess from Africa," I replied, all I could think of as we shook hands.

By the end of the convention, I had decided to make my resignation official, and I sent the following telex to President Museveni:

JULY 21, 1988

H.E. THE PRESIDENT OF UGANDA

I AM SENDING TO YOUR EXCELLENCY IN ADVANCE A COPY OF
A STATEMENT I SHALL RELEASE TOMORROW.

BUT ALLOW ME TO REITERATE WHAT A GREAT HONOUR IT
HAS BEEN TO SERVE THE PEOPLE OF UGANDA AND TO EXPRESS
MY GREAT RESPECT FOR YOU AS OUR LEADER.

RESPECTFULLY,

ELIZABETH NYABONGO

On the termination of my mission as Ambassador of
Uganda to the United States of America and my resignation from the public service of Uganda, I wish to make a
personal statement.

I know only one ideology—the ideology of patriotism—the love of my country and my people. My resignation from government service does not alter this fact.
It is intended strictly to give me a much needed break to
restore my personal life and my energy.

It is well known that in December 1986, at the very
beginning of my service as Ambassador to the United
States, Wilbur, my beloved husband, tragically died. At
the same time, I had to rebuild the Ugandan Embassy for
the beginning of a new chapter in our relationship with
the United States. These situations have taken a great toll
on my energy.

In the next two years I want to try to concentrate
myself and my efforts on contributing to ideas that will
help further shape the fundamental changes that have already engulfed Uganda and Africa. Part of this project,
which is already underway, involves the publication of
my autobiography. During this time I also want to read
and study in order to prepare for my return to the service of my beloved country, Uganda.

It is my hope that I can further cement the gains already made during my tenure as Ambassador of Uganda
to the United States of America, namely:
- there is a new awareness in America toward Uganda
- a new image of Uganda and Africa has been established
- bilateral relations between Uganda and the United
States of America are visibly improved

In this connection, I am deeply grateful for the support of the United States Government and the promo-
tional support of organizations such as *60 Minutes* and
The Washington Post, which have brought about a spe-

cial relationship with so many Americans and an increased knowledge about Uganda by the American public.

With respect to my recent appointment as Ambassador of Uganda to France, I am deeply honored by the confidence placed in me by President Yoweri Museveni. In addition, I am personally and deeply indebted to France for having defended me when I was under attack by Idi Amin. It would have been a very special honor and privilege to serve in this great country so important to Africa and the world. Thus, it was an agonizing decision for me not to accept this assignment.

I have instead decided to stay in the United States of America temporarily to pursue the matters described above. The dynamism and vitality here have already helped me to come to terms with my personal tragedy, and I believe that the environment in the United States of America uniquely lends itself to assist me in generating dynamic ideas consistent with the goals of assisting in the changes currently ongoing in Uganda.

At the end of this period of reprieve, I sincerely hope to re-enter the service of my country in order to assist it in its worldwide relations and its further economic development.

When the convention was over, I returned to Washington and moved to a new apartment, ready at last to begin to contemplate a future without Wilbur.

The philosophical African concept of time is not measured in years, months, hours, or minutes. An African elder never makes references to historical or past events by dating them. If the question "When?" is put to him, his answer will always be "*Ira naira*" or "*Ira muno,*" meaning "From the immense depths of time" or "From the most remote antiquity." For my people, life does not begin at conception, nor does it end with death. In turn, I have always seen my life not in fragments of time, but in cycles, like the phases of the moon. I have never celebrated birthdays, which Wilbur found amusing. I even rebelled against wearing a watch. An African elder would look to the heavens, not to his Timex.

This African timelessness, in which past, present, and future are interwoven, is born from the notion of spiritual identification with our ancestors. History is not just a vague concept; it is tangible and alive. We buried Wilbur at the base of the Mountains of the Moon, next to his father, his grandfather, and his great-grandfather, because Ibonde is not just a place but a binding force of the Abacaki—Wilbur's clanstock.

I was named Bagaaya after strong, fearless women who symbolized the spiritual and temporal well-being of our people. Throughout my upbringing, the stories of my ancestors instructed me: "You are Bagaaya." Thus my character, my actions, even my fate to some extent, have been consciously shaped by the legacy of my name. But the encounter with Wilbur transformed me from being a mere symbol to an individual protected by love. Moreover, his death opened me to a new dimension of life's mystery. I am freed from fear of anything, including death itself. As I forge ahead, I go on my own—entrusting the next cycle of my life to the hand of destiny.

Appendix
The Songs of Toro

The Poetic Song of Kaboyo Olimi V of Toro

He has rebelled, Kasunsu Nkwanzi*
He has rebelled, Kyayolire (Roaring mighty)
He has rebelled with his father's offspring
But not his mother's, ai!

He has rebelled, Kasunsu Nkwanzi
He has rebelled, the one I will never see!
The artistic tattoos over all his abdomen
They're so beautifully arranged and so perfect like the moon!

Around the neck of his stepmothers
He is like beautiful jewels
Saying good-bye to his father's Queen Consorts
He has rebelled, the one I'll never see again, mhu!

On the laps of his sisters-in-law

* Kasunsu Nkwanzi (Head-Tuft Plaited with Beads).

269

ELIZABETH OF TORO

Round the waists of his sisters-in-law
He is like their belts
He has gone, the one I will not see again, mhu!

Kapupa, my precious servant, wake up and sound the royal Drum!
Sound it specially and cunningly,
Make it sound like the one of exile,
Sound it like the one of rebellion,
Let's go home to Toro
Let's go to be saluted "Okali" (the royal salute)
Let's go to make a sacrificial ritual to the moon.

The fools of Kahuruge
The ignorants of Rwamwanja
They thought I was going to cattle graze
Yet I was going to rebel.

His wife Katutu said,
"Engaju* is in temper, what's up with Engaju?
This is not his usual mood. Why is he upset?"

Katutu, Katutu, the snow-teethed
It is morning time, go and bid them farewell
Those of Karuzika, go and bid them good-bye.
What kills me most are the young maids of Rwengo.
Get up early to gather baskets
He said: "Poor women can be cheated! You think flattery is love, mhu!"

I've gone, Rusule of Myeri, I've gone, Kasunsu Nkwanzi (Rusule—the
  unruly)
Who is never milked by the learners
I've gone to sound the Royal drum (Empango)
I've gone to be saluted, "Okali."

As he moved on he fell in the stream's quagmire,
That stream, he just turned round and gave it a cynical smile.
"Sire, may we block it or leave it alone?"
"Leave it alone. When else shall I come across it?"

And the ant hill that tumbled him, he just turned around and looked at it.
His entourage asked for permission to pull it out or leave it alone.
"Leave it alone, when else shall I again come across it?"

* Engaju (fair-skinned and beautiful, likened to the color of a brown cow).

The Songs of Toro

He said: "Ababito, fight for the throne.
If you don't fight for the throne, never come to Isansa.
Fight like a deserted man
Who has nowhere to go
My precious servant Kapupa
Take your shield and fight."

Sogahi River had never got dry
He dried it with his palm
They said, "We are yours" (The inhabitants around said: "We're your
  subjects")

He encouraged Bairu (peasants) to till the ground
And Abahuma (cattle owners) to water the cattle.

Adyeri hated the dull
He valued adventurers.
He hated the cowards
And loved the fighters.

Those who sided with Adyeri
They now live in big palaces.
Those who remained behind
Their children are in exile.

Let me mention Adyeri. It may rain
And the Virgins may conceive
Why not mention him
He has never been bad to me
Adyeri Busume, Mango Ibona
He makes me comfortable
He deserves my praises
They put him in flames
And found him safe
They put him in chicken (for divination)
He grieved people
Let me mention him last
Lest misfortune befalls me
Anyeri Busume, Mango Ibona.
The Royal Drum, Tibamulinde (irresistible)
Was found with Mugungu
The Royal Drum, Mutengesa
It found him at Buhungu

271

The Red Crown
Was found with Mugungu.
The Trumpet, Kimulikyokyamahauga (universal torch)
Has found him at Buhungu.
The Trumpet, Nyawanga
Was found with Mugungu.
The Spear, Kaitantahi (one which kills sparrows)
Has found him at Buhungu.
The bow, Nyampogo
Was found with Mugungu.
The throne, Kaizirokwera
Was found with Mugungu.
The basket for the beads, Kagole (the "kagole," bead-keeping basket)
Has found him at Buhungu.
The armlet of Wahemba
Was found with Mugungu.
The sandal, Biganja
Was found with Mugungu.
The flute, Tibarurra
Was found with Mugungu.
Eh! watch out, should you go on with
Mugungu the leader of the Abasulies (those who initiate)
You'll force him to wake up
And initiate the realm of the ancient kings.

NOTE: Most of the royal regalia mentioned above was brought to Kaboyo by Mugungu all the way from Bunyoro secretly. Kaboyo was at Buhungu when they were brought. This place is at Rusekere—overlooking Lake Albert and Butuku. Mugungu served all the kings of Toro from Kaboyo to Kyebambe. He belonged to the Abasegenya clan. He died at Buhungu in 1912.

Amoti Omujwiga—Poetic Song of Kasagama Kyebambe VI

Amoti's brave son, Omujwiga!
The one who swims the seas, Amoti Omujwiga!

He came at the time of confusion and upheaval, when he
went to rebel, Kanyesongoorre Rukirabasaija (Let me, in
songs, praise His Majesty).

Rubinga stayed in Ankole like all other children,
But hatred made him run to Buganda
Amoti's brave son, Omujwiga.

The Songs of Toro

He asked Byakuyamba his cousin; take me to
Toro I want to lay a claim
Byakuyamba I am telling you;
Take me to Toro I want to make a claim
Amoti's brave son, Omujwiga.

He told Kapere (Captain Lugard) the European, take me I want to make
   a case;
Amoti's brave son, Omujwiga,
Kapere I am telling you
Take me to Toro I must make a case.

He came amidst a crowd of Baganda fighters
He came with Nubian heads surrounding him ready to fight
Rukirabasaija Omujwiga.

He sailed over in metallic boats
Rowed with sparkling oars,
Rwoga Mayanja Omujwiga (The one who swims the seas).

The Abarugura at Katwe were hit by an eagle
Rukara rwa Magigi forgot his guns,
Rwoga Mayanja Omujwiga (The one who swims the seas).

The Bakonjo submitted with no problem,
Those who met him at Kanyanyange
Mistook him for a hunter,
Rwoga Mayanja the hunter.

Let Kisasa talk (the maxim gun) since all
The drums are collected together
And the usual fighter is now puzzled
He won't be able to stop them
Amoti's brave son, Omujwiga.

The Kasese vultures were dancing,
Hail you big king
Kill a bull for us to feast;
Amoti's brave son, Omujwiga.

When we reached Kisomoro at Nyakusarra's, fires blazed all night,
When he entered the place of the Abasoka, Queens offered productive
cows;
Chiefs brought calves.

ELIZABETH OF TORO

Carer for orphans, if I become cowardly
You take away your Nubians
Nyesongoorre Ibona mihanda (*Let me sing—praise the Pathfinder*).

Kanyesongoorre Omuteera-kaheeka
(*Let me sing-praise the industrious one.*)
Rwoga Mayanja Omujwiga
(*The one who swims the seas*).

He reached Kabarole and erected his spear,
Queens brought cows and chiefs calves.

When he reached Kabarole, planted his Mutoma (*barkcloth tree*)
The drums sounded and chiefs were appointed and confirmed.

Kabalega's General Rwabudongo came with desperation
Seeking a bond of friendship,
Declaring his submission,
Rukirabasaija Omujwiga.

When I don't chant his praises I get no peace;
After all there is nothing to prevent me
Since he has never mistreated me;
He handles me delicately.

The Kings of the Empire of Kitara, and Toro Kingdom After Secession

The Abatembuzi (First Dynasty)
Kintu
Kakama
Twale
Hangi
Ira Iya Hangi
Kazoba Ka Hangi
Nyamuhanga
Nkya I
Nkya II
Baba
Kamuli
Nseka
Kudidi
Ntozi
Nyakahongerwa
Mukonko
Ngonzaki Rutahinduka
Isaza Waraga Rugambanabato
Bukuku

The Abacwezi (Second Dynasty)
Ndahura
Mulindwa
Wamara

The Ababito (Present Dynasty)
Rukiidi I, Mpuga
   Kyeramaino Isamba Iya
   Nyatworo
Ocaki I
Oyo I
Winyi I
Olimi I
Nyabongo I
Winyi II
Olimi II
Nyarwa I
Chwa I
Masamba I
Kyebambe I
Winyi III
Nyaika Omuragwa
Kyebambe II
Ilimi III
Duhaga I
Olimi IV
Kyebambe III
   Nyamutukura
Kaboyo Olimi of Toro
Kazaana Ruhaga of Toro
Kasunga Nyaika Kyebambe IV of Toro

Kato Rukiidi I of Toro
Mukabirere Olimi VI of Toro
Muskarusa Kyebambe V of Toro
Isingoma Rukiidi II of Toro
Rububi Kyebambe VI of Toro
Kakende Nyamuyonjo of Toro
Dandi Kasagama Kyebambe
   VI of Toro
George David Matthew
   Kamurasi Rukiidi III of
   Toro
Patrick David Matthew
   Kaboyo Olimi VII of Toro

INDEX